# Truth, Faith, and Reason

# Truth, Faith, and Reason

## Scripture, Tradition, and John Paul II

## Kenneth M. Sayre

PICKWICK *Publications* · Eugene, Oregon

TRUTH, FAITH, AND REASON
Scripture, Tradition, and John Paul II

Pickwick Publications
An Imprint of Wipf and Stock Publishers
199 W. 8th Ave., Suite 3
Eugene, OR 97401

www.wipfandstock.com

PAPERBACK ISBN: 978-1-6667-3153-8
HARDCOVER ISBN: 978-1-6667-2413-4
EBOOK ISBN: 978-1-6667-2417-2

*Cataloguing-in-Publication data:*

Names: Sayre, Kenneth M., 1928–, author.

Title: Truth, faith, and reason : scripture, tradition, and John Paul II / Kenneth M. Sayre.

Description: Eugene, OR : Pickwick Publications, 2022 | Includes bibliographical references.

Identifiers: ISBN 978-1-6667-3153-8 (paperback) | ISBN 978-1-6667-2413-4 (hardcover) | ISBN 978-1-6667-2417-2 (ebook)

Subjects: LCSH: John Paul II, Pope, 1920–2005—Criticism and interpretation. | Catholic Church—Doctrines. | Faith and reason—Christianity. | Faith and reason. | Knowledge, Theory of (Religion).

Classification: BT50 .S28 2022 (print) | BT50 .S28 (ebook)

07/27/22

# Contents

# Preface

THE ENCYCLICAL *FIDES ET Ratio* by John Paul II begins with the proclamation: "Faith and reason are like two wings on which the human spirit
rises to the contemplation of truth" (*FIDES ET RATIO binae quasi pennae
videntur quibus veritatis ad contemplationem hominis attollitur animus*).
This encyclical was issued in the midst of a seemingly endless debate
among theologians regarding the respective natures of faith and reason,
and the contribution each makes to the disclosure of truth. The present study is not an attempt to engage in that open-ended and potentially
endless debate. The purpose of this study is to examine the encyclical on
its own merits from an unbiased viewpoint, and to consider its strengths
and weaknesses in the context of contemporary Catholic Christianity.

The viewpoint of this study is intended to be unbiased, first, in being historical rather than doctrinal. In preparation for examining the encyclical itself, the concepts of faith and reason are traced through earlier
stages of development within the context of the Catholic tradition. Major
stages in this development are the New Testament, the Neoplatonic period dominated by St. Augustine, the Aristotelian period dominated by
St. Thomas, and the pre-Vatican II period represented by Karl Rahner
and Bernard Lonergan. The viewpoint is intended to be unbiased also in
the sense of being objective, which in this case means dealing with it in its
own terms rather than as the product of a much-beloved saint. Although
the approach of this study is critical overall, criticism of the encyclical

itself is directed more toward its language and conceptual coherence than toward its doctrinal contents.

The contemporary Catholic Church, of course, exists in a much different intellectual milieu than those of the earlier authors mentioned. A consequence is that the very concepts of truth, of faith, and of reason, as we entertain them today, tend to differ substantially from the corresponding concepts in these earlier periods. To provide a background for understanding the development of these concepts and of their interrelations, the present study begins with a brief survey of their significance in contemporary English discourse. This survey is not intended to be exhaustive, or in any way definitive, but only to set the stage for the historical analysis of those concepts that follows.

The analysis overall takes the form of a detailed examination of relevant texts, quoted both in translation and (when relevant) in their original languages. When pertinent to the overall analysis, difficulties with arguments contained in earlier texts are pointed out, and the effects of these difficulties traced through later authors. Several such difficulties are shown to reappear in *Fides et Ratio*.

The present study employs neither footnotes nor specific in-text references. Quotations from original sources (e.g., the Bible, Augustine's *Confessions*) are documented in a standard fashion, but there are no quotations from secondary sources. Accordingly, there is no index of authors quoted. There also is no index of original sources. For the record, however, passages are quoted from all books of the New Testament, a dozen or so from the Old Testament (Septuagint), and several from the Apocrypha.

Three appendices examine various rationales behind use of Latin as the official language of the Catholic Church, trace some of the conceptual errors in the encyclical to their origin in this language, and consider ways in which the Church might benefit from divesting Latin of its official status.

# CHAPTER 1

# Contemporary Views of Truth, Faith, and Reason

## 1.1 Introduction

THERE ARE NO SINGLE standard contemporary understandings of the three main concepts involved in this study. It is feasible, nonetheless, to summarize the main interpretations of each among contemporary philosophers. Philosophy in recent decades is a multifaceted enterprise, with some branches more devoted to precision and clarity than others. Clarity and precision are important for present purposes. Among currently active branches, the most attentive to precision and clarity is what is known broadly as analytic philosophy. This branch of philosophy itself has various sub-branches, distinctions among which are not immediately relevant.

Views represented in current analytic philosophy, by and large, match corresponding views in other fields of study that use the relevant concepts in a disciplined manner. The main purpose of specifying these various contemporary views is for comparison with corresponding views in *Fides et Ratio*. Another purpose is for comparison with corresponding views in earlier stages of the developing Catholic tradition. As we move through various stages of this tradition, it will be helpful to proceed against a background providing fixed points of comparison.

In addition to the summary overviews of the concepts of truth, faith, and reason that follow, there is an overview as well of belief in contemporary philosophic thought. This latter is called for by the fact that Augustine confuses faith and belief in ways that not only are detrimental to the clarity of his own thought, but that reemerge in John Paul II's encyclical. Interesting in its own right is the fact that Aquinas keeps faith distinct from belief, and uses the distinction in clarifying the notion of an act of faith. Unfortunately, *Fides et Ratio* follows Augustine rather than Aquinas in this regard.

The following account of these several concepts as they figure in contemporary philosophy should not be taken as either complete or definitive. Philosophers can always find ways of objecting to accounts proposed by other philosophers. This is what keeps the profession in business. The purpose of the accounts of truth, faith, belief, and reason that follow, accordingly, is not to settle anything about them once and for all, but only to provide clear reference points for comparison.

## 1.2 Truth

In contemporary analytic philosophy, the noun "truth," along with its adjectival form "true," is generally used in connection with propositions. The propositional calculus, for example, is often referred to as truth-functional logic. This form of logic deals with propositions that admit only two truth-values, those of being true and of being false. Falsehood, accordingly, is one of two truth-values. A proposition is true if it represents something that in fact is the case; otherwise, it is false.

States of affairs (SOAs) are either the case or not the case. A SOA is an aspect of the world, either as it is (an actual SOA) or as it might be (a possible SOA). An actual SOA is typically referred to as a fact; and a fact (actual SOA) is often referred to as a truth (as in "the truth of the matter is that . . ."). A proposition thus is true just in case it represents a truth in this latter sense.

The nature of propositions, among contemporary philosophers, is a topic of ongoing dispute. Different schools of philosophy work with different concepts of propositions, and individual philosophers sometimes work with their own idiosyncratic conceptions. A requirement underlying all these conceptions, nonetheless, is that a proposition contains at least two essential components. First, a proposition represents a SOA (actual or possible). Second, a proposition assigns a status (being the case or not being the case) to the SOA it represents. A proposition in fact is true if the SOA it represents has the status it is represented a having; otherwise, it is false. The truth of propositions thus depends on truths contained in the actual world.

The noun "truth" also can apply to a true proposition itself. In act 2 of Shakespeare's *The Tempest*, for example, Gonzalo addresses Sebastian with the complaint "the truth you speak doth lack some gentleness." The truth spoken by Sebastian is particular, in the sense of being specific. A more general truth is illustrated by these words from the Declaration of Independence: "We hold these truths to be self-evident." An even more general sense is illustrated by the academic slogan that scholarship is dedicated to a search for the truth. A general sense of truth at odds with this slogan is evident in these well-known words from Johnathan Swift: "Falsehood flies, and truth comes limping after it."

The concept of truth in contemporary philosophy has been heavily influenced by developments in formal logic. Major works of relevance include Gottlob Frege's *Begriffsschrift* (1879), *Principia Mathematica* (1910–13) by Bertrand Russell and Alfred N. Whitehead, and Ludwig Wittgenstein's *Tractatus Logico-Philosophicus* (1921). Generally speaking, active concern with the nature of truth in contemporary philosophy goes hand in hand with interest in formal reasoning.

## 1.3 Faith and Belief

Terms roughly synonymous with "faith" in contemporary use include "trust," "confidence," and "belief." To have faith in one's doctor is to have trust in his or her skills and judgment. To have faith in one's investment portfolio is to be confident in its long-term performance. To have faith in one's college or university is to believe in its principles and educational policies.

As understood today, there is extensive overlap between uses of the expressions "having faith in" and of "believing in." To believe *in* something, of course, is quite different from believing *that* one or another proposition is true. The act of believing in something does not directly engage the question whether that thing is true or false. It might in fact be neither. One might believe in the fidelity of one's spouse, for example, without giving rise to the question whether fidelity and comparable virtues have truth-values.

To believe in the fidelity of one's spouse is to repose confidence in a particular SOA as being the case. Essentially the same attitude is expressed by saying one has faith in the fidelity (faith-worthiness) of one's spouse. In this case, having faith in and believing in are equivalent attitudes. A kindred confidence might be reposed in sources of information. For example, one might have confidence in the *New York Times* as a reliable source of information about current events. This confidence might be described either as believing in or as having faith in the *New York Times*. Comparably reliable as information-sources are newscasters in the mold of Walter Cronkite and Dan Rather. There is little difference between expressing faith in and expressing belief in such a commentator.

There are other common circumstances, however, in which believing in something is quite different from having faith in that thing. In the current political scene, for example, one might believe in democracy as the most equitable form of government. But one at the same time might have little faith in democracy as a de facto source of social equity. Another example of current relevance has to do with the likelihood of extraterrestrial life. People who believe that life exists elsewhere than on earth are commonly described as believing in life on other planets. But it is hard to imagine circumstances in which one might intelligibly be said to have faith in life outside the earth.

Like believing in democracy or in the *New York Times*, having faith in such things is an attitude of confidence regarding the thing in question. Believing in and having faith in are states of mind (like being satisfied) as distinct from mental activities (like seeking a satisfactory answer to a question). In particular, neither believing in nor having faith in is itself an activity capable of grasping new truths or of discerning new facts. The attitude of having faith in the *New York Times* bears no perspicuous relation to the faith described in *Fides et Ratio* as rising "to the contemplation of truth."

Further examination of salient differences between faith and belief will take place in chapter 3 on St. Augustine. As noted previously, Augustine conflates the two, to the detriment of his treatment of Christian faith.

## 1.4 Reason

Reason and reasoning are like perception and perceiving. The latter is the activity of applying the faculty of perception. Like perception, reason is a mental faculty. Reason is the faculty of tracing out connections among propositions or SOAs. Formal reasoning is the activity of tracing out truth-connections among propositions. As far as formal reasoning is concerned, discerning connections of truth and falsehood among propositions is an end in itself. Practical reasoning, on the other hand, is the activity of tracing out connections between propositions (e.g., premises in a practical syllogism) and SOAs (regarding action) that one should bring about as a consequence.

An example of a practical syllogism (adapted from Aristotle's *Nicomachean Ethics* 1147a29–31) is: (i) sweet things are taste-worthy (a general proposition), (ii) this food is sweet (a particular proposition), therefore (iii) I ought to bring about the SOA of eating this food (an action). A distinctive mark of a practical syllogism is that, whereas its premises are factual, in stating things that are the case, its conclusion is modal, in stating what ought to be done. Another distinctive mark is that its conclusion introduces a term not found in the premises. In the example from Aristotle, "eating" is a term in the conclusion not found in either premise.

In his *Whose Justice? What Rationality?*, Alasdair MacIntyre argues that conceptions of justice and of practical reasoning alike are relative to particular traditions. In discussing this theme, MacIntyre draws examples from the tradition of the ancient Greek polis, that of medieval thought culminating in Thomas Aquinas, and that of Scotland prior to the Enlightenment. The view that conceptions of practical reasoning are relative in this manner does not dictate that all are equally cogent and defensible. According to MacIntyre's account, the tradition of pre-Enlightenment Scotland was subverted from within by the skepticism of David Hume. The primary nemesis in this account is the liberalism of the Enlightenment which Hume represented. In MacIntyre's own estimation, the tradition of Augustine and Aquinas (i.e., the Christian tradition) is best equipped to overcome this liberalism and to rescue the modern world from its present incoherence.

The Thomistic tradition of practical reasoning endorsed by MacIntyre occupies a favored position as well in John Paul II's *Fides et Ratio.* MacIntyre's work serves as a reminder that other systems of practical reasoning are available as well, and that choice of the Thomistic system over the others requires justification. With regard to the encyclical in particular, another lesson to be drawn from MacIntyre is that practical reason by itself is not an instrument of discovery. Practical reasoning is a guide to action, but has

little to offer toward "the contemplation of truth." The *ratio* John Paul II had
in mind clearly is some variety of formal reasoning instead.

Following is a summary of the nature of formal reasoning in contemporary thought. Readers already acquainted with such matters may
wish to proceed directly to section 1.42.

### 1.4.1

In the loose sense intended, formal reasoning is based on form irrespec-
tive of content. Commonly recognized varieties of formal reasoning
include deduction and induction. Standard forms of deduction include
syllogistic logic and truth-functional logic. Deduction by syllogism involves inference from two premises (e.g., "All S is M" and "All M is P") to
a conclusion ("All S is P"). If both premises are true, the conclusion must
be true as well. If one premise is false, the conclusion might be either
true or false. Purporting to derive a conclusion that is false from two true
premises is an invalid inference. An inference from false premises to a
true conclusion, however, might nonetheless be valid. For example, it is
valid to infer "Socrates is a man" from "Socrates is a rabbit" and "All rab-
bits are men." A study of syllogistic logic is an investigation of syllogistic
forms that yield valid inferences.

Syllogistic logic originated in Aristotle's *Prior Analytics*. With further elaboration and development, it remained the dominant model
of formal reasoning through the following two millennia. Prominent
contributors to its development included Boethius in the sixth century,
Abelard in the twelfth century, and Ockham in the fourteenth century.
Although Aquinas himself was not a major contributor, he employed
syllogistic reasoning in his theological disputes. As evident in Kant's
*Critique of Pure Reason*, syllogistic logic was still the dominant form of
deductive reasoning in the late-eighteenth century.

Truth-functional logic (propositional calculus) originated with the
Stoics in the third century BC. It reached entirely formal status, however, only with the work of Augustus De Morgan, George Boole, and
Gottlob Frege in the nineteenth century. Whereas syllogistic logic treats
relations among terms in analyzed statements (e.g., S and M in "All S is
M"), propositional logic deals with connections among unanalyzed statements (e.g., "if p is true and q is true, then the conjunction p and q is also
true"). The elementary connectives of propositional logic correspond to

English expressions such as "and," "or," and "if-then." As demonstrated in Wittgenstein's *Tractatus* 5.101, sixteen truth-functional connectives can be defined on two propositional variables. Validity of a complex truth-functional statement consists in the statement being true for all combinations or truth-values admitted by its elementary components. Validity can be determined (among other means) by use of truth-tables that correlate the truth-values of complex statements with combinations of truth-values of their components.

Predicate calculus (quantification theory) is an extension of propositional logic to deal with relations among constituent terms of analyzed statements, in addition to their truth-functional interactions. While anticipations of quantification theory can be found in Leibniz and elsewhere, it came to flourish in the *Principia Mathematica* of Russell and Whitehead. Primitives of quantification theory include predicate terms ("B," "C," "M," "P," "S," etc.) representing properties or classes, to which variables ("x," "y," etc.) are appended. The expression "Bx," for instance, represents the SOA of a given thing x having the property B. The other primitives of predicate calculus are the quantifiers "(x)" and "(∃y)," which represent the range of the variable in question. The formula "(x)(Sx ⊃ [only if ] Mx)," for example, affirms that everything S is also M. The formula "(∃y)(My.[and] Py)," in turn, affirms that something exists that is both M and P.

It is clear that the formal aspects of syllogistic logic can be duplicated in the predicate calculus. Thus "All S is M" in syllogistic terms can be expressed as "(x)(Sx ⊃ Mx)." More complex versions of the predicate calculus can be applied to serve more complex purposes. As indicated by its title, the *Principia Mathematica* of Russell and Whitehead was an effort to show that mathematics can be deduced from principles of logic. A more recent book on the foundations of mathematics is *Mathematical Logic*, by Willard Van Orman Quine (a onetime teacher of mine).

A ground-breaking book (by another former teacher) is *Symbolic Logic* by Clarence Irving Lewis, written in collaboration with Cooper Harold Langford. Instead of truth-tables, this work employs an axiomatic method in its development of propositional logic. In this method, basic axioms and previously established postulates are employed to establish additional formulae. The same method is employed in the work's treatment of modal functions, which is its major contribution to formal logic. Modal functions treated include possibility, consistency, and necessity. The function "p is possible (self-consistent)" is formalized as "◇p." The function "p and q are consistent" is symbolized by "p∘q." In these terms, "◇p" can be shown equivalent to "p∘p." The relation of (strict) entailment is symbolized by "≺"; "p≺q" means that if p is true then necessarily q is true as well. The function "p is necessary," in turn, is rendered "-◇-p" or "-(-p∘-p)." An equivalent rendition is "-p≺p," meaning that the truth of p is entailed by its negation. The versatility of Lewis and Langford's modal formalism is extended by the employment of quantifiers. "There is at least one proposition that is necessarily true," for example, is rendered "(∃p)-◇-p," while "all necessary propositions necessarily are self-consistent" goes into "(p)((-◇-p)≺(p∘p))."


## 1.4.2

Inductive logic is foreshadowed toward the end of Aristotle's *Posterior Analytics* (100a15–100b5). In this passage, Aristotle is concerned with the origin of universal premises in the mind's perception of particular instances. The general idea is that repeated perceptions of particular cases prepares the mind to comprehend what those cases have in common. After numerous repetitions, the mind's grasp of particular cases evolves into a grasp of the truth that all exhibit the same universal property. The term Aristotle uses for this process is *epagōgē*, usually translated "induction."

This intuitive conception of induction prevailed through the Middle Ages until the seventeenth century, when it received more systematic treatment in Francis Bacon's *Novum Organon* (1620). Techniques of inductive reasoning were further developed in John Stuart Mill's *A System of Logic, Ratiocinative and Inductive* (1843). Subsequent studies of inductive reasoning were heavily influenced by probability theory. Work in probability theory during the eighteenth and nineteenth centuries, primarily by Bayes, Laplace, and Boole, led to John Maynard Keynes' *A Treatise on Probability* (1921) and Rudolf Carnap's *Logical Foundations of Probability* (1950). A central concern of probability theory is the degree of confirmation a general conclusion receives from its supporting data. Determining degree of confirmation typically involves statistical inference, which analyzes relevant properties of underlying probability distributions.

Regardless of complexity, inductive inference is a formal procedure. In simplest form, inductive reasoning is inference from characteristics of a sample set to characteristics of the population from which samples are drawn. For an example, consider the reasoning involved in the following situation: five hundred swans are examined over a period of time and are all found to be white, after which it is inferred that all swans are white. The general form of this inference is:

> In a random sample S of population P, all S have characteristic C
> Therefore, all members of P have C.

The reliability to this inference obviously depends on the extent of population P, the size of sample S relative to the size of P, and the proportion of S that exhibit C. In the example given, P is indefinitely large, S relative to P is correspondingly small, and the proportion of S that exhibit C is 100 percent. If that proportion were less, the inference to the conclusion would be unwarranted.

When the proportion of S exhibiting C is less than 100 percent, another form of inference might yield more favorable results. Consider circumstances in which: (1) fifty balls have been placed in an urn, colored both (a) black and (b) white; (2) ten balls are drawn from the urn, of which three are black and seven are white; from which it is inferred (3) that fifteen balls originally in the urn are black and thirty-five are white. In formal structure, this is the inference:

> In a random sample S of population P, S is one-fifth the size of P
> S is found to possess characteristic C (namely, being divided three to seven between features a and b)
> Therefore, P is characterized by C.

The relatively high ratio of size S to size P (one-fifth) indicates that the conclusion is highly probable. By very nature, however, inductive inference is never 100 percent reliable. This means that it is incapable of yielding general knowledge of what in fact is the case.

If inductive reasoning (counterfactually) were 100 percent reliable, it would provide an avenue for the discovery of new facts about the world. It would disclose aspects of reality that had not been known previously. In the case of the swans, for example, it might purport to disclose that all swans indeed are colored white, something that cannot be known as matters stand.

As matters stand, nonetheless, inductive reasoning is capable of leading to the disclosure of previously unknown facts. On the basis of repeated observations of abnormalities in the orbit of a given planet, for example, inductive reasoning might suggest that the planet is under the gravitational influence of a previously unknown body. This might lead to an astronomical investigation that brings the existence of the concerned body to light. The avenue of disclosure would not be limited to the process of reasoning itself, but rather consists of the investigation prompted by the inductive process. In this case, inductive reasoning brings about a situation in which novel aspects of reality come to be known. But the process of reasoning does not disclose the relevant facts on its own.

## 1.4.3

Contrary to what might appear at first, deductive reasoning also is incapable of disclosing new facts about the world. A fact is a state of affairs (SOA) that is the case. Needless to say, deductive reasoning cannot convert one set of facts into another. It is not a means of manipulating the actual world. More to the point, deductive reasoning, operating just by itself, is incapable of gaining knowledge about the actual world. Knowledge is a mental state in which the mind is directly aware of some actual SOA. And reasoning by itself cannot determine whether an actual SOA is directly present in the mind's awareness. To be sure, reason can specify circumstances in which one could determine on the basis of experience whether a given SOA is actually present. But knowledge of that SOA is gained only when the mind is aware of it directly, which is a state of mind that reason cannot verify on its own.

The nature of knowledge is a much-debated topic among contemporary epistemologists. The conception of knowledge expressed above joins Plato in rejecting the common view that knowledge is justified true belief. For Plato, belief occupies the underside of the Divided Line (in his *Republic*), whereas knowledge resides in the upper portion. No matter how strong its justification, belief cannot move from the lower to the upper part of the Line. Expressed in more recent terminology, the difficulty with the common view is that belief is directed toward propositional objects, whereas objects of knowledge are actual SOAs. And the propositional object of a belief cannot be transformed into a SOA, regardless of the degree to which the belief is justified.

By way of countering the view of knowledge above, someone might object that scientific reasoning is capable of producing knowledge of actual SOAs. From quantum physics and molecular biology, to astrophysics and general relativity, we have gained more knowledge through reasoning in science than in any other human enterprise. This undeniably is the case. In none of these theoretical disciplines, however, is knowledge achieved by reason alone. Knowledge comes when the results of reasoning are verified by observation. In typical cases, observation involves use of complex instruments. Even so, observation through instruments constitutes awareness of actual SOAs. Scientific reasoning yields knowledge only when backed up by empirical evidence.

There are ongoing debates in the philosophy of science regarding the character of what can be known through science. The debate hinges on the relation between theoretical constructs, like those of bosons in particle physics and microstates in thermodynamics, and the putative entities to which these constructs correspond. The concept of microstates, for instance, is an integral part of thermodynamic theory; but microstates as such cannot be observed. As scientific theories go, thermodynamics is a successful theory. At issue in the case of thermodynamics is whether success of the theory demonstrates that microstates actually exist. Does our knowledge of thermodynamics as a successful theory convey knowledge of microstates as unobservable entities?

There are two basic responses to this question, commonly known as scientific realism and instrumentalism. Realism holds that the concept (model, construct) of microstates corresponds to entities in the actual world, and holds further that the theory's de facto success is due to this correspondence. Instrumentalism, on the other hand, holds that all we actually know in this case is that the theory has proved successful in accounting for the empirical data on which it is based. As a result of extensive experimentation, the instrumentalist maintains, we have come to know that thermodynamics is a successful instrument for dealing with phenomena pertaining to the distribution of heat. The theory works for its intended purposes, namely to explain, to control, and to predict phenomena pertaining to heat. But why it works, the instrumentalist claims, is a question without a scientific answer, better left unanswered in the interest of clarity.

For present purposes, there is no need to take a stand on issues separating instrumentalism and scientific realism. It will join other forms of realism to be considered at subsequent stages of this study, including the metaphysical realism inherent in *Fides et Ratio*. The lesson to be retained for present purposes is that deductive reasoning, in the absence of empirical support, is incapable of disclosing new facts about the actual world.

This result rings a bell of warning for John Paul II's encyclical, which depicts a reason (*ratio*) capable of joining with faith (*fides*) in lifting the human mind (*mens*) to the "contemplation of truth" (*veritatis ad contemplationem*). To be sure, it accords with the view of knowledge put forth above that equates knowledge with the contemplation of truth. As depicted in the encyclical, however, knowledge is gained without support from empirical observation. This is a departure from the view regarding the origin of knowledge prevalent in empirical science.

### 1.4.4

In tentative defense of the encyclical, however, we should note the view once prevalent among logicians and mathematicians that formal reasoning can produce knowledge without empirical input. This view went hand-in-hand with efforts around the turn of the previous century to reduce mathematics to formal logic. Early contributions to this effort included Gottlob Frege's *Die Grundlagen der Arithmetik* (1884) and David Hilbert's *Grundlagen der Geometrie* (1899). Its landmark moment came with Russell and Whitehead's monumental *Principia Mathematica* (1910–13).

As described previously, *Principia Mathematica* purports to show that mathematics can be deduced from principles of logic. The logic in question is strictly formal, in the sense of being free of either intuitive or empirical content. For this to work, the logical system defined by these principles must be consistent (since any proposition can be deduced from an inconsistency). Another requirement is that the system must be complete, meaning that every formula expressible in the system is such that either it or its negation can be proved in the system. Difficulties arose for the system of the *Principia* with attempts to prove that it is complete.

These difficulties came to a head in 1931, with Kurt Gödel's proof that the completeness of the *Principia* system (and others capable of yielding basic arithmetic) in fact cannot be proved. Gödel's proof, as it is often designated, actually comprises two separate theorems. One is that any formal system capable of yielding basic arithmetic will contain a statement about numbers that is true but not provable in the system. The second is that no formal system capable of yielding arithmetic can prove its own consistency. On either count (since consistency is necessary for a productive system), arithmetic contains truths that cannot be demonstrated within an uninterpreted formal system.

Gödel's proof, in part, was motivated by his conviction that numbers exist independently of other entities. Among mathematicians, this position is known as "Platonic realism," after the view often attributed to Plato that numbers are Forms, and hence entirely separate from sensible things that exemplify them. For Gödel and other Platonic realists, numbers are entities existing on their own as parts of the objective world. No matter what happens in the empirical world, numbers would continue to exist as independent entities.

Gödel's realism led him to think of his proof as a demonstration of how things stand in the real world of mathematics. For those of Gödel's persuasion, mathematics is capable of disclosing new facts about the world of real objects. For a mathematical realist, in brief, reasoning conducted in terms of mathematics can sometimes lead to the disclosure of new facts about the world. Mathematical realism is still being debated by mathematicians and logicians. Even if realism were to prevail, however, it would bolster *Fides et Ratio* only to the extent that the *ratio* of the encyclical is like reasoning in mathematics and logic.

The primary purpose of this brief overview of formal reasoning has been to enable comparison of (1) the reason said in John Paul II's encyclical to team with faith in yielding a contemplation of truth with (2) forms of reasoning pursued by logicians and scientists among his contemporaries. When time comes for detailed comparison, it will be seen that the reason championed in the encyclical has no place among forms of reason studied professionally in the twentieth century.

Having examined concepts of truth, faith, and reason current among John Paul II's contemporaries, we turn next to an examination of those concepts in the context of the New Testament.

CHAPTER 2

# The New Testament

## 2.1 Greek Text and Translations

ALL NEW TESTAMENT (NT) translations in this study are accompanied by
the original Greek texts. The Greek source is the fourth revised edition
of *The Greek New Testament* printed in 2012 (which is not copyrighted).
Translations are my own responsibility. In preparing my translations, I
frequently consulted several previous translations that are available on
the Internet. In some cases, my translations matched those of standard
NT editions. My translations often resemble those of the English Standard
Version in particular, with which I had longstanding familiarity. I made a
point of always comparing my translations with those of Douay-Rheims
Bible, to make sure there were no subtleties in the Latin Vulgate that my
translations overlooked. The point remains, however, that all translations
in this study are my own.

There are occasions on which the Greek yields no fully satisfactory
translation. When that happens, an attempt is made to clarify the text
by tracing other uses of the recalcitrant terminology in the NT. An example comes with the definition of faith in Heb 11:1. For reasons to be
examined in due course, problems arise with that definition that are only
exacerbated in the verses following.

In point of fact, there are several distinct uses of the term *pistis*
(faith) in the NT, each calling for its own definition. A basic sense is faith
in the Christian belief-system, labeled "the doctrine of the Lord" in Acts

14

13:12. It comes as no surprise to find that faith in this sense does not figure in the Gospels, inasmuch as there was no such belief-system until after Christ's death. Faith in this sense was introduced in Acts, with further references in Paul's letters, and in the later letters.

The term *alētheia* (truth), however, occurs in each of these distinctive contexts, the Gospels included. Examination of the concepts of truth, faith and reason in the NT begins with the treatment of truth in the Gospels.

## 2.2 Truth in the New Testament

In Greek, the language of the New Testament, the term *alētheia* has two distinct meanings. One is truth (1) as it pertains to accurate discourse (spoken, written, or in the mind). The other is truth (2) as reality, in the sense of the way things are. An example of the first is found in Plato's *Republic* 537D, where Socrates is describing "the power of dialectic" (*tē tou dialegesthai dunamei*) to go beyond sense perception to "being itself in company with truth" (*auto to on met' alētheias*; see also *Phaedo* 65B, 90D). In this passage, truth in discourse is explicitly contrasted with what is real (being itself). An example of truth (2) is found in *Republic* 527D-E, where Socrates speaks of a "particular mental organ" (*organon ti psuchēs*) everyone has which "alone can see reality" (*monō . . . autō alētheia horatai*; see also *Phaedo* 65B, 99E). The *organon* in question is the faculty that enables the study of reality in geometry and other branches of mathematics. Although Plato wrote in classical Greek, these two senses carry over into the koine of the NT.

This second sense of *alētheia* helps clarify the seeming redundancy in the Nicene Creed about the descent of the Son from the Father. God the Son comes from God the Father (*Deum de Deo*). Furthermore, the Son who descends from the Father is *really* God and the Father is *really* God as well (*Deum verum de Deo vero*). In reality (*verum*), that is to say, the first two Persons of the Trinity are the Father and his begotten Son. So at least one affirms in reciting the Nicene Creed.

The sense of *alētheia* as reality also helps decipher John 14:5–6, where Thomas asks Jesus the way to where he is going. Jesus' response is: "I am the way, and the truth, and the life" (*Egō eimi hē hodos kai hē alētheia kai hē zōē*). Put otherwise, Jesus' response is that he is the being (*alētheia*) whose presence gives (everlasting) life (*zōē*), as well as the access (*hodos*) to that state of existence. Regarding access, Jesus continues with the explanation that "No one comes to the Father except through me" (*oudeis erchetai pros ton patera ei mē di' emou*). What Jesus says, in other terms, is that eternal life is the state of being with the Father, and that he is the way of achieving that state.

### 2.2.1

There are roughly ten dozen occurrences of the noun *alētheia* in the NT, distributed through all its major books. It is worth the effort to categorize these occurrences. Among senses in the NT, those of discursive truth (1) and of reality (2) are both well represented. As will be seen shortly, there are other prominent senses of *alētheia* in the NT as well.

Notably missing among senses of truth in the NT, however, are those pertaining to propositions. Before the medieval period, philosophic traditions with an interest in propositions were limited to those explicitly concerned with logic (e.g., Stoicism). Needless to say, the authors of the NT were not explicitly concerned with logic. A related disinterest among NT authors has to do with falsehood as the opposite of truth. The few occurrences of the term *pseudos* (falsehood, lie) in the NT pertain to the activity of lying rather than to falsehood as a truth-value. In Rom 1:25, for example, Paul berates those who exchange "the truth about God for a lie" (*tēn alētheian tou theou en tō pseudei*).

Truth in the above sense (1) of true (non-propositional) discourse, however, is spoken of frequently in the NT. At John 16:7, Jesus says to the disciples "I tell you the truth" (*egō tēn alētheian legō humin*) in explaining why he must leave them. In Acts 26:25, Paul assures Festus that he (Paul) is "speaking truth and good sense" (*alētheias kai sōphrosunēs hrēmata*) in his testimony to King Agrippa. In these two cases, true discourse takes the form of spoken words. This seems to be the case with Galatians (Gal) 2:5 as well, where Paul speaks of "the truth of the gospel" (*hē alētheia tou euangeliou*). The reasonable assumption here is that the *euangeliou* in question is the "good news" exchanged orally among the disciples, rather than one of the Gospels we have in written form. This accords with the likelihood that the contents of our written Gospels were circulated orally among the original disciples.

Turning now to *alētheia* in the sense (2) of reality (being, what is), we recall the previous example of John 14:6, where Jesus affirms "I am the way, the truth, and the life" (Greek above). As parsed previously, this is an affirmation that Jesus himself is the way to the state of being with the Father that constitutes eternal life. Obviously parallel in sense (2) is another affirmation by Jesus in John 8:31–32, saying that those who "abide in my word" (*meinēte en tō logō tō emō*) "will know the truth, and the truth will set [them] free" (*gnōsesthe tēn alētheian, kai hē alētheia eleutherōsei*). Those who abide in the truth which is the *logos* of Jesus, that is to say, will be freed by that truth from time-bound existence.

The theme of Jesus as true being is continued in Eph 4:21–22, where Paul tells his audience that "the truth is in Jesus" (*estin alētheia en tō 'Iēsou*), and that they should set aside their "old way of life" (*tēn proteran anastrophēn*). In 1 Tim 2:3–4, for yet another example, Paul asserts that "God our savior" (*sōtēros hēmōn theou*) desires "all people to be saved and to come to the knowledge of the truth" (*pantas anthrōpous thelei sōthēnai kai eis epignōsin alētheias elthein*). In each of these cases, Jesus is identified as the real being whose truth provides the way to human salvation.

Of particular interest for the present study are several senses to the term *alētheia* that seem to have been initiated by NT authors. While senses (1) and (2) appear in the NT, they also are found elsewhere in then-current Greek literature. A new sense appearing for the first time in the NT is truth in the sense (3) of Christian teaching or Christian faith. Uses of the term in this sense occur frequently throughout the letters, including both those of Paul and those that come later. A clear illustration of this sense is found in Paul's first letter to Timothy. In this epistle, Paul reminds Timothy how to behave in the church (*ekklēsia*), which is "the household of God" (*oikō theou*), further described as "a pillar and mainstay of truth" (*stulos kai hedraiōma tēs alētheias*, 3:15). The church, in other words, is the foundation of truth, specifically the truth taught by Christ. This advice is reinforced in 2 Tim 3:8, where Paul warns of men who "oppose the truth" (*anthistantai tē alētheia*) and are "disqualified with regard to faith" (*adokimoi peri tēn pistin*). By opposing the truth of sense (3), that is to say, these men are defective in the faith.

A similar message is conveyed in Heb 10:26. If we continue to sin deliberately "after receiving the knowledge of the truth" (*meta to labein tēn epignōsin tēs alētheias*), the author warns, "there no longer remains a sacrifice for sins" (*ouketi peri hamartiōn apoleipetai thusia*). Put otherwise, Jesus' sacrifice on the cross is of no avail to those who deliberately ignore the truth of his teaching. A less ominous reminder of Christ's teaching is conveyed in the first chapter of 2 Peter. Following a long list of attributes befitting a believer in Christ (faith, virtue, knowledge, self-control, etc.), the author reminds his audience of these attributes at 1:12. He hastens to acknowledge, however, that his audience already "knows them" (*toutōn . . . eidotas*) and is "established in the presence of the truth" (*estērigmenous en tē parousē alētheia*). Once again, the truth here is the teaching of Christ's church.

The truth taught by the church is truth in sense (3). The requisite response to truth (3) is the faith of acceptance (*pistis* at 2 Tim 3:8). The NT also speaks of a truth that requires acts of obedience. The two responses are not the same, given that someone could preach the faith of Christ for perverted reasons and fail to abide by its dictates. Paul complains of such circumstances in Phil 1:17, speaking in the first person of people who "proclaim Christ out of selfish ambition, thinking to stir up affliction for me in my imprisonment" (*ex eritheias ton Christon katangellousin . . . oiomenoi thlipsin egeirein tois desmois mou*). Paul's predicament aside, sincere acceptance of Christ's faith engages some form of action. There is a truth in the NT that inspires an active response beyond mere acquiescence. We may refer to it as truth in sense (4), a truth that inspires obedience.

The truth (4) that inspires obedience is clearly illustrated by Jesus' declaration at John 3:21. "Whoever does what is true" (*ho de poiōn tēn alētheian*), Jesus says, comes to the light, "so that his works may be manifested as having been carried out in God" (*hina phanerōthē autou ta erga hoti en theō estin eirgasmena*). Truth here is something one does, and the doing of it constitutes homage to God. Obedience to truth in sense (4) is stressed in Rom 2:6–9, where Paul chastises those whose works (*ta erga*, 2:6) are contentious (*ex eritheias*, 2:8). These people, Paul warns, "disobey the truth but obey unrighteousness" (*apeithousi tē alētheia peithomenois de tē adikia*, 2:8), which will lead them to "tribulation and distress" (*thlipsis kai stenochōria*, 2:9). Another example provided by Paul comes as part of the glorious paean to love in 1 Cor 13. Among the excellent features of love recited there is that it "does not rejoice at wrongdoing but rejoices with the truth" (*ou chairei epi tē adikia, sunchairei de tē alētheia*, 13:6). By doing right, that is to say, love celebrates truth in sense (4).

This sense of truth also was acknowledged by later authors of the NT. The author of 1 Peter relates truth in this sense to the second great commandment. Having purified your soul "by obedience to the truth" (*en tē hupakoē tēs alētheias*), he writes, "love one another earnestly with a pure heart" (*ek . . . kardias allēlous agapēsate ektenōs*, 1:22). The act of obeying truth in sense (4) allegedly prepares one for the practice of brotherly love. Obeying truth in this sense is also connected with the second commandment by the author of 2 John. Speaking to the "elect lady" (*eklektē kuria*, 1) and her children, the author commends them for "walking in the truth" (*peripatountas en alētheia*, 4), and advises that they "love one another" (*hina agapōmen allēlous*, 5). "And this is love" (*kai hautē estin hē agapē*), he adds, "that we walk according to his [the Father's] commandments" (*hina peripatōmen kata tas entolas autou*, 6). A reprise on the theme of dedicated walking occurs in 3 John 4, where the author commends Gaius for "walking in the truth" (*en tē alētheia peripatounta*). These passages from 2 John and 3 John both speak (figuratively) of dedicated walking as something to be done in obedience to truth in sense (4).

## 2.3 Belief in the New Testament

The NT word for faith is *pistis* (rendered *fides* in Latin). Authorities are divided on whether it stems from *peithō* (to persuade) or *pisteuō* (to believe). (Liddell and Scott, *A Greek-English Lexicon*, 1883, is indecisive on the issue.) As far as the NT is concerned, there is little overlap between circumstances described in terms of *pistis* and those described in terms of *peithō*. For purposes of understanding the faith extolled in the NT, accordingly, there is little insight to be gained by thinking of faith as a consequence of being persuaded. More useful toward that end is to focus on passages describing what the early Christians are said to have believed, and to compare these with passages regarding faith. Belief and faith in the NT are not the same; but as far as faith is concerned, their interactions can be informative.

In the Septuagint, *pisteuō* covers a range of meanings most readers today would find familiar. One such is that of *believing that something is the case*, exemplified at Job 9:16 where Job says he "could not believe that [God] was listening to my voice" (*ou pisteuō hoti eisakēkoen mou*). Another is that of *believing in persons*, as when Job says that he "does not reside trust in his servants" (*kata paidōn autou ou pisteuei*, Job 4:18). That of *believing in information sources* is illustrated in Ps 106:12, where the psalmist addresses the Lord saying that his fathers "believed his [the Lord's] words" (*episteusan en tois logois autou*). Given the institutional character of God's commands in the Old Testament (OT), we might even consider the topic of Ps 119:66 an instance of *believing in institutions*;

for here the psalmist says "that he believes in his [the Lord's] command-ments" (*hoti tais entolais sou episteusa*). Not surprisingly, all these mean-ings are retained in the NT.

Uses of the noun *pistis* in the Septuagint are more difficult to clas-sify. Not infrequently, it is used as an adverb or adjective rather than a noun. Use as an adverb occurs in 2 Chr 31:15, where various people were faithfully (*en pistei*) assisting Kore in his priestly duties. Use as an adjec-tive is illustrated in (apocryphal) Wis 22:23, where the wise man is urged to be "faithful to his neighbor" (*Pistin . . . tou plēsion*) in his poverty. More frequently, however, *pistis* serves as a noun, in keeping with its grammati-cal form. In Deut 32:20, for instance, it carries a sense close to "faithful-ness" in English. Here Moses quotes God as disdaining the children of Jeshurun, describing them as "children in whom there is no faithfulness" (*huioi hois ouk estin pistis en autois*). The same sense is carried by the term in Hos 2:20.

Not to be overlooked in the case of Hos 2:20 is that the *pistis* in question is faithfulness on the part of the Lord himself. Speaking to the house of Israel, the Lord says: "I will betroth myself to you in faithfulness" (*mnēsteusomai se emautō en pistei*, Hos 2:20). Another passage attribut-ing faithfulness to the Lord is Deut 32:4, where by self-ascription he is "a faithful God" (*Theos pistos*). In these contexts, faithfulness is a variant of fidelity, a character trait both possessed by God and desired by God in his people.

Mutual agreements are solidified when all parties commit them-selves with fidelity. Such an agreement is described in Nehemiah (Neh) 9:38, where the enslaved Israelites envisage a "covenant in writing" (*pis-tin . . . graphomen*) with their oppressors. Here the faithfulness required by the hoped-for agreement is referred to simply as *pistis* (fidelity) itself. A similar abbreviation is employed at (apocryphal) Wis 27:16, which warns that "whoever discloses secrets" (*Ho apokaluptōn mustēria*) will "lose his credit" (*apōlese pistin*). The credibility here at stake is designated by the single term *pistis* (credit). The meanings "covenant" and "credit" are departures from the standard meaning of *pistis* in the Septuagint of fidelity or faithfulness.

Idiosyncratic meanings such as "covenant" and "credit" do not carry over into the NT. Strictly understood, the standard meaning of "fidelity" is confined to the Septuagint as well. Faith in the NT is a mental state, in contrast with an active exercise of the will or mind. As will appear mo-mentarily, the meaning of *pistis* in the NT most closely related to fidelity of the Septuagint is a mental state that can wax and wane. The desideratum for a Christian is that his or her faith progresses from waning to a waxing state. While character traits like fidelity might change with time, they do not wax and wane in the manner of faith. This underscores the essential difference between faith (the mental state) and fidelity (the character trait).

As we shall see, there are several other key senses of *pistis* in the NT that are not anticipated in the Septuagint. One is *pistis* in the sense of an abstract belief-system in which individual people might participate. Let us turn to examine uses of the verb *pisteuō* (to believe) in the NT, prior to an examination of the noun *pistis* itself.

### 2.3.1

There are 248 occurrences of the verb *pisteuō* in the NT, many of which can be classified under three headings identified in chapter 1): (i) believing that something is the case, (ii) believing in persons, and (iii) believing in sources of information. Given the institutional status of the church, it is noteworthy that believing in institutions is not mentioned in the NT. In its place is what might be described as (iv) believing in abstract belief-systems. The belief-system primarily in question, of course, is the set of beliefs that came to identify the followers of Christ after his resurrection.

Acts of believing under these categories exhibit a pattern of stage-wise development in the NT. To display this development, examples will be drawn from four stages: (a) the Gospels, (b) the book of Acts, (c) Paul's letters, and (d) letters of the later authors. In what follows, we shall examine occurrences (if any) of *pistieuō* under each of the four headings in each of the four stages, beginning with (i) believing that something is the case in the context (a) of the Gospels.

### 2.3.2

In Matt 9:28, Jesus asks two blind men seeking healing: "Do you believe that I am able to do this?" (*Pisteuete hoti dunamai touto poiēsai;*). When they answered affirmatively, Jesus touched their eyes and they were healed on the spot. In Mark 11:23, Jesus assures Peter that someone with "no doubt in his heart" (*mē diakrithē en tē kardia autou*) can move mountains on command if "he believes that what he says will come to pass" (*pisteuē hoti ho lalei ginetai*). (The Gospel record suggests that Peter did not respond but remained speechless.) In the passage before Mary's Magnificat in Luke, Elizabeth (bearing John the Baptist) proclaimed: "Blessed is she who believed that there would be a fulfillment of what was spoken to her by the Lord" (*makaria hē pisteusasa hoti estai teleiōsis tois lelalēmenois autē para kuriou*, 1:45). In John 11:26, Jesus asks Martha whether she believes that all who believe in him shall never die, to which Martha responds: "Yes, Lord; I believe that you are the Christ, the Son of God" (*Nai kurie, egō pepisteuka hoti su ei ho Christos ho huios tou theou*, 11:27). Grammatically and in content, these all are examples of (i) believing that.

As just indicated, John 11:26 provides an illustration of (ii) believing in persons; namely, with Jesus' query whether Martha believes that "all who believe in me shall never die" (*pas . . . pisteuōn eis eme ou mē pothanē*). Among numerous other examples provided in John is the interesting variant believing in Jesus' name. John 2:23 mentions that "many believed in his name" (*polloi episteusan eis to onoma autou*) when they saw the signs Jesus worked. And John 3:18 refers to those who are condemned because they "do not believe in the name of the only Son of God" (*mē pepisteuken eis to onoma tou monogenous huiou tou theou*). Turning to earlier Gospels, we find Jesus' warning in both Matt 18:6 and Mark 9:42 to a man who causes a little child "who believes in me" (*tōn pisteuontōn eis eme*) to sin. Both passages continue with Jesus' admonition that it would be better for such a man to drown at sea with a millstone around his neck. These appear to be the only instances in these two Gospels of believing in persons. The Gospel Luke contains none at all. Of roughly three dozen cases in the Gospels of believing in persons, most by far occur in the Gospel John.

Belief in information sources (iii) is sparsely represented in the Gospels, and typically is expressed without use of a preposition (use of *en* in Mark 1:15 is an exception). In Matt 21:32, the information source is John the Baptist. Whereas tax collectors and prostitutes believed John's message, the Jewish authorities whom Jesus is addressing did not afterwards change their minds and come "to believe him" (*pisteusai autō*). John's message is alluded to in Mark 1:15, where Jesus proclaims "the kingdom of God is at hand, repent and believe in the gospel" (*ēngiken hē basileia tou theou˙ metanoeite kai pisteuete en tō euangeliō*). The words of Gabriel are featured in Luke 1:20, where the archangel deprives Zechariah (John's father) of speech because the old man "did not believe his [my] words" (*ouk episteusas tois logois mou*) foretelling John's birth. The writings of Moses come to the fore in John 5:47, writings which Jesus tells the authorities concern Jesus himself. "If you do not believe his [Moses'] writings" (*ei de tois ekeinou grammasin ou pisteuete*), Jesus asks, "how can you believe the words that I am speaking?" (*pōs tois emois hrēmasin pisteusete*).

As might be expected, believing in abstract belief-systems (iv) is not represented in the Gospels. The set of beliefs that came to typify Christianity began to coalesce only after Christ's ascension. Over a dozen probable allusions to a Christian belief-system, however, can be found in the book of Acts.

*2.3.2.1*

Throughout Acts, by and large, reference to what Christians believe is expressed elliptically. A distinct exception appears in 13:12. The scene is set in 13:7–11, telling of Paul's encounter with a magician who was trying to steer proconsul Sergius Paulus away from "the faith" (*tēs pisteōs*, 13:8). With an incantation evoking "the hand of the Lord" (*cheir kuriou*, 13:11), Paul struck the magician blind. Thereupon, the proconsul believed (*episteusen*), because "he was astonished at the doctrine of the Lord" (*ekplēssomenos epi tē didachē tou kuriou*, 13:12). The doctrine that the proconsul came to believe was the set of teachings by which he subsequently would be identified as a Christian. This doctrine was the "word of the Lord" (*ton logon tou kuriou*), which the Gentiles in Acts 13:48 are said to believe (*episteusan*). What here is designated "the word of the Lord" is also referred to as "the word of the gospel" (*ton logon tou euangeliou*) in Acts 15:7.

To (iv) believe in the teachings of Jesus is not the same as believing (ii) in Jesus himself, and is obviously different from believing (iii) in Jesus as an information source. The passages cited above refer to belief in the word of the Lord explicitly. There are numerous other passages in Acts where believing in sense (iv) is clearly intended, but is expressed in truncated form as simply "believing." The book's first example of elliptical reference is in 2:44, which reports that "all who believed were together and had all things in common" (*pantes de hoi pisteuontes ēsan epi to auto kai eichon hapanta koina*). As with most other examples in Acts, reference here is to a group of believers who have banded together for a common purpose. An exception regarding belief of an individual apart from a group is found in 8:13, which reports that "Simon himself believed" (*ho de Simōn . . . autos episteusen*), and after being baptized continued with Philip on his journey.

Contention among believers, indicated in 15:5–11, is said to have been incited by "some believers who belonged to the sect of the Pharisees" (*tines tōn apo tēs aireseōs tōn Pharisaiōn pepisteukotes*, 15:5). The issue was whether Gentiles had to be circumcised to join the faith. In arguing that they did not, (Simon) Peter avowed that God had chosen him as messenger from whose mouth "the Gentiles should hear the word of the gospel and believe" (*akousai ta ethnē ton logon tou euangeliou kai pisteusai*, 15:7). Supported by James, Paul, and Barnabas, Peter eventually prevailed. Other passages in Acts with references to Christian believers include 4:4, 32; 5:14; 13:39, 48; 14:1; 18:27; 19:2; 21:20, 25.

Senses of believing other than (iv) are less frequently mentioned in Acts. Believing that something is the case (i) is clearly indicated in 9:26, which reports the disciples' lack of belief (*pisteuontes*) regarding Saul (Paul) "that he was a disciple" (*hoti estin mathētēs*). Several passages concern believing in persons (ii), almost always in Jesus Christ. A dramatic example comes in the midst of Paul's address to the Jewish crowd in chapter 22, in which he tells of his encounter with (the voice of) Jesus on the roads to Damascus, of the consequences of this encounter, and of his subsequent baptism by Ananias. Paul also tells of a trance in which the Lord advised him to leave Jerusalem, and of his contrite response that he had imprisoned and beat "those who believed in you" (*tous pisteuontas epi se*, 22:19). According to Paul's report (22:21), the Lord told Paul to leave promptly on his mission to convert the Gentiles.

Another dramatic example (within an implausible time frame) concerns Paul's reaction when an earthquake opened the doors of the prison in which he was incarcerated with Silas. When the doors sprang opened, instead of escaping, Paul reassured the jailer, preached the word of the Lord to him, and went with him to his house to baptize his family and to have a late-night meal. As Paul recounts, the jailer "rejoiced with his entire household that he had believed in God" (*ēgalliasato panoikei pepisteukōs tō theō*, 16:34). The event-packed night ended with Paul dutifully returning to prison. Other passages in Acts concerning belief in the Lord include 9:42; 10:43; 14:23; 18:8.

Regarding believing in sources (iii), Acts provides only a handful of cases. Acts 8:12 reports that people in Samaria "believed Philip" (*episteusan tō Philippō*) when he preached the good news about God's kingdom, thereby drawing attention away from the magic worker Simon. And in one of his run-ins with Roman authorities, Paul tells procurator Festus about a question he had addressed to King Agrippa: "King Agrippa, do you believe the prophets? I know that you believe" (*pisteueis, basileu 'Agrippa, tois prophētais; oida hoti pisteueis*, 26:27; see also 24:14).

In upshot, the Book of Acts is concerned mostly with believing in sense (iv), which is belief in Christian doctrine, and less with believing in the other three senses.

### 2.3.2.2

Paul as author occasionally employs locutions signifying believing (i) that something is the case. In Rom 6:8, for example, he encourages his audience with the words: "Now if we have died with Christ, we believe that we will also live with him" (*ei de apethanomen sun Christō, pisteuomen hoti kai suzēsomen autō*). Other examples are found in 1 Cor 11:18 and 1 Thess 4:14.

There are many more references in Paul's letters to believing (ii) in God or in Christ. Of some interest, perhaps, is that Romans includes six references to believing in God, but none to believing in Christ. In 4:24, for instance, Paul promises favor to those "who believe in him who raised Jesus our Lord from the dead" (*tois pisteuousin epi ton egeiranta 'Iēsoun ton kurion hēmōn ek nekrōn*; see also 4:3, 5, 17; 10:14). In the remaining letters of Paul, on the other hand, there are six references to believing in Christ but none to believing in God. Galatians 2:16, for instance, reminds its audience: "we have believed in Christ Jesus, in order to be justified by faith in Christ and not by works of the law" (*hēmeis eis Christon 'Iēsoun episteusamen, hina dikaiōthōmen ek pisteōs Christou kai ouk ex ergōn nomou*; see also Eph 1:13; Phil 1:29; 1 Tim 1:16; 2 Tim 1:12).

Paul provides several references to believing (iii) in sources of information. Included among these sources are "the gospel" (*tō euangeliō*, Rom 10:16), God (*tō theō*, Gal 3:6), and (more frequently) the teaching or testimony of Paul himself. An instance of the latter is found in 1 Cor 15:2, where Paul expresses hope that the Corinthians are being saved "by the word I preached to you" (*logō euēngelisamēn humin*), assuming "it was not believed in vain" (*mē eikē episteusate*; see also 1 Cor 15:11; 2 Thess 1:10).

More numerous by far are references to believing (iv) in the abstract belief system by which Christianity was coming to be known. This is the belief-system referred to as "the doctrine of the Lord" (Greek above) in Acts 13:12. Paul presumably has this in mind when he says in Rom 1:16: "For I am not ashamed of the gospel, for it is the power of God for salvation for everyone who believes" (*Ou gar epaischunomai to euangelion, dunamis gar theou estin eis sōtērian panti tō pisteuonti*). In 1 Cor 1:21, a falsely-modest Paul brags a bit in saying: "it pleased God through the foolishness of what we preach to save those who believe" (*eudokēsen ho theos dia tēs mōrias tou kērugmatos sōsai tous pisteuontas*). In 1 Thess 2:13, for another example, Paul smugly describes his testimony as the "word of God, which is at work in you who believe" (*logon theou, hos kai energeitai en humin tois pisteuousin*). Other passages regarding believing in sense (iv) include Rom 3:22; 4:11; 10:4; 13:11; 15:13; 1 Cor 3:5; 2 Cor 4:13; Eph 1:19; 1 Thess 1:7; 2:10.

### 2.3.2.3

There are approximately one and one-half dozen occurrences of the verb *pisteuō* in the later letters of the NT. They occur at a frequency of less than one-half per standard page, compared with more than one per page for Acts and Paul's letters. These figures gain interest in contrast with frequencies of the noun *pistis*, to which we turn presently. The noun occurs about one and one-half times per page in the later letters, compared with only one-half per page in Acts. It appears that the authors of the later letters were more interested in the Christian faith generally than in what individual Christians happened to believe.

Of the several occurrences of the verb in the later letters, some pertain to believing in sense (i). First John 5:5, for example, affirms that the world can be overcome only by one "who believes that Jesus is the Son of God" (*ho pisteuōn hoti 'Iēsous estin ho huios tou theou*; see also Heb 11:6; Jas 2:19). Others pertain to believing in sense (ii). The person believed is either God (under various descriptions) or his Son. An example of the first occurs in Jas 2:23, harking back to the fact that "Abraham believed God" (*Episteusen de 'Abraam tō theō*) and hence "was called a friend of God" (*philos theou eklēthē*; see also 1 Pet 2:6, 7; 1 John 4:16; 5:13). An example of believing in the Son occurs in 1 Pet 1:8, commending its audience for "believing in Christ even though you do not now see him" (*eis hon [Christou] arti mē horōvtes pisteuontes*; see also 1 John 5:10; Jude 5).

A probable case of believing (iii) in sources is offered by 1 John 4:1, containing advice "not to believe every spirit" (*mē panti pneumati pisteuete*) since many false prophets are found in the world. Believing in sense (iv) most likely is intended in Heb 4:3, which refers to "the rest" (*tēn katapausin*) mentioned in Ps 95:11. In the passage from Hebrews, the author assures his audience that "we who have believed enter that rest" (*eis [tēn] katapausin hoi pisteusantes*).

### 2.3.2.4

By way of overview, the NT contains roughly five dozen occurrences of the verb *pisteuō* that can be classified with confidence under the four categories: (i) believing that something is the case, (ii) believing in persons, (iii) believing in sources of information, and (iv) believing in the complex set of beliefs with which early Christianity came to be identified. It is apropos at this point to compare tallies from the four sections into which the NT was divided for the preceding analysis. The four sections, again, are (a) the Gospels, (b) the book of Acts, (c) Paul's letters, and (d) letters following Paul's in the standard canon.

To be compared are frequencies of occurrence per unit length of each sense of *pisteuō* for each of the four sections involved. For example, the Gospels combined are 102 pages long (relative to other lengths in my copy of the NT), and contain 47 occurrences of *pisteuō* in sense (i). Accordingly, there are roughly 0.46 occurrences per page of *pisteuō* (i) in the Gospels overall.

The Gospels's 0.46 per page is much larger than the corresponding figures for the other sections of the NT concerned, each of which is close to 0.1. This might be expected, inasmuch as the Gospels are more concerned than the other portions with what happened and when in Jesus' earthly life. To believe in sense (i) is to take a stand on factual matters, and the authors of the Gospels were obviously concerned with making their stands known on the facts of Jesus' personal life.

With 55 occurrences of (ii) believing in persons, the Gospels score 0.55 per page under this category. This is roughly double the scores of the other three portions, which are 0.23 for Acts, 0.2 for Paul's letters, and 0.22 for the later letters. Again, this is not surprising, given the concern of the Gospel writers to make the commitment inspired by interaction with Jesus a matter of public record. The great innovation of the Gospel writers was to replace commitment to the punitive God of the OT with commitment to the NT God who loved the world enough to give his only begotten Son for its salvation. In the words of Matt 5:16, the preoccupation of the Gospels writers is with the light they want "to let shine before men" (*lampsatō . . . emprosthen tōn anthrōpōn*), inspiring others with "the good works" (*ta kala erga*) that accompany it. This goes a long way toward explaining the dominance of the Gospels in their reference to believing (ii) in persons.

The NT contains roughly two dozen occurrences of *pisteuō* in the sense (iii) of believing in sources. These are distributed to yield scores of 0.1 or less for each of the four portions of the NT. Regarding sense (iii), there is nothing distinctive about any of the four portions under consideration. Nor is there any reason to think there should be.

Regarding sense (iv) of believing in the doctrinal system of Christianity, the score for Acts of 0.47 occurrences per page is double that of 0.23 for Paul's letters. The later letters in turn score only 0.02. What is distinctive under this category is that no occurrences at all appear in the Gospels. This is predictable on the (probable) grounds that formulation of the Christian belief-system did not begin until sometime after Christ's tenure on earth. It was noted previously that nomenclature for this belief-system is introduced in Acts. Among terms there introduced are "doctrine of the Lord" (13:12), "the word of the Lord" (13:48), and "the word of the gospel" (15:7). The fact that Acts has the highest ratio of occurrence per page in sense (iv) reinforces the likelihood that the Christian belief-system began to take shape during the period covered by this book.

Acts' score of 0.47 in category (iv) not only is highest among the four portions under consideration; it also is highest within the four categories for the book Acts itself. Next highest is 0.23 for category (ii) of believing in persons, followed by 0.1 each for (i) believing that something is the case and (iii) believing in information sources. This further enhances the conjecture that consolidation of the Christian belief-system was an implicit accompaniment of the activities reported in the book of Acts.

## 2.4 Faith in the New Testament

Despite the affinity in spelling between *pisteuō* (the verb, to believe) and *pistis* (the noun, faith), the meanings they carry in the NT are essentially disparate. English versions of the NT seldom translate the verb as "to have faith in"; and *pistis* is never properly translated "belief." In point of fact, there is no term properly translated "belief" in the vocabulary of the NT.

Given this disparity in meaning, there is no neat correspondence between the senses of *pisteuō* distinguished above and senses of *pistis* to be examined below. There is no use of the noun in the NT inviting a translation like "faith that such-and-such is the case." Likewise, there are no occurrences of *pistis* meaning faith in information sources. Accordingly, there are no analogues to *pisteuō* in senses (i) and (iii) above that are relevant to the examination that follows.

Cases of having faith in persons, however, occur frequently in the NT. Sense (ii) of *pisteuō* thus carries over as a relevant analogue. There also is a very important sense of *pistis* analogous to (iv) believing in abstract belief-systems. The abstract system in which Christians believe is often referred to directly as "the Christian faith." For following purposes, the *pistis* version of category (iv) will play a major role. In the forthcoming discussion, the noun *pistis* in sense (iv) will be used to designate the Christian faith specifically.

In the preceding study of the verb *pisteuō*, the NT was divided into four sections: (a) the Gospels, (b) Acts, (c) Paul's letters, and (d) letters after those of Paul. The same divisions will be used in the following study of the noun *pistis*. We proceed with an examination of (ii) faith in persons and of (iv) faith in the Christian belief-system in each of these four sections.


2.4.1


Of 244 occurrences of *pistis* in the NT, only twenty-four are found in the Gospels. The Gospels also contain six occurrences of the noun *oligopistos*, which means "lack of faith." In each of these (combined) thirty occurrences, the faith in question is a mental or spiritual state. Having faith is akin to being confident, in that both are states or stances a person occupies rather than something a person does. As already observed, by contrast, believing is something a person does. "To believe" *(pisteuō)* is an active verb, designating an action (the act of belief) taken toward one or another object. The noun "faith" *(pistis)*, on the other hand, does not designate an action. It rather designates a passive stance directed toward a person or other object of faith. Most references to faith in the Gospels pertain to a stance taken either toward God or toward Jesus Christ. The remaining pertain to a general stance of acceptance with no indication of a specific object toward which that faith is directed.

An example of faith (ii) in God is found in Mark 11:22. An earlier verse in Mark (11:14) depicts Jesus putting a curse on a barren fig tree. A day or so later, Peter pointed out to Jesus that the affected tree had already withered. Jesus answered; "Have faith in God" (*Echete pistin theou*, 11:22), adding that someone "without doubt in his heart" (*mē diakrithē en tē kardia autou*, 11:23) could successfully command a mountain to be thrown into the sea. Lack of faith in God is the topic of Luke 12:28, where Jesus admonishes the disciples, saying "O you of little faith" (*oligopistoi*), for not trusting God to supply their needs, as he does for the lilies and the grass in the field.

Faith (ii) in Jesus is illustrated in Matt 8:8, where Jesus responds to the centurion's request for the healing of his servant. When Jesus offers to heal him person-to-person (8:7), the centurion replies (using words to be repeated countless millions of times over the centuries) "Lord, I am not worthy to have you come under my roof, but only say the word and my servant will be healed" (*Kurie, ouk eimi hikanos hina mou hupo tēn stegēn eiselthēs, alla monon eipe logō, kai iathēsetai ho pais mou*). Hearing this response, Jesus turned to the crowd, saying "nowhere in Israel have I found such faith" (*oudeni tosautēn pistin en tō 'Israēl heuron*, 8:10; see also Luke 7:9).

Another illustration is in Mark 2:1–5, which tells of a paralytic being lowered through the roof of the room where Jesus was preaching. When "Jesus saw the faith" (*idōn ho 'Iēsous tēn pistin*) of those lowering the afflicted man, he said to the man: "Son, your sins are forgiven" (*Teknon, aphientai sou hai hamartiai*, 2:5), followed by "rise, pick up your bed, and return home" (*egeire aron ton krabatton sou kai hupage eis ton oikon sou*, 2:11; see also Matt 9:2–7; Luke 5:18–25). In Luke 22:32, for yet another example, Jesus tells Simon Peter: "I have prayed for you that your faith may not fail" (*egō de edeēthēn peri sou hina mē eklipē hē pistis sou*), so that Peter might strengthen the other disciples with his renewed faith in Jesus.

Most of the remaining occurrences of *pistis* in the Gospels (none occur in John) pertain to faith not directed toward specific persons. Almost without exception, however, such faith is mentioned in words spoken by Jesus himself. An example is found in Matt 17:20, where Jesus explains why the disciples were unable to cure the boy with epilepsy. His explanation is "Because of your little faith" (*Dia tēn oligopistian humōn*). Jesus goes on in the same verse to say (parabolically) that if they had "faith like a mustard seed" (*echēte pistin hōs kokkon sinapeōs*) they would be able to move mountains. Another "mustard seed" instance is recorded in Luke 17:5–6, where some unnamed apostles beseech Jesus: "Increase our faith" (*Prosthes hemin pistin*). Jesus responds (again parabolically): "If you had faith like a mustard seed" (*Ei echete pistin hōs kokkon sinapeōs*), you could command a mulberry tree to be transplanted in the sea. Jesus then adds "and it would obey you" (*kai hupēkousen an humin*).

Taken together, the twenty-four cases involving *pistis* in the Gospels have in common the status either of faith directed toward a divine person or faith urged upon the disciples by Jesus himself. As such, they correspond closely to cases of *pisteuō* in sense (ii) of believing in persons. There are no cases of *pistis* in the Gospels corresponding to sense (i) of believing that something is the case, or to sense (iii) of believing in sources of information. Most notably, there are no cases corresponding to sense (iv) of believing in the abstract belief-system of Christianity. The belief-system soon to be known as the Christian faith had yet to take shape during the time of Jesus' life recorded in the Gospels.

2.4.2

The noun *pistis* occurs only sixteen times in Acts. Of these, four designate faith (ii) in Jesus Christ. In 20:21, for example, Paul testifies to the church of Ephesus regarding "faith in our Lord Jesus" (*pistin eis ton kurion hēmōn 'Iēsoun*; see also 24:24; 26:18). A variant under this category regards faith in Jesus' name. Thus 3:16, where Peter, after berating his audience for killing the one "God raised from the dead" (*ho theos ēgeiren ek nekrōn*, 3:15), calls attention to the lame man who had been healed "by faith in his name" (*epi tē pistei tou onomatos autou*).

Acts contains five references to *pistis* in sense (iv) of the Christian belief-system (noted above as missing from the Gospels). Some occur in chapter 6, regarding a rapid increase in number of disciples. A substantial contribution to this increase came with the conversion of many priests in Jerusalem. As recorded in 6:7, "a great many of the priests became obedient to the faith" (*polus te ochlos tōn hiereōn hupēkouon tē pistei*). Then, in chapter 13, we hear of the encounter between Paul and the magician Bar-Jesus, in behalf of the proconsul Sergius Paulus. By striking Bar-Jesus blind, Paul saved the proconsul from "perverting the faith" (*diastrepsai . . . tēs pisteōs*, 13:8). The expression *tē pistei* (with article) in these passages refers to the belief-system to which the priests were converted. Other locutions in Acts referring to this belief-system, noted previously, are "the doctrine of the Lord" (13:12, Greek above), "the word of the Lord" (13:48, Greek above), and "the word of the gospel" (15:7, Greek above).

The faith designated "the doctrine of the Lord," or "the word of the Lord," is manifested in individuals who participate in it. Stephen (the first martyr) is described in 6:5 as "a man full of faith" (*andra plērēs pisteōs*). Stephen's faith was an individual case of the faith in which he participated. Also "full of faith" (*plērēs . . . pisteōs*, 11:24) was Barnabas, who vouched for Paul before the disciples after Paul's conversion (9:26–27). In the same vein, there is the achievement of Paul himself wherein he "opened the door of faith to the Gentiles" (*ēnoixen tois ethnesin thuran pisteōs*), as recorded in 14:27.

Contrary to the general disparity between believing and having faith, faith in sense (iv) is also expressed in terms of believing. The passages reporting the proconsul incident end by noting that the proconsul believed (*episteusen*, 13:12) as cited above. In another previously cited example, Peter came to believe (*episteusan*, 8:12) in the good news (*euangelizomenō*) preached by Philip, whereupon he joined Philip in his mission to Samaria.

### 2.4.3

Viewed statistically, Paul's letters are appreciably more preoccupied with faith than are other sections of the NT. Whereas there is roughly one occurrence per page of the noun *pistis* in the NT overall, there are nearly two per page in the letters of Paul. This contrasts with about one-quarter per page for the Gospels and one-half per page for Acts. Among Paul's letters, moreover, the one addressed to the Romans contains roughly three and one-third occurrences per page in itself. Given our immediate purpose of analyzing use of *pistis* in Paul's letters, Romans seems a good place to start.

Faith in sense (ii) is mentioned in Rom 3:22, where Paul avers that the righteousness of God is brought to bear "through faith in Jesus Christ for all who believe" (*dia pisteōs 'Iēsou Christou eis pantas tous pisteuontas*). This probably is the faith alluded to in 3:25 as well, where Paul speaks of the reception by faith (*dia tēs pisteōs*) of God's sacrifice of his Son. These are the only references in Romans to faith in sense (ii).

Faith (iv) in the abstract belief-system of Christianity is mentioned in Rom 1:8 and 10:8. In 1:8, Paul thanks God in behalf of the Romans "because your faith is proclaimed through all the world" (*hoti hē pistis humōn katangelletai en holō tō kosmō*). And in 10:8, he joins his audience in identifying "the word of faith that we proclaim" (*to hrēma tēs pisteōs ho kērussomen*) as the word that is near you, "in your mouth and in your heart" (*en tō stomati sou kai en tē kardia sou*, quoting Deut 30:14).

There is a clear distinction between Christian faith (iv) per se and the collaborative faith of those who participate in it. The latter is illustrated in 1:12, where Paul speaks of his faith in conjunction with the faith of his brothers (*adelphoi*, 1:13) in Rome. Paul here expresses his hope that they may be comforted together "by each other's faith, both yours and mine" (*en humin dia tēs en allēlois pisteōs humōn te kai emou*). Another illustration appears in 10:17, where Paul asserts that "faith comes from hearing, and hearing through the word of Christ" (*hē pistis ex akoēs, hē de akoē dia hrēmatos Christou*).

The faith of individuals such as Paul belongs in a category by itself. Let us refer to it as faith in sense (v). A distinctive feature of individual faith (v) is that, unlike faith of a group (iv), it is subject to increase and diminution. In Rom 4:19, Abraham is said "not to weaken in faith" (*mē asthenēsas tē pistei*) after being told that, despite his advanced age and the barrenness of Sarah, he would become "father of many nations" (*patera pollōn ethnōn*, 4:18). Romans 4:20 continues with the message that Abraham "instead grew strong in his faith and gave glory to God" (*all' enedunamōthē tē pistei, dous doxan tō theō*). Another example of varying degrees of faith (v) is found in 12:3–6. In 12:3, Paul advises the Romans to think soberly about their own worth, "each according to the measure of faith that God has apportioned" (*hekastō hōs ho theos emerisen metron pisteōs*). This advice is extended in 12:6, where he says they should use God's various gifts "in proportion to their faith" (*kata tēn analogian tēs pisteōs*), gifts such as prophecy, teaching, and exhortation.

Another notable feature of faith (v), as distinct from faith (iv), is its being the faith the salvific importance of which vies with that of law in the NT. Although hinted at in Acts, (13:39; 15:5), the quarrel comes to the surface in Paul's letter to the Romans. Paul's stance on the matter is stated in 3:28: "For we hold that one is justified by faith apart from works of the law" (*logizometha gar dikaiousthai pistei anthrōpon chōris ergōn nomou*).

In 4:13, he traces the origin of the dispute to a faulty interpretation of God's promise to Abraham. Paul's view is that this promise "did not come through the law but through righteousness produced by faith" (*Ou . . . dia nomou . . . alla dia dikaiosunēs pisteōs*). For if heirs to the kingdom are "adherents of the law" (*hoi ek nomou klēronomoi*, 4:14), "faith is null" (*kekenōtai hē pistis*) and God's promise is void. Moses laid down the law on Mount Sinai; and as the history of the Jewish people illustrates, "the law brings wrath" (*ho . . . nomos orgēn katergazetai*, 4:15). Needless to say, these are strong words for the traditional Jews in Paul's audience.

Paul's view of Mosaic law is equally harsh in 9:30–32. In his words, the "Israel that pursued the law [aimed at] righteousness did not achieve that law" (*'Israēl de diōkōn nomon dikaiosunēs eis nomon ouk ephthasen*, 9:31). The reason is "because they did not pursue it by faith, but as if it were based on works" (*hoti ouk ek pisteōs all' hōs ex ergon*, 9:32). Paul's verdict is that they "have stumbled over the stumbling stone" (*prosekopsan tō lithō tou proskommatos*, 9:32) mentioned in Isa 8:14–15. Understanding the "stumbling stone" as the law of Moses is reinforced in Acts 13:38–39 and 15:5. The former affirms that everyone who believes (*ho pisteuōn*) in Jesus is freed "from everything from which you could not be freed by the law of Moses" (*apo pantōn hōn ouk ēdunēthēte en nomō Mōüseōs*). The latter tells of the Pharisees who insisted that Gentile converts should be circumcised "to keep the law of Moses" (*tērein ton nomon Mōüseōs*).

As indicated in Rom 3:28, Paul ties the dispute between faith and works to the nature of justification. To repeat from above, Paul holds that "one is justified by faith apart from works of the law." The point is reiterated in 3:30, which says more specifically that God (being one, *heis*) "will justify the circumcised by faith and the uncircumcised through faith" (*hos dikaiōsei peri tomēn ek pisteōs kai akrobustian dia tēs pisteōs*). A further statement regarding the dispute comes in 4:13, saying that God's promise that Abraham's offspring would "be heir to the world" (*to klēronomon . . . einai kosmou*) did not come "through the law but through the righteousness of faith" (*Ou . . . dia nomou . . . alla dia dikaiosunēs pisteōs*).

God's grace becomes part of the controversy in Rom 5:1–2. "Not only have we been justified by faith" (*Dikaiōthentes oun ek pisteōs*), Paul says, "we also have gained access by faith into this grace in which we stand firm" (*tēn prosagōgēn eschēkamen (tē pistei) eis tēn charin tautēn en hē estēkamen*). Romans 6:14 and 11:5 are interesting in this regard, inasmuch as they seem to substitute grace for faith in its opposition to works. Regarding sins of the body, the former reads: "For sin will have no dominion over you, since you are not under law but under grace" (*hamartia gar humōn ou kurieusei˙ ou gar este hupo nomon alla hupo charin*). Romans 11:5, in turn, is immediately preceded by Paul's allusion to the seven thousand faithful men of 1 Kings (1 Kgs) 19:18, saying that a remnant of this group "has been chosen by grace" (*kat' eklogēn charitos gegonen*). Paul then adds (11:6): "But if it is by grace, it is no longer on the basis of works; otherwise grace would not be grace" (*ei de chariti, ouketi ex ergōn, epei hē charis ouketi ginetai charis*).

Faith is opposed to works of OT law in Rom 4:13 and 9:32. In Rom 6:14 and 11:6, the opposition is between works and grace instead. An obvious question in this regard is that of the relation between faith and grace. Is grace a precursor of faith, making faith itself a gift of grace? Or is grace a gift that God might bestow on his faithful, making faith a precursor of grace? There is ample grist here for potentially endless theological debate. Paul's letter to the Romans raises the question, yet does not provide a definitive answer. Romans 5:1–2, nonetheless, seems to support the view that faith comes first. As translated above, 5:1 affirms that Paul and his audience are justified by faith, followed by an affirmation in 5:2 that their faith has provided access to grace. There is nothing to gainsay this in the other letters written by Paul.

### 2.4.3.1

Paul's other letters contain approximately two uses of *pistis* per page, distributed more or less evenly from 1 Corinthians to Philemon. More than a dozen of these pertain to faith in sense (ii), in contrast with the two such occurrence in Romans. A majority of these uses mention faith (ii) in Jesus Christ. Early in his message to the Ephesians, for example, Paul tells them: "I have heard of your faith in the Lord Jesus" (*kagō akousas tēn kath' humas pistin en tō kuriō 'Iēsou*, 1:15; see also Gal 3:22, 26; Col 1:4; 2:5). Less frequently mentioned is faith (ii) in God (instead of Jesus), as in Col 2:12 and 1 Thess 1:8.

Apart from a few that are difficult to classify, the remaining occurrences of *pistis* in Paul's letters are more or less evenly split between use in sense (iv) and use in sense (v). By way of reminder, faith in sense (iv) is the Christian faith, understood as an abstract set of essential beliefs, while faith in sense (v) is participation in (acceptance of) that set of beliefs by individual believers. Faith (iv) is the object toward which the personal state of faith (v) is directed, whereas faith (iv) itself is impersonal and without a proper object.

A few examples of each are in order, beginning with faith (iv). In 1 Cor 16:13, Paul urges his audience: "Be watchful, stand fast in the faith" (*Grēgoreite, stēkete en tē pistei*). In 2 Cor 13:5, he advises: "Examine yourselves, [to see] whether you are in the faith" (*Heautous peirazete ei este en tē pistei*). In his letter to the Ephesians, he urges its recipients to persevere "until we all attain to the unity of the faith and to knowledge of the Son of God" (*mechri katantēsōmen hoi pantes eis tēn enotēta tēs pisteōs kai tēs epignōseōs tou huiou tou theou*, 4:13). And in his first letter to Timothy, Paul describes him as "being trained in the words of the faith and of the good doctrine that you have followed" (*entrephomenos tois logos tēs pisteōs kai tēs kalēs didaskalias hē parēkolouthēkas*, 4:6). In each of these cases, the term *pistis* is preceded by a definite article, making "the faith" a natural translation.

Faith (v) is a personal attitude directed toward a specific object. In the following cases, it is directed toward the Christian faith (iv). One such occurs at 2 Cor 1:24, in the apology of Paul and Timothy for their appearing overly concerned with the faith of the recipients. As Paul puts it: "Not that we [want to] lord it over your faith" (*ouch hoti kurieuomen humōn tēs pisteōs*), but we work with you joyously "because you stand firm in that faith" (*tē gar pistei estēkate*). In his first letter to the Thessalonians, for another example, Paul says he sent Timothy "to confirm you and to exhort you in your faith" (*eis to stērixai humas kai parakalesai huper tēs pisteōs humōn*, 3:2). And in greeting the Thessalonians for a second time, he compliments the recipients by saying: "your faith is growing abundantly" (*huperauxanei hē pistis humōn*, 1:3). As is typical with *pistis* in sense (v), the noun is modified by a personal pronoun (thus *hē pistis* at 1:3). Whereas the belief-system which is faith (iv) does not "belong" to particular believers, the faith of individual Thessalonians is theirs specifically.

2.4.3.2

While Acts contains occasional references to Christian faith in sense (iv), Paul's letters contain more the three dozen such references. Some of these are discussed above. Beyond these, Paul has a good deal to say about what he considers to be mandates associated with that faith. Indeed, Paul's letters are a primary source of that faith's content in the NT. The gospels, of course, contribute as well. Nonetheless, as far as Christian faith (iv) is concerned, we rely heavily on Paul's letters for information about what that faith entails.

As present day readers of his letters commonly realize, however, Paul was an author preoccupied with various personal issues. He also was a man with biases and personal obsessions. These factors influence both the subject-matter and the rhetoric of his letters. As a consequence, it is not always easy to distinguish between advice regarding the de facto behavior of his recipients and advocacy of doctrines that belong to an enduring Christian faith. An example of the former appears in 1 Cor 16:1–3, In which Paul insists that the Corinthians put money aside each week to be delivered "to the saints" (*eis tous hagious*, 16:1) in Jerusalem with whom he was currently concerned. An example of the second is the statement of the second great commandment and its ramifications in Rom 13:8, where Paul urges that the Romans "love each another, for the one who loves another has fulfilled the law" (*allēlous agapan· ho gar agapōn ton heteron nomon peplērōken*).

Notable among Paul's biases was his disrespect for women. A striking illustration is his analogy in 1 Cor 11:3, insisting that "the head of a wife is her husband" (*kephalē de gunaikos ho anēr*), just as the head of every man is Christ. Another instance is his pompous dictate at 1 Cor 14:34 that "women should keep silent in the churches" (*hai gunaikes en tais ekklēsiais sigatōsan*). This because they "are not permitted to speak, but should be [kept] in obedience" (*ou gar epitrepetai autais lalein, alla hupotassesthōsan*). For this particular prohibition, he claims the backing of Gen 3:16, where God says to Eve "your husband shall rule over you" (*ton andra sou . . . autos sou kurieusei*). A similar prohibition is imposed in 1 Tim 2:11, where women are instructed to "learn silently in all submissiveness" (*en hēsuchia manthanetō en pasē hupotagē*). Paul continues in the next verse, saying: "I do not permit a woman to teach or to exercise authority over a man" (*didaskein de gunaiki ouk epitrepō oude authentein andros*). It is not known today whether Paul was ever married. First Corinthians 7:8 suggests he may have been a widower. In any case, it appears that his experience with women inclined him to distrust them.

Paul also was uncomfortable with sexuality itself. First Corinthians 7:9 and 1 Thess 4:4–5 both recommend resisting passion with self-control. Advising the single men and women to which it is addressed, the first passage says that "if they cannot exercise self-control, they should marry. For it is better to marry than to burn [with passion]" (*ei de ouk enkrateuontai, gamēsatōsan, kreitton gar estin gamēsai ē prousthai*). In rank order, this passage indicates that burning with passion is morally worst, that marital sex is better, but that control of passion (without succumbing to it) is best of all. Paul's advice to the Thessalonians, in turn, urges "that each one of you know how to possess [to control] his own vessel [body]" (*eidenai hekaston humōn to heautou skeuos ktasthai*, 4:4), not giving in to "the passion of lust" (*mē en pathei epithumias*, 4:5). Once again, self-control should make exercise of sexuality unnecessary, with no mention in this case of the marital alternative.

Paul apparently considered both marital sex and abstinence to be morally acceptable. His main preoccupation with sexuality in 1 Cor is with behavior that is unjust (*adikoi*) and unworthy of "the kingdom of God" (*theou basileian*, 6:9). Included among people given to culpable behavior of this sort are fornicators (*pornoi*), adulterers (*moichoi*), effeminate males (*malakoi*), and sodomites (*arsenokoi*, 6:9). Another list of "dishonorable passions" (*pathē atimias*) is given in Rom 1:26–27. This list includes women engaged in relations "contrary to nature" (*tēn para phusin*), men "inflamed with passion for one another" (*exekauthēsan en tē orexei autōn eis allēlous*), otherwise described as "men committing shameful acts with men" (*arsenes en arsesin tēn aschēmosunēn katergazomenoi*). Paul's condemnation of homosexuality had precedent in the OT. Leviticus 18:22 depicts God proclaiming "you shall not lie with a male as with a woman; it is an abomination" (*kai meta arsenos ou koimēthēsē koitēn gunaikeian, bdelugma gar estin*; repeated at Lev 20:13).

In 2 Cor 12:7, Paul avers that he has been given a "thorn in the flesh" (*skolops tē sarki*) to keep him from becoming conceited because of "the surpassing greatness of the revelation" (*tē huperbolē tōn apokalupseōn*) to which he bears witness. Although the nature of that "thorn" probably will never be known, commentators never tire of making educated guesses. A plausible guess is that it has something to do with sexuality. His harsh condemnation of homosexuality in the passages above can be interpreted to two ways. Either he is using strong language to chastise a proclivity of his own; or else he is condemning an "abomination" practiced among his audience, by which he is not burdened himself. The vehemence of his condemnation of homosexuality seems to favor the former alternative, making it likely that Paul himself was homosexual. Being unmarried (as we know from 1 Cor 7:9), however, he would have been unable to quench a "fire of passion" by marital intercourse. Homosexual or not, Paul's thorn may well have been a sexual appetite he could not satisfy by morally acceptable means.

## 2.4.4

In retrospect, we should realize that the mandates and instructions dictated in Paul's letters were not automatically incorporated into the emerging Christian faith (iv). Presumably it was never a matter of faith (iv), for instance, that women should not speak in church. And men who dress in soft clothing (*malakoi,* mentioned in morally neutral terms at Matt 11:8 and Luke 7:25) are not excluded from the fold as a matter of course. On the other hand, there are mandates articulated in Paul's letters that undoubtedly were central to the Christian faith in its formative years. An obvious example is the second great commandment, featured in Rom 13:8 and 1 Thess 3:12. The centrality of this commandment is affirmed by several passages in the Gospels (Matt 22:39; Mark 12:31; John 13:34; 15:12), where Christ himself expresses it as a mandate for his followers to obey.

Other doctrines in Paul's letters that are central to the faith concern Christ's death and resurrection. In 1 Cor 15:3, Paul affirms that "Christ died for our sins in accord with the scriptures" (*Christos apethanen huper tōn hamartiōn hēmōn kata tas graphas*). Then in 1 Thess he attests that "we believe that Jesus died and rose again" (*pisteuomen hoti 'Iēsous apethanen kai anestē,* 4:14). Christ's death is authenticated as a central doctrine by its prominent mention in Matt 27:46; Luke 23:33; John 19:30. The centrality of Christ's resurrection, in like fashion, is authenticated in Matt 28:6; Mark 16:6; Luke 24:6; John 20:9.

Although certain doctrines, such as Christ's death and resurrection and the two great commandments, were central to the Christian faith from the beginning, others were added more gradually. There is evidence that first generation Christians were actively involved in this process. According to Acts 16:6–10, the Holy Spirit was involved as well. Having been forbidden by the Holy Spirit (*hagiou pneumatos*) from "speaking the word" (*lalēsai ton logon,* 16:6) in Phrygia, Galatia, and Bithynia, a vision came in Paul's dreams urging him and his companions to go help out in Macedonia. Obediently, they went to Macedonia to "preach the gospel" (*euangelisasthai,* 16:10) there. As a result of this evangelizing, it may be assumed, the developing faith of the Macedonians took more determinate shape.

More concrete evidence that the early Christians contributed actively to the development of their faith is found in Acts 19:18. When Paul was in Ephesus, he performed extraordinary acts of healing, and became known to all who lived there. Spurred by Paul's presence, "many who had believed" (*polloi te tōn pepisteukotōn*) gathered together, "confessing [their faith]" (*exomologoumenoi*) and "divulging their practices" (*anangellontes tas praxeis autōn*). Reading *praxeis* here as "practices" (rather than "deeds") stresses things they do regularly in practicing their faith, instead of things they might do on this or that occasion. The people involved in this meeting were practicing Christians. And the purpose of the meeting was to inform each other of their practices. In doing so, it may be presumed, they hoped to consolidate these practices and to make them more uniform. Emerging from NT times, nonetheless, the character of Christian faith (iv) remained in flux.


2.4.5

Hebrews 11:1 contains an explicit definition of *pistis* (faith). According to this definition, faith is "the assurance of things hoped for, the conviction of things not seen" (*elpizomenōn hupostasis, pragmatōn elenchos ou blepomenōn*). The term *elenchos* in the second clause is often translated "evidence," but this is misleading. The only other time *elenchos* is used in the NT is at 2 Tim 3:16, where it is usually translated "reproof" or "rebuke." What Paul considered rebuke can scarcely count as evidence for things unseen.

Conviction here is a mental or spiritual state. This state might result from relevant evidence; but the state and what causes it are quite distinct. The state of *elenchos* in the second clause matches the state of *hupostasis* (assurance) in the clause preceding. Inasmuch as we often hope for things not immediately present to sight, there is a match as well between the condition of not being seen in the second clause and the condition of being hoped for in the first. The parallel grammar of the two clauses invites reading them as parallel in content as well. Comparing the terminology of the two clauses is a step toward discerning the significance of this elusive definition.

Like the noun *elenchos* (conviction) in the second clause, the noun *hupostasis* (assurance) in the first occurs only rarely in the NT. The only other occurrence in which *hupostasis* carries unmistakably the same sense is in Heb 3:14, which reads: "for we have come to share in Christ, if indeed we hold our original assurance firm to the end" (*metochoi gar tou Christou gegonamen, eanper tēn archēn tēs hupostaseōs mechri telous bebaian kataschōmen*). In phrasing 11:1, the author of Hebrews employed these two nouns in senses that are distinctly idiosyncratic. This prevents the meaning of the definition from being initially self-evident.

The verb *elpizomenōn* (hoped for) in the first clause also carries an unusual meaning. In most of its two dozen or so NT uses, *elpizō* means something close to trust in persons or states of affairs (e.g., its meaning in "Moses, in whom you trust," *Mōusēs, eis hon humeis ēlpikate*, at John 5:45). Generally speaking, things you trust are not things you hope for (one does not "hope for" Moses). There is one other NT passage, however, in which the term carries the same sense as at Heb 11:1. Having observed in Rom 8:24 that no one "hopes for what he sees" (*blepei tis elpizei*), Paul instructs his audience: "if we hope for what we do not see, we wait for it with patience" (*ei de ho ou blepomen elpizomen, di' hupomonēs apekdechometha*, 8:25).

Romans 8:25 has obvious ties with Heb 11:1, not only in their shared sense of the verb *elpizō* but also in their shared pairing of things hoped for with things not seen. There of course are many references in the NT to things not seen. An example of immediate relevance appears at 2 Cor 4:18, where Paul states that (as Christians) "we look not to the things that are seen but to the things that are unseen" (*mē skopountōn hēmōn ta blepomena alla ta mē blepomena*). He then continues: "for the things that are seen are temporal, but the things that are unseen are eternal" (*ta gar blepomena proskaira, ta de mē blepomena aiōnia*). Although expressed in different terms, this extends the reference of the second clause of Heb 11:1 from the temporal to the timeless. Faith is conviction regarding things not seen, which is to say things not temporal but rather eternal.

A probable illustration of such conviction is the often-cited "doubting Thomas" episode in John 20:24–29. Upon hearing from the other disciples that they had seen the Lord, Thomas said he would not believe unless he saw for himself. Appearing in his presence eight days later, the risen Jesus told Thomas to look at his hands and to feel his side, then bade him: "be not faithless but believing" (*mē ginou apistos alla pistos*, 20:27). Without touching or feeling, Thomas said "My Lord and my God" (*Ho kuriois mou kai ho theos mou*, 20:28). Jesus responded: "Have you believed because you have seen me? Blessed are those who have not seen but have believed" (*Hoti eōrakas mē pepisteukas; makarioi hoi mē idontes kai pisteusantes*, 20:29). Those who believe without seeing would exemplify the faith defined as conviction of things not seen in Heb 11:1.

But what kind of faith is this? The unseeing believers of John 20:29 do not exemplify faith (iv) in the sense of a belief-system. This because the Christian belief-system was not established until after Christ's ascension, and the doubting-Thomas episode occurred before that event. For the same reason, they do not exemplify faith (v) in the sense of participating in that belief-system. At first glance, it may seem they exemplify faith (ii) in the risen Jesus himself. But the faith defined in Heb 11:1 constitutes assurance of things hoped for. And since he was standing in Thomas' presence, Jesus could not have been something hoped for, either by Thomas or by subsequent unseeing believers.

Uncertainty about the nature of the faith in Heb 11:1 is compounded by the examples that follow. Cited as paragons of faith are numerous OT characters (Abel, Abraham, Moses, et al.) and groups of people (nameless prophets, those who safely crossed the Red Sea) who accomplished what they were known for by faith. Sarah, for instance, though barren, "by faith, received power to conceive seed, when she was past age" (*Pistei . . . dunamin eis katabolēn spermatos elaben kai para kairon hēlikias*, 11:11). When Jericho fell, for another example, "By faith, Rahab the prostitute did not perish with those who were disobedient" (*Pistei Hraab hē pornē ou sunapōleto tois apeithēsasin*, 11:31). In Sarah's case, however, it seems unlikely that she consciously hoped for fertility before receiving it. And Rahab's being spared surely was not something she did not see. As far as Abel, Abraham, and Moses are concerned, they are described in 11:13 as having "all died in faith, not having received the things promised, but having seen and greeted them from afar" (*Kata pistin apethanon houtoi pantes, mē labontes tas epangelias alla porrōthen autas idontes kai aspasamenoi*). Mention of their having seen these promised things actually contradicts the definition of faith as directed toward things unseen.

Viewed overall, the eleventh chapter of Hebrews is problematic in several respects. For one, the definition of faith in 11:1 is formulated in terms that are idiosyncratic and difficult to understand. For another, the twenty or so examples occupying the rest of the chapter are mostly at odds with the definition they purport to illustrate. This list suggests that the author viewed major events in the OT generally as enabled by faith, presumably faith in the OT God. Other anomalies follow in this regard.

Chapter 11 of Hebrews contains more occurrences of *pistis* by far than any other chapter in the NT. A further incongruity of this chapter is that none among these many occurrences pertains to faith in Jesus Christ, which is central to other books of the NT. The audience of Hebrews presumably consists of Jewish converts to Christianity. But the milieu that provides context for the book overall is less evocative of their Christian present than of their Jewish past.

Although chapter 11 of Hebrews contains an explicit definition of *pistis*, along with many putative illustrations, the definition is problematic in several respects. It is difficult to discern its exact meaning. And it is followed by examples at odds with the definition itself. Hebrews 11:1 contributes less than often thought to our understanding of faith in the NT.

## 2.4.6

Let us summarize this section on faith in the NT. Use of the noun *pistis* (faith) has been examined against the background of a previous survey of the verb *pisteuō* (to believe). Four senses of the verb were previously identified: (i) believing that something is the case, (ii) believing in persons, (iii) believing in information sources, and (iv) believing in the abstract Christian belief-system. Relevant uses of the verb in these senses were examined in four specific contexts: (a) the Gospels, (b) Acts, (c) Paul's letters, and (d) subsequent letters in the NT.

Uses of the verb exhibited a stage-wise development in this sequence of contexts. Of the four senses in question, all but sense (iv) are present in the Gospels. Inasmuch as the Christian belief-system did not begin to take shape until the period covered by Acts, this might well have been anticipated. In Acts, all four senses are represented, with sense (iv) most dominant. This accords with the primary topic of Acts, which is deeds done under inspiration of the emerging belief-system. Paul's letters are concerned primarily with believing (iv) in this emerging system. Paul not only contributed substantially to the development of that system, but also provided a terminology for referring to it specifically. Among such terms are "the gospel," "the word of God," and "the doctrine of the Lord." While all four senses are represented in the later letters, sense (ii) seems to dominate in these writings. This may be due to a common concern with believing in Christ, accompanied by a lack of homogeneity regarding other concerns.

It was noted that there is no term in the NT corresponding to the English noun "belief." Despite its morphological overlap with *pisteuō*,

English translations almost invariably render *pistis* as "faith." Regarding the relation between faith and believing, the former occasionally but not always is a concomitant of the latter. There is no use of the noun in the NT inviting the translation "faith that such and such is the case," and none signifying faith in information sources. This eliminates correlatives of believing (i) and believing (iii) from further consideration. In addition to the remaining faith (ii) and faith (iv), there is a further faith (v) that plays a central role in the NT. Faith (v) is a personal participation in the Christian belief-system, which is to say a personal acceptance of what Paul termed "the doctrine of the Lord." Elimination of forms of faith correlative to believing (i) and believing (iii) left uses of faith (ii), faith (iv), and faith (v) to be traced in their development through the NT. Development of each was traced through (a) the Gospels, (b) the book of Acts, (c) Paul's letters, and (d) the letters after Paul's.

As with the verb *pisteuō*, these uses of *pistis* were found to exhibit a stage-wise development. Faith (ii) in both Jesus and God is amply illustrated in the Gospels. Since the Christian belief-system had yet to emerge, however, there are no examples there of faith (iv) or faith (v). It was noted, as a matter of curiosity, that the noun *pistis* does not appear in the Gospel John. The noun *pistis* also appears infrequently in Acts, although senses (ii), (iv), and (v) are all represented. Acts provides the first NT context in which faith (iv) is referred to explicitly.

Preoccupation with matters of faith came to a peak in Paul's letter to the Romans. This letter contains more than three occurrences of the noun *pistis* per page, in contrast with roughly one per page for the NT overall. Faith (ii) and faith (iv) figure clearly in Romans, but its emphasis is on the faith (v) of those who participate in the belief-system faith (iv). Romans anticipates the controversy between faith and works that figures prominently in Galatians and James. For Paul, the conflict is between the faith (v) of NT Christians and the works called for by the Mosaic laws of the OT. Paul's other letters contain an average of about two uses per page. All three senses are present in these other letters, but senses (iv) and (v) predominate. Paul's letters overall are a major source of the content of faith (iv), details of which are considered briefly above.

Among the later letters, Hebrews has most to say about the nature of faith, but what it has to say is problematic. Its primary contribution is an explicit definition of faith as "the assurance of things hoped for, the conviction of things not seen." After a detailed examination of this definition, and of the examples offered by way of illustration, it was concluded that the faith in question does not fall under the any of the standard senses (ii), (iv), or (v). Although these standard senses are all found in the books following Hebrews, no further clarification of faith is found in these later letters.

## 2.5 Reason in the New Testament

While both truth (*alētheia*) and faith (*pistis*) are discussed at length in the NT, little is said there about either the nature of or the use of reason. The standard term for reason in the Greek of that period is the noun logos. Although this term occurs more than three hundred times in the N'I, and covers almost a dozen different senses, it is never used there to designate the faculty of reason as such. There is one occasion, however, when verbs for reasoning figure in the narrative. Mark 11:27–33 and Luke 20:1–7 tell of the time when chief priests, scribes, and elders of the temple in Jerusalem "reasoned among themselves" (*dielogizonto pros heautous* in Mark 11:31, *sunelogisanto pros heautous* in Luke 20:5) about how to respond to Jesus' trick question whether John's baptism was backed by heavenly or human authority. The decision they reached, on grounds of prudence, was to say simply that they did not know.

Apart from this single exception, the topic of reason is not a factor in the discourse of the NT. Reason does not become a factor in the developing Christian story until theologians enter the scene a century or two later. The daunting task faced by theology when this happens is to give a rational account of a story with an origin to which reason was not a contributing factor.

CHAPTER 3

# St. Augustine and the Platonic Tradition

## 3.1 Theology before Augustine

JOHN PAUL II's *FIDES et Ratio* opens with the affirmation that faith and reason enable the human spirit to achieve contemplation of truth. For a credible reading of this affirmation, the key concepts of truth, faith, and reason must be understood as endowed with specific theological meanings. A primary purpose of the present essay is to trace the development of these concepts, beginning with the NT and proceeding through salient stages in the evolution of western Christianity. After the NT, the major stages of development to be examined are those dominated by St. Augustine and Neoplatonism, those dominated by St. Thomas Aquinas and Scholastic Aristotelianism, and those typified by the Transcendental Thomists (Joseph Maréchal, Karl Rahner, and Bernard Lonergan) around the turn of the last century. We proceed now to consider the concepts of truth, faith, and reason in the context dominated by Augustine and Neoplatonism.

St. Augustine (AD 354–430) was preceded by a new breed of theologians, represented primarily by Tertullian and Origen, and by participants in the First Ecumenical Council of Nicaea (325). He emerged as a prominent Christian author with the completion of the *Confessions* in 400, shortly after the First Council of Constantinople (381). Augustine's philosophic views were heavily influenced by the Neoplatonists Plotinus and Porphyry.

Augustine's theological antecedents were marked by a radical departure from the NT. Whereas reason had no major role in the discourse of the NT, it was employed with apparent abandon by the newly-fledged theologians. Origen's *On First Principles* contains a section entitled "On Rational Natures" in which the author claims that "logical reasoning" (*ratio intelligi*, 1.5.3) will compel (*coget*) admission that the Prince of Darkness was doomed to fall by his very nature. Origen also relied on so-called "reason" to prove that God created the souls of all intelligent beings before he created the material universe, and that these souls subsequently fell away from God and were relegated to physical bodies. Using reason to address the same topic, but arriving at quite different conclusions, Tertullian previously had concluded that individual souls are created on the occasion of being born (*De Anima* xxvii), and that they are capable of escaping the bondage of Satan by voluntarily calling on God (*De anima* xii).

As suggested by existing fragments, there was no attempt by either author to explain what it is about reason that endows it with such extraordinary powers. The authors of the NT had little need for rational inference in their mission of spreading the gospel, whereas these early theologians treated reason as a potent instrument for disclosing divine truths. In their application of this instrument, they engaged in reasoning that is hard to comprehend.

Regarding the topic of truth itself, however, nothing distinctive emerges from scholarship on their existing works. Both Tertullian and Origen wrote in Greek, but none of the former's Greek works survive. Although several Latin titles by Tertullian are still available for study, scholarship on these works has not focused on what they have to say about truth. The same may be said regarding their treatment of faith. In light of the common view among Tertullian scholars that his views were often unorthodox, it may be that faith was not among his primary concerns.

The orthodoxy of Origen has also been questioned, but for reasons of hermeneutics rather than content. A skilled rhetorician, Origen interpreted certain key passages of the Bible as figurative rather than literal. He viewed the Garden of Eden sequence, for example, as an allegory with spiritual rather than historical significance. He interpreted the refining fire of Mal 3:2–3 and 1 Cor 3:13, for another example, not as actual fire but as the inner anguish of realizing one's sinful state. Although Origin's interpretive principles have ramifications for the truths to which faithful Christians subscribe, his surviving works share with those of Tertullian an apparent lack of concern with the nature either of Christian truth or of Christian faith.

Whereas the theologians are noteworthy for their seemingly unbridled confidence in what Origen calls "logical reasoning," nothing is said about reason in the reports of the early councils. The terminology of truth, moreover, appears only in the expression "true God from true God" (*theon alēthinon ex theou alēthinou; deum verum ex deo vero*), which is found in both the Greek and the Latin versions of the Nicene creed. As previously explained, *alētheia* here means "real" rather than "truth" as it pertains to propositions. The Son who comes from the Father is really God and the Father is really God as well. Apart from this, documents from the councils provide no insight into the concepts of truth and reason that were inherited by Augustine of Hippo.

The NT terminology of faith (*pistis*), on the other hand, was retained essentially unchanged in the reports of these councils. The NT distinction between the noun *pistis* and the verb *pisteuō* (to believe) is maintained in the report from Nicaea. The verb introduces the creed in question, namely: "We believe in one God the Father all powerful" (*Pisteuomen eis hena Theon patera pantokratora*), the Latin version of which is *Credimus in unum deum patrem omnipotentem*. This expression from the Nicaean creed is repeated verbatim at the beginning of the report from the subsequent First Council of Constantinople.

The verb also figures in the letter from the bishops of Constantinople to the bishops of Rome. Referring to the creed, the former remark to the latter that it tells how "to believe in the name of the Father and of the Son and of the Holy Spirit" (*pisteuein eis to onoma tou patros kai tou huiou kai tou hagiou pneumatos, credere in nomine Patris, et Filii, et Spiritus Sancti*). Immediately following in this letter is the claim that the creed supports "our believing . . . that the Father, the Son and the Holy Spirit have a single Godhead and power and substance" (*theotētos kai dunameōs kai ousias mias tou patros kai tou huiou kai tou hagiou pneumatos pisteuomenēs; Divinitatem, et virtutem, atque substantiam unam Patris, et Filii, et Spiritus sancti credimus*) comprising "three perfect persons" (*trisi teleiotatais prosōpois; tribus perfectis personis*). These occurrences exhaust the use of *pisteuō* in the reports of these two councils.

As far as the noun *pistis* (faith) is concerned, the document from Constantinople is more revealing than the one from Nicaea. The only use of *pistis* in the latter comes in Canon 11, which allows that "those of the faithful" (*hoi pistoi*) who transgress and genuinely repent should be shown mercy and eventually be readmitted to the fold. In the Latin version, *fideles* replaces the Greek *hoi pistoi*.

Regarding the more extensive use of *pistis* in the report from Constantinople, a feature of particular interest is the retention of the two uniquely Christian senses of faith initiated in the NT. One sense, it may be recalled, is that of faith as the abstract belief-system in which individual Christians participate. An example occurs in the letter to the Roman bishops from their counterparts in Constantinople. In a gesture of good will, the latter invoke "the account of the faith agreed between us" (*tēs pisteōs sumphōnēthentos logou*; *verbo fidei concordante*). Another instance comes with the reference in canon 6 to those who endorse a "faith that is sound" (*tēn pistin . . . tēn hugiē/ sanam . . . fidem*). The other relevant sense of faith is the participation of individual believers in this shared belief-system. In their letter to the bishops of Rome, the bishops of Constantinople allude to their "confessed faith" (*tēn pistin hōmologēsamen*; *fidem professi*) which they think their Roman counterparts will find heartening. Canon 6 then refers warily to those who claim "to confess" (*homologein*; *confiteri*) the sound faith in question but may have strayed from orthodoxy.

Before turning to the works of Augustine himself, let us summarize the treatments of truth, faith, and reason by the theologians and church councils that preceded him. Tertullian and Origin had little to say about either truth or faith, but exhibited a seemingly unbridled use of reason in their theological speculations. On the other hand, nothing is said about either truth or reason in the reports of the two Ecumenical Councils held during Augustine's lifetime. The terminology of faith developed in the NT, however, was preserved in the reports of both councils, albeit more prominently in the report from Constantinople. A salient fact in that regard is that the Constantinople report maintains the NT distinction between faith as an abstract belief-system and the faith of individual believers who participate in that system.

## 3.2 Truth in the *Confessions*

St. Augustine flourished as a Christian writer around the turn of the fourth century AD. Following his *Confessions* in 400, his *The City of God* appeared in 426. Of particular interest for present purposes is his *The Teacher* (*De Magistro*), written between 388 and 391. Other prominent works include *The Enchiridion on Faith, Hope, and Love* (c. 420), *On Christian Doctrine*

(397–426), and *On the Trinity* (400–416). In addressing Augustine's work, our concern will be limited to his views on the topics of truth, faith, and reason, as evident in the *Confessions* and *The Teacher* specifically. Little will be said about the general contents of these works, beyond what is necessary by way of context for these particular topics.

If Augustine's theological views were of primary interest, books such as *On Christian Doctrine* and *On the Trinity* would need to be consulted. Inasmuch as our present interest is limited to the specific topics of truth, faith, and reason, however, examining a larger sampling of Augustine's works would be superfluous. We begin with his use of the term *veritas* (truth) in the *Confessions*.

The *Confessions* is no less prolific in its deployment of the terminology of truth than the early theologians were in their application of so-called "reason." The nouns *veritas* and *vera* occur over 150 times, and cognate terms (e.g., the adjective *verax* and the adverb *veraciter*) occur over eighty times in addition. This adds up to almost one occurrence per page in the 249-page Latin text on my desk. The terminology of truth in the *Confessions* also conveys a variety of unmistakably different meanings. Some of these are generic (e.g., the truth of propositions), some were introduced in the NT (e.g., the truth that is Christian teaching), and some (such as God's own Truth) apparently were initiated by Augustine himself.

Propositional truth is clearly illustrated in section 42 of book XII, chapter xxxi (abbreviated XII.xxxi.42), where Augustine discusses alternative readings of a claim (unspecified) in Genesis attributed to Moses. Hesitant to "set down one true opinion on this matter" (*unam veram sententiam ad hoc apertius ponerem*) as his own, Augustine acknowledges that there might be several truths blended (*temperavit*) by God into the contents of the relevant passage. Pertaining to the same "diversity of true opinions" (*diversitate sententiarum verarum*) in an earlier passage (XII. xxx.41), he petitions "Truth itself [God] to beget concord" (*concordiam pariat ipsa veritas*) among them. No less than ten instances of propositional truth are listed in nearby XII.xix.28, where he affirms, for example, "it is true, O Lord, that you have made heaven and earth" (*Verum est enim, Domine, fecisse te caelum et terram*). Propositional truth appears to be involved as well in XII.xxi.30; XII.xxv.34; and XII.xxvii.37.

The spoken word can be true in ways distinct from that of the propositions it might be used to articulate. Discourse might be considered true if it occurs at the right time, in a suitable place, and under an appropriate set of circumstances. An example cited previously from the

NT is in Acts 26:25, where Paul responds to Festus's challenge by insisting that he is speaking "words of truth and good sense" (Greek above). A comparable instance is found in *Confessions* XI.iii.5, where Augustine specifies circumstances in which he can confidently say of Moses "You speak the truth" (*Verum dicis*). Another parallel between texts in this regard pertains to the Good News of the Gospel. In Gal 2:5, Paul alludes to the spoken words that constitute "the truth of the gospel" (Greek above); whereas Augustine, in *Confessions* VI.iii.4, tells of his beloved Ambrose "rightly dispersing the word of truth" (*verbum veritatis recte tractantem*) to those who listen. Other probable cases of circumstantially true discourse are found in *Confessions* X.xxiii.34; XII.xxx.41; and XIII.xxv.38.

Truth in the sense of what is taught by the Church is sometimes mentioned in the *Confessions*, albeit less frequently than in the NT letters of Paul. A paradigmatic case of the latter occurs in 1 Tim 3:15, where Paul refers to the Church as "the household of God" and as "a pillar and mainstay of truth" (Greek above). An obvious parallel occurs at *Confessions* V.x.19, where Augustine despairs of "finding the truth" (*inveniri verum*) which resides in God's Church. The Catholic Church is mentioned specifically in this regard in VII.v.7. "Fearing that I might die before I discovered the truth" (*de timore mortis et non inventa veritate*), Augustine says, he credits faith in Christ "as maintained in the Catholic Church" (*haerebat . . . in catholica Ecclesia*) with providing nourishment to sustain him in the quest. Another source of truth in this sense is mentioned in VI.v.8, namely the written Bible. Seeing that "we were too weak by unaided reason to find out the truth" (*cum essemus infirmi ad inveniendam liquida ratione veritatem),* Augustine acknowledges that "for this work we needed the authority of the holy Writings" (*ob hoc nobis opus esset auctoritate sanctarum Litterarum*).

We turn next to senses of truth that figure prominently in the *Confessions* but lack precedent in the NT. There are roughly two dozen passages in which Augustine speaks of Truth (capital "T") and God as identical. A few examples should suffice to make this sense apparent. Addressing the Lord in IV.v.10, Augustine makes the blanket request: "May I learn from you, who is Truth?" (*Possumne audire abs te, qui veritas es . . . ?*). In X.xli.66, he shows reverence for God in proclaiming: "You are the Truth, who presides over all things" (*Tu es veritas super omnia praesidens*). In XIII.xxix.44, the truth of scripture is explained in these words: "you truly are, and being Truth have produced it" (*tu verax et veritas edidisti eam*). A more effusive affirmation to this effect appears in III.vi.10, where Augustine praises the Lord saying that he "verily is the Truth" (*vere veritas est*) and characterizes him as "supremely good, beauty of all things beautiful" (*summe bone, pulchritudo pulchrorum omnium*). The paean culminates with "O Truth, Truth! How inwardly did the marrow of my soul pant after thee" (*O veritas, veritas, quam intime etiam tum medullae animi mei suspirabant tibi*). A small sampling of other passages equating Truth with God includes IV.xvi.31; X.xl.65; XII.xxv.35; and XIII.xxv.38.

There is a distinction between the Truth that is identical with God and a truth belonging to God. Regarding the latter, the truth is either a feature of God himself or something that God possesses. An analogous distinction is that between a good man and a man who owns a good home, a good car, or suchlike. While the difference between feature and possession is sometimes obscure in the *Confessions*, the two senses appear with approximately equal frequency in Augustine's text.

Addressing God in II.vi.13, Augustine speaks in praise of "your truth, bright and beautiful above all" (*prae cunctis formosa et luminosa veritas tua*). What is bright and beautiful here seems to be the truth that characterizes God, rather than something God possesses. Such is the case as well with the truth of God mentioned in VI.x.16, which Augustine recognizes as the source of good faith. Attesting to the existence of such faith, he says to God that "nothing could be void which proceeds from the mouth of your truth" (*nec ullo modo erit inane, quod tuae veritatis ore processit*). The truth that escapes voidance here must be a property of God the creator, not a truth he possesses. Another reference to truth as a property of God is found in XII.xxviii.38, where Augustine affirms that people "rejoice in the light of your [God's] truth" (*gaudent in luce veritatis tuae*) when they see the beautiful things that God has made. Other passages apparently referring to truth as a feature of God include IV.xv.26 and XI.xxx.40.

Truth as a possession of God, on the other hand, may be understood in light of Matt 22:21, where Jesus says "render to Caesar the things that are Caesar's, and to God the things that are God's" (*Apodote oun ta Kaisaros Kaisari kai ta tou theou tō theō*). One thing due God according to this instruction is to serve one another, after the fashion of 1 Pet 4:10, which reads: "as each has received a gift [from God], use it to serve each other" (*ekastos kathōs elaben charisma eis heautous auto diakonountes*). Obedience to the second great commandment is God's due, and in Matt 22:21, Jesus advises those listening to render God his due.

Possessions of God generally are things God has created, some of which have been placed at human disposal. One such is time, which is a major concern of Augustine in the *Confessions*. In the midst of his acute but burdensome musings on time (XI.xv.18), Augustine expresses his resignation to an inconclusive outcome in the words: "O my Lord, my light, even here might not your truth ridicule man?" (*Domine meus, lux mea, nonne et hic veritas tua deridebit hominem?*). The source of his discouragement is not a property of God, but rather one of God's creations, namely time. In XII.xxiii.32, for another example, Augustine discusses Moses and his testimony in scripture, remarking on the nourishment that comes with truly understanding it. Augustine numbers himself among beneficiaries of this testimony, asking God that he might "delight in you with those who feed on your truth" (*delecter cum eis in te, qui veritate tua pascuntur*). The nourishment in which he delights is not a feature of God, but rather God's word as expressed by Moses. In yet another example featuring nourishment at XIII.xxx.45, Augustine speaks of "tasting a drop of sweetness from your [God's] truth" (*elinxi stillam dulcedinis ex tua veritate*). What Augustine speaks of tasting here is not a characteristic of God, but instead the many manifest works of God (*opera tua*), including the orderly movement of heavenly bodies. Other passages mentioning truth in God's possession include II.v.10; X.xxxvi.59; and XIII.xx.27.

There are several passages in the *Confessions* alluding to a Truth that is immutable and eternal. A prime candidate for such is the Truth identical to God himself. The eternity of the Truth that is God is featured in VII.x.16, where Augustine refers to God as the Light "who made me" (*quia . . . fecit me*), and then proclaims that "someone who knows Truth knows that Light" (*Qui novit veritatem, novit eam*) and thus "knows eternity" (*novit aeternitatem*). It is by Love, he goes on to say, that this Light is known, a thought that prompts him to exclaim "O Eternal Truth, and true Love, and dear Eternity!" (*O aeterna veritas et vera caritas et cara aeternitas!*). The immutability of the Truth that is God is the focus of XII. xxv.35, where Augustine addresses those who agree with him regarding the preeminence of the "Light of the Lord our God" (*Domini Dei nostri luce*). Their agreement, he says, is not founded on the truth they speak to each other, but rather "on the unchangeable Truth itself, which is above our minds" (*in ipsa quae supra mentes nostras est incommutabili veritate*). Other passages that seem to allude to the eternity of the Truth that is God include VII.iii.4; XI.xxx.40; XII.xv.18; and XII.xxix.40.

There is a truth distinct from God himself that is characterized as eternal in XI.viii.10. This is the truth of the Christian belief-system, as articulated and taught in the Gospels. Also referred to as "your [God's] word" (*Verbum tuum*), the "Good News may be found in the Eternal Truth, where the good and only master teaches all his disciples" (*Evangelio . . . inveniretur in aeterna veritate, ubi omnes discipulos bonus et solus magister docet*). Other passages in which the Christian belief-system is characterized as either eternal or immutable truth include VII.xviii.24; XI.vi.8; and XIII.xx.27.

Beyond God himself, there are passages where the other two Persons of the Trinity are designated truth as well. In VII.xix.25, Christ is referred to as "a personification of truth" (*persona veritatis*). And in IX.iv.9, the Paraclete (*Paracletum*; i.e., the Holy Spirit) is designated "the Spirit of truth" (*spiritum veritatis*).

## 3.3 Faith and Belief in the *Confessions*

The vocabulary of faith in the *Confessions* includes the noun *fides*, which occurs approximately three dozen times, along with a few occurrences of the adjective *fidelis* (faithful) and the adverb *fideliter* (faithfully). As might be expected, there is no verb that would invite an aberrant translation like "to faith." A quite distinct vocabulary of belief is based on the verb *credere* (to believe). Although our primary interest in this section is with Augustine's understanding of faith, there are salient connections here between faith and belief that warrant attention to his vocabulary of belief as well.

It may be recalled that in the NT there is no noun corresponding to the verb *pisteuō* (to believe), and no verb corresponding to the noun *pistis* (faith). In Augustine's Latin, however, there are standard forms of the active verb *credere* that serve as nouns designating belief. Among such are the participle (*credens, credendi*, etc.), the gerund (*credendi, credendo*, etc.), and the infinitive (*credere*) itself. In each of these cases, the activity of the verb carries over to the object designated, meaning that the belief designated by these predicate nominatives lacks the static character of a typical mental state. By way of contrast, conviction and certitude, near synonyms of belief, are fixed rather than fluid in character.

Four distinct senses of believing are evident in the *Confessions*. Three standard senses include believing that something is the case, believing in persons, and believing in information sources. An example of the first is found in VII.iii.4, where Augustine reports that he needed to seek out the cause of evil to avoid attributing it to God and thereby "to believe that the immutable God is mutable" (*Deum inconmutabilem mutabilem credere*). The second is exemplified in I.xi.17, where Augustine attributes his "believing in Christ" (*in Christum crederem*) to his mother's piety, despite the fact that his father at the time "had not yet believed" (*nondum crediderat*). The third is illustrated in XII.x.10, with Augustine's simple declaration to God: "I have believed in your books, and their words are very deep" (*Credidi libris tuis, et verba eorum arcana valde*).

Although the senses of belief illustrated by these examples are quite ordinary, however, it may be noted that they all pertain to extraordinary topics. They all are spiritual in orientation, in a manner suggesting that the beliefs in question are endowed with a specifically religious significance. This significance is made apparent in VI.v.8, which begins with reference to Augustine's once sporadic believing (*credidi*) that God exists and cares for his people. Turning to the topic of the scriptures, he proceeds by acknowledging that "the authority of the sacred Writings" (*auctoritate sanctarum Litterarum*) bespeaks God's "desire to be believed in and thereby sought" (*tibi credi et per ipsam te quaeri voluisses*). God desires to be believed in, which constitutes a special instance of believing in persons. Even more, God desires that believing in him leads the believer to seek him.

Seeking something is tantamount to looking for it. But looking for something can be understood in two senses, depending on the consequences of finding it. Suppose someone (e.g., a comparison shopper) goes to a grocery store looking for radishes. Seeing some on the produce shelf, the person notes their availability and moves on to check other items. Alternatively, the person might be interested actually in buying radishes, rather than merely finding out whether the store has them in stock. In this latter case, the radishes are purchased and carried out of the store. Now owning them, the radishes are the person's own.

In VI.v.8, where Augustine depicts God as desiring to be sought, the sense is that God desires to be made the believer's own. Believing in God could amount to nothing more than acknowledging God's existence, analogous to noting that the store has radishes. The God who desires to be sought, however, wants to be "owned" by the believer. He wants to be made the believer's own.

This is the fourth sense of belief acknowledged by Augustine. To believe God in this sense is to accept God as one's own. This means accepting God as an integral part of one's own life. It means making God part of the configuration of factors that establishes a person's own self-identity.

### 3.3.1

In contrast with Augustine's multifold use of the verb *credere* in the *Confessions*, his use of the noun *fides* is limited to only two distinct senses. Both senses occur frequently in the NT, primarily in the book of Acts and in the letters of St. Paul. One is the faith constituted by the Christian belief-system. This sense is exemplified in IV.xvi.31, which anticipates the imagery of wings bearing the human spirit aloft in *Fides et Ratio*. Beseeching the Lord in behalf of the Lord's "little ones" (*parvulos*), Augustine asks that they "might safely become fledged in the nest of your Church, and might nourish the wings of charity by the food of a sound faith" (*in nido Ecclesiae tuae tuti plumescerent et alas caritatis alimento sanae fidei nutrirent*). In most of the dozen or so passages referring to faith in this sense, the noun *fides* is accompanied by a confidence-inspiring adjective. Sections V.x.20; VI.xi.18; and VII.xix.25 identify the faith as Catholic (*catholica fides*); V.xi.21 and VI.xi.19 call it Christian (*Christianae fides*); whereas VIII.ii.5 and VIII.vi.14 declare it true or right (*fidem veracem, fide recta*).

The other sense of faith in question is that of participation in the Christian belief-system. Put otherwise, it is the personal faith of a Christian believer. An example is given in the first section of the book, where Augustine proclaims "Lord, my faith calls on you" (*Invocat te, Domine, fides mea*). Personal faith can be either firm (*fide solida*; VI.xi.20) or flimsy (*infirmum . . . in fide*; VIII.xii.30). Firm or flimsy, faith in the second sense is a matter of taking part (participating) in certain beliefs.

The fact that there are two senses of faith in the *Confessions*, in contrast with four senses of belief, leaves open the possibility that Augustine thought of faith and belief as different mental postures. There are passages, nonetheless, in which he seems to treat them as equivalent. Section (XIII.xxi.29), for example, first denies that "faith caused by great miracles" (*nec magnalia mirabilium . . . quibus fiat fides*) is necessary for "entrance into the kingdom of heaven" (*intratur . . . in regnum caelorum*). But the section then continues with essentially the same point phrased in terms of belief: "for it [the living soul] is not such that it will not believe unless it has seen signs and miracles" (*neque enim nisi signa et prodigia viderit, non credit*). As far as this disclaimer is concerned, faith's independence from prodigious events is no different from the equivalent independence of belief.

Another passage that seems to equate faith and belief is VI.iv.6, in which Augustine addresses the unhealthy state of his soul. He admits to God initially that there is "no other way to be healed than by believing in" (*nisi credendo sanari non poterat*) "your truth" (*veritatem tuam*). Then he continues in the same sentence by describing this remedy as "the medicine of faith" (*medicamenta fidei*).

Perhaps needless to say, there are many passages in which Augustine mentions belief but not faith, and vice versa. But there are no other texts counter to the joint implication of XII.xxi.29 and VI.iv.6 that he conflates faith and belief. If he indeed did conflate them, which seems on balance to be correct, this is the first case we have encountered in the Christian tradition of a major figure who treats them as equivalent. Augustine's apparent conflation of faith and belief returns with a vengeance in later contexts, notably including John Paul II's encyclical *Fides et Ratio*.

## 3.4 Reason in the *Confessions*

Augustine's uses the term *ratio* (reason) in the *Confessions* both in a basic literal sense and in various extended senses that appear to be figurative. In its basic sense, *ratio* is a faculty possessed exclusively by embodied human beings. In VII.xvii.23, he designates it the "capacity of reason" (*ratiocinantem potentiam*) and describes it as the faculty "to which whatever is received from the senses of the body is referred to be judged" (*ad quam refertur iudicandum, quod sumitur a sensibus corporis*). Section X.vi.10 states that "animals great and small" (*Animalia pusilla et magna*) have bodily senses, but save in the case of humans the sense faculties involved are "not empowered with reason" (*Non . . . praeposita . . . ratio*). This precludes other animals from making rational judgments.

Given the characterization of VII.xvii.23, it follows that disembodied entities, which lack bodily sensation, cannot possess reason in this basic sense. When Augustine refers to "the rational and intellectual mind of your [God's] chaste city" (*mens rationalis et intellectualis castae civitatis tuae*) in XII.xv.20, accordingly, he must be using the term *rationalis* in a

figurative sense. A further indication here that this attribution of rationality to the "chaste city" is metaphorical is his description of the city as
"eternal in the heaven of heavens" (*aeterna in . . . caeli caelorum*). Since
eternal entities do not have bodies, they cannot possess reason in the
basic sense.

This must be the case as well with the "eternal reason" (*aeterna
ratione*) attributed to God in XI.viii.10. In the gospel (*Evangelio*) there
mentioned, to be sure, God speaks "through the flesh" (*per carnem*, presumably that of the evangelists), which Augustine describes as God's "re-
sounding outwardly in the ears of men" (*insonuit foris auribus hominum*).
Although the evangelists, being incarnate, might speak with the voice of
reason in its basic sense, the "eternal reason" attributed to God must be
reason in an extended sense. To be eternal is to exist outside of time; and
since bodies are essentially temporal, the attribution of reason to God in
XI.viii.10 must be figurative rather than literal. This is a counterintuitive
consequence of Augustine's definition of basic reason.

Reason in its basis sense is an effective instrument in mental en-
deavors. In XIII.xxiv.37, Augustine cites "the fruitfulness of reason" (*rationis fecunditatem*), describing it as "a power and faculty" (*facultatem
ac potestatem*) granted by God as an aid to understanding. Drawing on
his own experience for an example, Augustine credits "true reason" (*vera
ratio*, XII.vi.6) with persuading him to stop trying to understand God's
creation as proceeding from matter "conceived wholly without form"
(*prorsus informe cogitare*). Augustine appears to stumble, however, in
describing humankind's "powers of reason and understanding" (*rationis
et intellegentiae virtute*, XIII.xxxii.47) as an "image and likeness" (*imagi-
nem et similitudine*) of the corresponding powers of God. Regardless of
context, it is hard to conceive how reason in the basic sense could be an
image and likeness of the reason metaphorically attributed to God.

The context that brings this apparent anomaly into focus is a theory
Augustine devised about God's role in the reasoning process. This theory
is more fully developed in *The Teacher*, to which we turn shortly. Some
of its main features, however, are sketched in book IV of the *Confessions*.
While trying to understand "the nature of the mind" (*animi naturam*,
IV.xv.24), Augustine tells his reader, "the very power of truth forced itself
on my gaze" (*inruebat in oculos ipsa vis veri*). Things came together in
a kind of unity, in which he "conceived that wherein the rational soul
and the nature of truth and of the chief good consist" (*mens rationalis
et natura veritatis ac summi boni . . . esse videbatur*). As disclosed in *The*

*Teacher* (written before the *Confessions*), possession of these superlative qualities entails the active presence of God (or Christ) in the mind. Thus situated, God acts as a criterion by which reason can discern the truth. Given the benefits resulting from this discernment, God's active presence in this capacity is the "chief good" (summun . . . bonum) of man.

This account of God's role in the process of reasoning throws additional light on previously noted passage VI.v.8, in which Augustine attests that "we were too weak by unaided reason to find out the truth" (ess*emus infirmi ad inveniendam liquida ratione veritatem*). Beyond the faculty of reason itself, arriving at truth requires God being present in the mind as the criterion by which truth can be identified. This account also clarifies Augustine's admission to God in V.vi.10: "nor of truth is there any other teacher than you" (*nec quisquam praeter te alius doctor est veri*). The manner in which God teaches truth is not like that in which Augustine taught (his natural son) Adeodatus, but rather that of enabling the mind to identify truth by the light of his presence. This account of God's presence as an inner light in the mind is often referred to as Augustine's "theory of illumination."

According to this account, a mind is healthy to the extent that it willingly accedes to God's presence as a criterion of truth. "If the rational mind itself is depraved" (*si rationalis mens ipsa vitiosa est*, IV.xv.25), however, "errors and false opinions contaminate the life [in question]" (*errores et falsae opiniones vitam contaminant*). In Augustine's view, human reason generally is contaminated by original sin. Christ's death on the cross not only gained eternal life for his faithful; it also enabled their minds to participate in eternal truths revealed by the light of his interior presence.

Augustine's theory of Illumination itself throws light on his treatment of the concepts of truth, faith, and reason, the topics of primary interest in the present study. This theory is both described and illustrated in his carefully reasoned work entitled *De Magistro* (*The Teacher*). The main tenets of the theory itself will be identified, before we consider its relevance to these featured topics.

## 3.5 The Illumination Theory of *The Teacher*

*The Teacher* was written approximately a decade before the *Confessions*. It consists of a dialogue between Augustine and his natural son Adeodatus. The general topic of their discussion is what, if anything, can be learned directly from a teacher. A summary of Augustine's answer is that human teachers can provide an occasion for learning, but that God is the only teacher by whom true knowledge is imparted to man. Precedence for this view (as acknowledged in a later work *Retractiones*, I.xii) is Matt 23:10, saying "for you have one teacher, the Christ" (*hoti kathēgētēs humōn estin heis ho Christos*).

The main outlines of the illumination theory are laid out in a soliloquy by Augustine occupying the final four chapters of *The Teacher*. Premises of his argument, established earlier in the dialogue, are (1) that knowledge is a state in which the object known is directly present to the knowing mind; (2) that both names of things and things themselves can be known, but that knowledge of things is superior to knowledge of mere names; and (3) that learning is a process through which an object of knowledge becomes present to a knowing mind. As expositors of the theory generally recognize, there are parallels between this account and the so-called "theory of recollection" found in several of Plato's dialogues.

In point of fact, this similarity between the illumination theory and the theory of recollection is only a superficial aspect of the overlap between Augustine's views and dominant themes in the Platonic dialogues. Commentators on Augustine commonly stress his dependence of the Neoplatonist authors Plotinus and Porphyry. The illumination theory, however, shares more with Plato's dialogues than could likely have been filtered through the Neoplatonists. The extent to which Augustine had direct access to Plato's works is unclear. He did not read Greek; and only the *Timaeus* at the time had been translated into Latin. It is possible that the extensive overlap between his views and those of Plato was only coincidental. The points of overlap, nonetheless, are complex, and should be studied in separate stages.

3.5.1

Let us begin with a comparison of the illumination theory with Plato's theory of recollection. According to the theory of recollection, the human soul first gains knowledge of the timeless Forms while directly in their presence before incarnation. Upon birth, the soul is beset with a rush of distracting sensations, which eradicate the knowledge gained previously and replace it with a motley of false opinions. Learning constitutes a reinstatement of the Forms in the soul of the learner, which is accomplished by removing the false opinions that stand in its way. False opinion is removed by a process known as elenchus or refutation, applied by someone like Socrates (in the *Meno*) or the Eleatic Stranger (in the *Sophist*; see 242B). Recollection figures explicitly in the *Meno*, the *Phaedo*, and the *Phaedrus*, but is never pictured as resulting in a full return to knowledge.

Augustine's account is similar to Plato's in (1) portraying knowledge as direct apprehension of eternal objects, and (2) characterizing learning as gaining a state of knowledge aided by some form of human assistance. Illumination differs from recollection, however, in several substantial respects. One is that Plato's account, unlike Augustine's, is premised on a soul (or mind) that exists before being incorporated in a body. Another is that Augustine's account, unlike Plato's, features a divine agency (God, Jesus Christ) that works within the mind, guiding it in its pursuit of truth. Yet another is that Augustine attributes capacities to the soul beyond those involved in recollection. In particular, the individual mind can judge the truth of its contents with reference to an internal criterion. This internal guide to truth is comparable to Socrates's "divine sign" (*tou theou sēmeion, Apology* 40B) which steered him away from moral wrongdoing. Socrates's sign, however, was more an ethical guide than a guide to inner truth.

Moving beyond recollection as such, we find extensive parallels between Augustine's illumination theory and the account of the Good in the *Republic*. The latter account features an analogy between the Good in the realm of intelligible Forms and the sun in the realm of visible objects. Besides rendering objects visible by its light, the sun provides the energy by which visible objects on earth are brought into being. In similar fashion, the Good is responsible both for the intelligibility of the Forms and for their being Forms as such. Since knowledge for Plato is a direct apprehension of Forms, it follows that the Good is the source of knowledge as well. Inasmuch as the Good "gives truth to the objects of knowledge and enables the power of knowing them" (*tēn alētheian parechon tois gignōskomenois kai tō gignōskonti tēn dunamin apodidon*), Plato says in *Republic* 508E, "one must conceive it as being the cause of knowledge and of truth as far as known" (*aitian d' epistēmēs ousan kai alētheias, hōs gignōskomenēs men dianoou*).

What Plato says about the Good in the *Republic* is closely matched in *The Teacher* by its discourse on God. In XII.40, Augustine refers to God as "the inner light of truth" (*interiore luce veritatis*). In his role as inner light, God both sheds light on truth and is identical with the Truth that provides illumination. God is identified with Truth in VIII.21 with its reference to "God, that is Truth itself" (*Deo . . . id est ipsa veritate*), and again in XI.38 which refers to "the truth that presides inwardly over the mind itself" (*intus ipsi menti praesidentem . . . veritatem*). God's illumination of truth is illustrated by Augustine's observation in XII.40 that when Augustine conveys a truth to another person, that person is taught not by his words but by "things themselves made manifest when God displays them within" (*sed ipsis rebus, Deo intus pandente, manifestus*).

Parallel to the Good's role as the source of knowledge, God is responsible for the mind's ability to judge the veracity of putative truths presented to it. As Augustine puts it in XIV.45, when students "consider within themselves whether truths have been stated" (*utrum vera dicta sint . . . considerant*), they judge by "looking upon the accessible inner Truth" (*interiorem scilicet illam veritatem*) insofar as they are able. The inner Truth that is God serves as a criterion by which the authenticity of other truths can be established. Truth itself, that is to say, certifies the veracity of truths presented externally to a learner on the path to knowledge.

Augustine's account of God's inner presence as a criterion of truth takes its title from the inner light of XII.40 by which truth is revealed as genuine. Another striking parallel with Plato links Augustine's inner light with a similar image in Plato's Seventh Letter. Speaking of the knowledge (*eidenai*, 341C) at which philosophy aims, Plato says that, after a long period of preparation, knowledge "is generated suddenly in the soul, like a torchlight kindled by a leaping flame, and forthwith becomes self-sustaining" (*exaiphnēs, hoion apo puros pēdēsantos exaphthen phōs, en tē psuchē genomenon auto heauto ēdē trephei*, 341C-D). The onset of this leaping flame seems similar to the "onset of a trembling glance" (*ictu trepidantis aspectus, Confessions* VII.xvii.23) by which Augustine says invisible things "come to be understood" (*sunt intellecta*). (The term *ictu* actually is rendered "flash" in J. G. Pilkington's 1876 translation.)

More is said about preparing for Plato's luminous event in Seventh Letter 344A-B. In addition to a good memory and native intelligence, a candidate for illumination must have a natural (*sungeneis*) affinity with "justice and other such fine things" (*dikaiōn te kai tōn allōn hosa kala*). These traits are necessary for "understanding the truth about virtue" (*mathōsin alētheian aretēs*), which is preliminary to inquiry into "both falsehood and truth regarding being overall" (*to psuedos hama kai alēthes tēs holēs ousias*). This inquiry is conducted under tutelage of an expert in elenchus, which is described as "benevolent cross-examination by question and answer without ill-will" (*eumenesin elenchois elenchomena kai aneu phthonōn erōtēsesin*). Then, if all goes well, "wisdom and intelligence shine forth regarding the defining features of each object, which involves the utmost exertion of which mankind is capable" (*apokrisesin chrōmenōn, exelampse phronēsis peri hekaston kai nous, sunteinōn hoti malist' eis dunamin anthrōpinēn*).

As with Augustine's illumination theory, the truth-revealing light of the Seventh Letter comes from within. It is also self-generating, and thus independent of external causes. Yet another similarity is that, in both the Seventh Letter and in Augustine's theory, moral requirements must be met for illumination to take place. Augustine characterizes this prerequisite in terms of the will. In XI.38 he affirms that "the everlasting Wisdom" (*sempiterna Sapientia*) of God is available for "all rational souls to consult" (*omnis rationalis anima consulit*), but is disclosed to a given person only to the extent that "his bad or good will" (*sive malam sive bonam voluntatem*) enables it. In Plato's case, wisdom comes to a mind in accord with "virtue and other fine things" (Greek above).

## 3.6 Truth, Faith, and Reason in *The Teacher*

Several distinct senses of truth were identified in the NT. One (i) is that of standard propositional truth, which is a property propositions gain by affirming what is the case or denying what is not the case. Another (ii) pertains to discourse that is appropriate or timely. Words of truth in this sense are words that are right for the occasion at hand. A third sense (iii) is that of the truth found in the Bible or taught by the Church, a sense that became prominent in the letters of St. Paul.

Beyond these are senses of truth that figure prominently in the *Confessions*, but are not foreshadowed in the NT. Among such is (iv) truth as a property of God, along with other attributes such as wisdom and goodness. The most preeminent among these other senses, however, is (v) the Truth identified with God himself. The Truth that is God is characterized as unchangeable (*inconmutabilis*, XII.xxv.35) and eternal (*aeterna*, VII.x.16). Yet another truth characterized as eternal is (vi) the belief-system of Christianity taught in the Gospels. In *Confessions* XI.viii.10, for example, Augustine speaks of the Gospel (*Evangelio*) as an "eternal truth" (*aeterna veritate*).

Augustine's dialogue *The Teacher* contains several of these senses. Propositional truth (i) appears at IX.26. Augustine has been explaining some of his views on temperance to Adeodatus, after which he says "if these things are true, as you know they are" (*si haec vera sunt, sicuti esse cognoscis*), you will see that words are less valuable than what we use them for. The truth of the words in question is propositional truth. (In this dialogue throughout, the noun *vera* rather than *veritate* is used to designate propositional truth.) Propositional truth (i) also appears in XIII.41 and XIV.46.

Truth (v), which is God, is mentioned in VIII.21, where Augustine says he wants his son and himself to be led to eternal life by "God, that is Truth itself" (*Deo . . . id est ipsa veritate*). Although the Truth identical to God figures in the *Confessions*, a set of new roles is attributed to divine Truth in *The Teacher*. To serve in these roles, divine Truth has to be internalized within the mind of the individual person. Augustine refers to this as the "inner truth" (*interiorem . . . veritaem*) in XIV.45. This internalized Truth is different enough from truth (v) to be assigned a category of its own, namely truth (vi).

Another name for truth (vi) in *The Teacher* is the "inner light of Truth" (*interiore luce Veritatis*, XII.40). As this designation suggests, the inner light of XII.40 is light at the core of the illumination theory. Augustine's illumination theory is discussed at some length in the previous section. The several roles served by truth (vi) are those identified in this previous discussion. Let us return to this topic by way of elucidating truth (vi).

In the path toward understanding, Augustine says in XI.38, we consult "the Truth that presides inwardly over the mind" (Latin above) rather than tutors who instruct us verbally from outside. Nonetheless, the words of these tutors "might prompt us to consult" (*consulamus admoniti*) this inner Truth. Section XII.40 expands on this theme with reference to Augustine's own vocation as a tutor. When he "states truths" (*vera dicens*) to someone, Augustine says, the person looking on these truths is taught "not by my words (*non verbis meis*), but rather "by things made manifest within when God discloses them" (*ipsis rebus, Deo intus pandente, manifestis*).

Another role assigned to this inner Truth is that of criterion by which things stated in words by their tutors can be verified. When those who have been tutored "consider whether truths indeed have been stated" (*utrum vera dicta sint . . . considerant*), they do so "by looking upon the inner Truth according to their abilities" (*inrteriorem scilict illam veritatem pro viribus intuentes).* When they "inwardly discover that truths have been stated (*vera dicta esse intus invenerint*), "that is the point at which they learn" (*Tunc ergo discunt*). No other senses of truth we have been considering appear in *The Teacher.*

## 3.6.1

A notable truth about *The Teacher* is that the noun *fides* (faith) is used only three times, two of which have nothing to do with religious faith. In X.31, which is concerned generally with the distrust of reason, Augustine laments that when reason is suspect "confidence might be withheld" (*ne . . . fides habenda*) from plain truth itself. In this case, "confidence" seems to be a better translation of *fides* than "faith." A second instance occurs in XIII.44, where he talks about mistaking the term *fidem* (faith) for *pietatem* (piety) due to poor hearing. Here the meaning of the term *fidem* is irrelevant. The only case having to do with religious faith as such comes in XI.37. This is the case of the three boys (Ananias, Azarias, and Misael) who escaped the fire of King Nebuchadnezzar by exercising their "faith and religion" (*fide ac religione*). As readers of scripture, Augustine affirms, we accept (*accepimus*) this story by believing (*credimus*) it. This he claims to be in accord with the relevant part of Isa 7:9, which he translates *Nisi credideritis, non intelligetis* (Unless you believe, you will not understand; italicized in Latin).

## 3.6.2

There are roughly a dozen occurrence of the term *ratio* in *The Teacher.* On one hand, there are a few uses referring either to the faculty of reason or to its exercise. Section X.31 warns of "falling into hatred or distrust of reason" (*odium vel timorem rationis incidamus*). This pertains to the faculty, namely the ability to reason. In XII.39, the term pertains to the exercise of the faculty. This is the passage in which Augustine speaks of "consulting the inner Truth by means of reason" (*interiorem veritatem ratione consulimus*) regarding things that are understood.

On the other hand, there are several passages in which *ratio* refers to specific arguments, namely to results achieved by exercising the faculty for particular purposes. In V.15, for instance, Augustine presents an argument purportedly demonstrating that every part of speech signifies something. When Adeodatus demurs on the authority of unnamed objectors, Augustine asks him whether "the argument itself seems less adequate once the authorities are set aside" (*Minus enim idonea . . . idonea, remotis auctoritatibus, ipsa ratio*). Other passages in which *ratio* refers to particular arguments include VI.8; X.31; and XI.32.

## 3.7 Summary of Chapter

Augustine introduces several senses of truth beyond those found either in common discourse or in the NT. He appears to stumble, however, in improperly conflating faith and belief. His account of reason, furthermore, has untoward consequences for reason in the mind of God. More promising is his illumination theory, which approximates various views of Plato. Expanding on these points will yield a summary of what Augustine had to say about truth, faith, and reason, the primary topics of this study.

The term *veritas* occurs frequently in the *Confessions*, anticipating its extravagant use in John Paul II's *Fides et Ratio*. In addition to propositional truth, Augustine speaks of the truth taught by the Church and the truth constituted by the Catholic belief-system. These senses of truth are carried over from the NT. Augustine extends the concept to cover truth associated in various ways with God. Concerning truth associated with God, paramount is the Truth that is God, which is eternal and the source of truth in other forms. In addition, there is the truth possessed by God, the truth personified by Christ, the Spirit of Truth (the Paraclete), and the inner truth providing illumination.

In one form or another, several of these truths associated with God are passed on to St. Thomas. Although Aquinas does not adopt the truth of illumination for his own purposes, he is aware of its importance to Augustine. Whereas these several senses of divine Truth are delineated more or less clearly by Augustine, however, they lose their sharp boundaries by the time they reach John Paul II and his encyclical *Fides et Ratio*.

Augustine's apparent conflation of faith and belief was a mistake waiting to happen. The distinction between them was firmly established in the (koine) Greek of the NT. The noun *pistis* means "faith," and the verb *pisteuō* means "to believe." NT Greek has no verb to be translated "faithing," and no noun for "belief." In Augustine's Latin, however, there are no corresponding grammatical barriers between faith as a (inactive) mental state and the activity of believing. Latin grammar provides various verbal nouns, which have the force of designating objects. In the case of *credere* (to believe), one noun form is *credendum*, which can serve either as a participle or a gerund. By way of illustration, Augustine admits in VI.iv.6 that "by belief he might have been healed" (*sanari credendo poteram*) if his soul had been directed toward God's Truth. The term *credendo* here combines the action of the English "to believe" with the referential force of "belief."

With forms of *credere* functioning as nouns, there is no grammatical barrier to keep these nouns distinct from *fides* in its various forms. An additional conceptual hazard is imminent when faith and belief are assimilated. To believe is to engage in an activity. In the case of verbal nouns deriving from *credere*, the active force of believing carries over to the beliefs themselves which they designate. This is illustrated by the belief of VI.iv.6. The additional hazard is that when faith is assimilated with belief, faith itself assumes active powers. Faith by itself (apart from belief) is a passive state of the mind or soul. When assimilated with belief, however, it takes on active powers of its own, and becomes part of the causal order. This seems to have happened in VI.iv.6, where Augustine speaks of applying the "medicines of faith" (*medicamenta fidei*) to the maladies of the world at large.

Reason is characterized in the *Confessions* as a faculty based on bodily sensation VII.xvii.23. The soul receives representations of external objects through the senses, which representations are passed on to reason for judgment. If a given representation is judged to be accurate, it receives the status of being intelligence in the soul. According to this account, reason is a faculty of a soul endowed with sensation, which precludes its possession by entities without bodies. Reason attributed to eternal entities, such as the "rational mind" (*mens rationalis*, XII.xv.20) of Augustine's eternal City, thus must be figurative rather than literal.

A more serious consequence of Augustine's account of reason is that the "eternal reason" (*aeterna ratione*) attributed to God in XI.viii.10 must be figurative as well. Bodies with sensations are essentially temporal. And since what is eternal is not in time, reason cannot be attributed to God in a literal sense. This poses problems for Augustine's depiction in XIII. xxxii.47 of human rationality as an image (*imagine*) of "God's excellence of reason and intelligence" (*rationis et intelligentiae virtute*). The actual reason that distinguishes humans from other animals cannot credibly be thought of as an image of a reason that is only figurative.

As laid out in *The Teacher*, Augustine's illumination theory bears a surprisingly close resemblance to themes developed by Plato. The resemblance seems too close to be attributed solely to Augustine's reading of Neoplatonists such as Plotinus and Porphyry. Since Augustine did not read Greek, however, and since Latin translations of the Platonic corpus were not available until roughly a century after the *Confessions* was written, the close resemblance may have been coincidental. Nonetheless, the parallels between the illumination theory and Plato's Seventh Letter seem too close to be attributed to chance.

Particularly striking is the imagery shared by these two accounts. As Plato puts it in the Seventh Letter, knowledge, after a long period of preparation, "is generated suddenly in the soul, like a torchlight kindled by a leaping flame, and forthwith becomes self-sustaining" (Greek above). For Augustine, in turn, knowledge is authenticated by the inner Truth that is God. In both accounts, knowledge is internal to the soul. For both Augustine and Plato, moreover, there is a suddenness in the onset of knowledge. As Augustine puts it in VII.xvii.23 (Latin above), understanding arise with the "onset of a trembling glance." In the Seventh Letter, finally, once knowledge is kindled in the soul, it sustains itself in existence. Being divine, the inner Truth responsible for understanding in the illumination theory also is self-sustaining.

Whether these similarities are coincidental could be determined only by a study of Augustine's indebtedness to Proclus and Porphyry, which is beyond the scope of a project focused on truth, faith, and reason.

# CHAPTER 4

# St. Thomas and the Aristotelian Tradition

## 4.1 Life and Writings

THOMAS AQUINAS (1225–74) WAS born into a noble family. His father was the Count of Aquino, his mother the Countess of Teano. He was distantly related to Emperor Frederick II ("Frederick Barbarossa"). His family initially planned for him to become abbot of the famed Monte Casino, where he began to study at age five. At age ten, he was sent to study at the University of Naples. Ten years later, he went to the University of Paris to study with Albert the Great.

While at Naples, Thomas decided to join the Dominicans, a newly founded order dedicated to poverty and preaching. Since this was contrary to his family's plans, they locked him up in a tower with the intent of dissuading him. After more than a year in captivity, his brothers hired a prostitute "to bring him back to reality." As the story goes, he drove the woman away with a hot poker, and escaped through a window to join a group of Dominicans waiting below. The remainder of his life was spent preaching, teaching, and writing treatises.

During the roughly thirty years of life remaining, Thomas wrote at a rate of what we might count as ten to fifteen pages a day. In a typical writing session, he would dictate to several scribes simultaneously, speaking more rapidly than any one of them could write. Most of his works were clearly reasoned, and some were used as reference books by other theologians during his lifetime. According to some accounts, he could continue to dictate even when momentarily falling asleep. It might be surmised that certain less clearly written pieces were dictated under such conditions.

Aquinas' writings include the monumental *Summa Contra Gentiles* (1259–65) and *Summa Theologica* (1965–74), seven disputations on specific topics, and roughly two dozen commentaries. Longest by far is the (unfinished) *Summa Theologica*, which includes 614 Questions divided into 3,125 Articles, each several pages long. Prominent among the disputations are those on truth, on mind, on evil, on faith, and on charity. Among commentaries, in turn, are several on Aristotle, one each on Boethius, Pseudo-Dionysius, and Proclus, and a considerable number on various books of the Old and New Testaments. Prominent among the latter are several commentaries on the letters of St. Paul.

Regarding commentaries on Aristotle and biblical authors, it is noteworthy that Aquinas did not work with the original Greek. In the case of Aristotle in particular, he relied on the translation from Greek into Latin by William of Moerbeke, his rough contemporary. St. Thomas' language was Latin. He had a reputation for remaining silent when he was not dictating or lecturing. Idle conversation was not part of his agenda.

There was an occasion late in life when Aquinas apparently was in direct communication with God. According to an often-repeated account, Thomas was attending Mass on the feast day of St. Nicholas in 1273. During Mass, he had an experience that left him in ecstasy. A Brother Reginald who was with him eventually suggested that perhaps he should return to his writing. Thomas' verbatim response was not recorded, but was to the effect that all he had written previously seemed like "so much straw." St. Thomas had been writing non-stop about God for almost thirty years, and apparently had just found himself in God's presence directly. A few months later, Thomas was summoned to the Second Council of Lyon. He died on the way after hitting his head on a fallen tree.

The main concern of the present essay is with Questions 1, 14, and 15 of *De Veritate*, his disputation on truth, which consists of twenty-nine questions in all. Questions 1 and 14 are on the topics of truth and faith respectively, each comprising twelve articles. Question 15 is concerned with the nature of reason, and contains five articles in all. Each article under each question deals with a specific aspect of the topic concerned. In overall structure, each article is divided into (a) difficulties with the position Aquinas will defend, (b) a general exposition of his position, and (c) his response to the difficulties item by item. Difficulties might be drawn from several sources, including previous theologians and conversations with his students. Aquinas' own views are laid out in (b) and (c) together, which in what follows will be referred to simply as his response (R). References to the text of *De Veritate* will cite the work (V), the question (e.g., 1), the article (e.g., 2), and (generally) the response (R). In the format employed below, this would be designated "V.1.2.R." References to the *Summa Theologica* are necessarily more complicated, and will be explained when need arises.

## 4.2 Truth in *De Veritate*

From the perspective of ordinary discourse, the least esoteric sense of truth is probably that pertaining to propositions. Apart from controversies of contemporary truth-theory, it is easy for someone to understand the remark that the proposition "snow is white" is true just in case snow is white. Aquinas deals extensively with propositional truth in *De Veritate*, and most of what he says there is relatively straightforward. Let us begin with his understanding of propositions, then move on to his treatment of propositional truth.

In V.14.2.R, Aquinas characterizes propositions obliquely as what is proposed in particular circumstances by particular acts of the will. "Moved by the good" (*mota a bono*), he says, "the will proposes as worthy of assent" (*Voluntas . . . proponit . . . dignum . . . assentiatur*) something "not naturally apparent to the intellect" (*intellectui naturali non apparens*). The verb *proponere* (to set forth, propose) appearing here yields the noun *propositione*, which is one of Aquinas' most frequently used words for proposition. Thus, for example, he speaks in V.14.1.R of circumstances in which "the truth of propositions is unmistakably clear" (*veritas propositionum . . . infallibiliter apparet*).

Another frequently used term for proposition is *enuntiatio* (assertion). In Question 1 and Question 14 of *De Veritate* taken together, this term is used approximately forty times, compared with approximately thirty for *propositione*. A less frequently used term for proposition is the noun *complexe* (complex), as for example in V.14.8.R which notes that "faith deals with propositions" (*fidei . . . sit complexorum*). This locution is especially revealing as an indication of the composite character of propositions. In basic form, a proposition is composed of a subject and a predicate, as in "Socrates is mortal," a staple of syllogistic logic.

Propositions themselves are structured to serve as components of syllogisms. Syllogistic reasoning is the basis of what Aquinas calls *scientia* (science). Given premises which themselves are known, valid syllogistic reasoning yields scientific knowledge of the conclusion. A classic example is: given "Socrates is a man" and "All men are mortal" as known, the proposition "Socrates is mortal" is scientifically known as well. This understanding of reasoning as basically syllogistic traces back to Aristotle, and remained prevalent up through Kant in the eighteenth century. In dealing with propositional truth as understood by Aquinas, we should bear in mind that the bearers of truth are compound assertions of relations between subjects and predicates. As Aquinas points out in V.14.12.R, the composition of propositions is changed "because of changes in subject and verb" (*per alia accidentia verbi et nominis variari*).

Another relevant feature of propositions for Aquinas is their location in the mind or intellect. As indicated in V.1.3.R, the "joining and separating" (*compositione vel divisione*) of subject and predicate inherent in a proposition takes place "in the intellect" (*intellectus*). It is with respect to this joining and separating, he goes on to say, that "truth is predicated" (*veritatis praedicationem*). The location of truth in the intellect accords with the assertion in Aristotle's *Metaphysics* that "truth and falsity are not in things, but in thought" (*ou gar esti to pseudos kai to alēthes en tois pragmasin . . . all' en dianoia*, 1027b26–28), translated by Aquinas as *verum et falsum non sunt in rebus, sed in mente*.

Essential involvement of the intellect is reaffirmed in the opening remarks of Article 3, which also clarifies how "things" (*res*) contribute to truth. In what amounts to a definition of truth, Aquinas says: "the true is a conformity of thing and intellect" (*verum est adaequatio rerum et intellectus*). The noun *adaequatio* is used over a dozen times in Question 1, always in reference to the relation between intellect and things that yield truth. While in most cases the intellects involved are those of human creatures, yielding the "created truth" (*veritatem creatam*) of V.1.5.R, there is also occasional reference to the conformity of God's mind to the world he created. In V.1.7.R, for instance, Aquinas speaks of "the truth of the divine intellect [consisting in] its conformity to created things" (*veritas intellectus divini secundum quod adaequatur rebus creatis*).

Commentators often trace Aquinas' conception of truth as adequation back to Aristotle's definition in *Metaphysics* 1011b26–27. As Aristotle puts it, "to say of what is that it is not, or of what is not that it is, is false; and [to say] of what is that it is, and of what is not that it is not, is true" (*legein to on mē einai ē to mē on einai pseudos, to de to on einai kai to mē on mē einai alēthes*). Although this is a version of the correspondence theory of truth, broadly conceived, there is nothing in Aristotle's definition about the truth-making relation between what is said and the corresponding matters of fact. As a consequence, here is nothing in Aristotle's definition to help clarify St. Thomas' conception of truth as adequation.

A more helpful comparison is with the picture theory of Wittgenstein's *Tractatus*. The relation of adequation in Aquinas is like Wittgenstein's relation between facts (*Tatsachen*) and reality (*Wirklichkeit*). In the *Tractatus*, a fact is an existing state of affairs (*Sachverhaltes*), which latter is a combination of entities *(Sachen)* or things *(Dingen)*. A picture (*Bild*), in turn, is a "model of reality" (*Modell der Wirklichkeit*, 2.12) which has elements corresponding to those of the objects (*Gegenständen*) it represents. According to 2.1514, "the pictorial relation consists of the correlations of the picture's elements with things" (*Die abbildende Beziehung besteht aus den Zuordnungen der Elemente des Bildes und der Sachen*). What a picture and thing depicted must share for this correlation to occur is labeled "pictorial form" (*Form der Abbildung*) in 2.17. The upshot is that the relation of shared pictorial form in the *Tractatus* corresponds to the relation of adequation in Question 1 of *De Veritate*.

Because of their shared pictorial form, moreover, a picture "is laid against reality like a measure" (*ist wie ein Masstab an die Wirklichkeit angelegt*, 2.1512). The same analogy is used by Aquinas in V.1.5.R. The adequation in question is there referred to as a commensuration (*commensurationem*), and likened to "a body measured by an intrinsic measure such as line, surface, or depth" (*Mensuratur . . . corpus . . . mensura intrinseca, ut linea, vel superficie, vel profunditate*).

With this elucidation of adequation in mind, let us return to the definition of propositional truth at the beginning of Article 3. Replacing "conformity" with "adequation," we have "the true is an adequation of thing and intellect" (Latin above). Truth is tantamount to a relation between intellect and things that is adequate to render the intellect capable of grasping how things stand in the world. In a true proposition, its elements (subject and predicate) are related in such a way as to display how things are related in the state of affairs it represents. A proposition is true just in case its elements are so ordered to make this occur.

Propositional truth occurs primarily in the mind or intellect. This occurrence is private. But as Aquinas notes in V.1.3.R, truth can occur also in the public behavior ("words and actions," *dicit vel facit*) of the person involved. In a full statement to that effect, he says: "For truth can be predicated of words in the same way as of the [ideas of] intellect they convey" (*Voces autem eodem modo recipiunt veritatis praedicationem, sicut intellectus quos significant*). The conformity with things that produces propositional truth, in brief, can occur either privately in the intellect or publicly in words expressing what the person involved has in mind.

### 4.2.1

Aquinas deals with truth in a variety of different forms, the most concrete of which is propositional truth. Most abstract, in turn, is what he labels "First Truth" (*veritate prima*). This Latin expression occurs more than two dozen times in Question 1 of *de Veritatis*. Other expressions designating the same entity are "Divine Truth" (*veritate divina*), "Eternal Truth" (*veritate aeternitate*), "Immutable Truth" (*veritate immutabile*), and "Highest Truth" (*veritate summa*). The entity these expressions designate, of course, is the Truth that is God. Augustine often spoke of a Truth identical to God, and Thomas Aquinas followed suit.

Most of what Aquinas says about propositional truth seems commonsensical and relatively straightforward. This is not the case, however, when it comes to First Truth. His treatment of First Truth seems counterintuitive and sometimes unintelligible. One difficulty is that First Truth is said to be the source of all other truths, a thesis which Article 8 of Question 1 is dedicated to defending. As stated in V.1.8.R, this is the thesis that "all other truth is from the First Truth, which is God" (*omnis alia veritas est a prima veritate, quae est Deus*). The context makes clear that this claim pertains not only to the source of propositional truth, but extends to the truth of things (*res*) as well. This is stated explicitly in his remark that "truth is found both in things and in the intellect" (*invenitur veritas in rebus et in intellectu*).

The notion that things (other than propositions) might be true poses problems on its own. The sense seems to be that the way things are disposed in the world should be acknowledged as part of the truth-making relation. A proposition is true just in case the arrangement of its components conforms to the arrangement of components in the corresponding state of affairs. Aquinas accordingly choose to speak of the objective (non-mental) part of the conformity as true itself, along with the part situated in the intellect. That this was a deliberate move on his part is indicated in the opening remarks of Article 8: "a transition can be made from the truth of a proposition to the truth of what is said, which in turn expresses the truth of the thing" (*fiat descensus a veritate propositionis ad veritatem dicti, quae exprimit veritatem rei*).

The effect of this move is to admit an ambiguity in the Latin *veritate* matching the dual meaning of *alētheia* in Greek. In classical as well as NT Greek, *alētheia* means reality as well as truth. Our discussion of the NT term above focused on John 14:5–6, where Jesus responds to a question by Thomas saying "I am the way (*hē hodos*), and the truth (*hē alētheia*, and the life (*hē zōē*)." In this response, Jesus is not describing himself as a truth-value. He is describing himself rather as the personal being that provides the pathway to eternal life. It is reasonable to view the opening remark of Article 8, quoted above, as making a similar linguistic move. The thing (*rei*) that establishes the truth of a proposition is not literally a truth in its own right, but rather a real entity contained in the world as it is.

Accepting this truth of things as included in the "other truth" of V.1.8.R, what sense can be made of the claim that all other truth comes from the First Truth which is God? A broad hint is offered in the same passage, to the effect that other truth comes from First Truth in the same manner that "all created goodness comes from the first uncreated goodness, which is God" (*omnis bonitas creata, est a prima bonitate increata, quae est Deus*). Invoking Plato, we should find it natural to think of good things in the created realm as coming from participation in an uncreated Good. Since created truth incorporates the truth of created things, it comes from the source of created things. Aquinas himself completes the inference in V.1.6.R, with an account of how true things change in their relation to First Truth. What this comes down to, he explains, is that "created things change in their participation in First Truth" (*res creatae variantur quidem in participatione veritatis primae*), which latter itself "does not change in any way" (*nullo modo mutatur*). The uncreated First Truth identical with God is the source of all created being, which includes the things that underlie propositional truth.

Another initially puzzling thesis in Aquinas's account has to do with the way First Truth participates in affairs of the intellect. As stated in V.1.4.R, "all created truths manifest themselves in the intellect by virtue of First Truth" (*omnes veritates creatae se intellectui exprimant virtute primae veritatis*). The apparent claim here is that First Truth enables the manifestation of created truths, and that this occurs within the confines of the (created) intellect. What is not immediately apparent is the manner in which First Truth supports the human intellect in its awareness of created truth.

An initial step toward resolving this issue is to note that Aquinas understands mind or intellect to be the seat of faith. This is stated explicitly in V.14.2.R, where he defines faith as "a mental habit" (*habitus mentis*) that "makes the intellect assent to things that do not appear" (*faciens intellectum non apparentibus assentire*). A further step is to note the relation of First Truth to faith stated in the preliminary remarks of Question 14, Article 8, where the relation is likened to that of vision to light. Aquinas's full statement of this likeness is: "First Truth is related to faith as light is to vision (*veritas prima sic se habet ad fidem sicut lumen ad visum*). The force of the analogy here is to depict First Truth as a source of illumination. First Truth supports the human intellect by providing the light that enables its awareness of created truth.

Article 1 of Question 14 begins with several references to Augustine, all pertaining in some manner to the earlier philosopher's views on faith and truth. As noted previously, a key component of these views is his so-called illumination theory. A fresh look at Augustine's illumination theory serves as the concluding step toward understanding the relation between First Truth and created truth laid out in Question 1, Article 4, of *De Veritate*.


4.2.2

The illumination theory receives its name from the phrase "the inner light of Truth" (*interiore luce veritatis*) in XII.40 of *The Teacher*. God is identified as the source of this inner light in VIII.21, with its reference to the "guidance of God, namely Truth itself" (*Deo duce, id est ipsa veritate*). God not only is the source of this inner light. In some manner or another, the Truth that is God is instantiated within the individual mind. This inner truth serves as a criterion by which truths of external origin are judged and verified. The role of inner truth as criterion is exemplified in XI.iii.5 of the *Confessions*. Speaking hypothetically about truths passed on in the words of Moses, Augustine asks himself "how would I know whether what he said is true?" (*unde scirem, an verum diceret?*). The answer, Augustine assures himself, is that "truth, within the chamber of my thought" (*in domicilio cogitationis . . . veritas*) would say "he speaks the truth" ("*Verum dicit*").

The issue in question from Aquinas's *De Veritate* is how First Truth supports the intellect in its pursuit of created truth. The issue is resolved by the highly plausible assumption that Aquinas was aware of Augustine's illumination theory, and ready to adopt it for his own purposes. As with Augustine's Truth who is God, Aquinas' First Truth supports the human intellect in two distinct roles. For one, First Truth is instantiated in the intellect as a criterion by which created truth of external origin can be assessed. In V.1.4.R, accordingly, Aquinas affirms that "First Truth is the truth by which the mind passes judgment on all things" (*veritas secundum quam anima de omnibus iudicat, est veritas prima*). The second is that First Truth is the source of the light in which that judgment occurs. As Aquinas notes explicitly in V.1.4.R, "intelligible light is an exemplification of divine light" (*lumen intelligibile exempletur a lumine divino*). It may be assumed that intelligible light here includes the internal illumination of the human intellect. The way First Truth supports the intellect in its pursuit of created truth, accordingly, is by internal illumination.


### 4.2.3

A second, and seemingly more intractable, problem with Aquinas's doctrine of First Truth has to do with the incomposite character of the divine intellect. The problem is encapsulated in this stark statement: "the divine intellect, to which all things are conformed, is one; and on its part, there is one conformity with all things" (*intellectus . . . divinus, cui omnia adaequantur, est unus; et ex parte eius est una adaequatio ad res omnes*, V.1.4.R). The First Truth residing in the divine intellect, moreover, is one as well. This is affirmed in V.1.5.R: "First Truth must be one for all things" (*veritas prima non potest esse de omnibus nisi una*). In this, First Truth contrasts with truths of the human intellect, which are multiple both in diversity of subject matter and in diversity of tense modality. "In divine cognition," Aquinas goes on to say, "neither form of diversity can be found" (*modorum diversitatis inveniri non potest in divina cognitione*). Both divine intellect and the First Truth within it are one in the sense of lacking diversity.

The problem already should be evident. Truth essentially is a conformity (*adequatio*) of intellect with the actual world. Conformity consists of a shared arrangement of constituents in the intellect and in the corresponding state of affairs. But if the intellect lacks diversity, it also lacks constituents, which precludes it from having constituents arranged in ways that might conform to the world as it is.

Yet Aquinas speaks repeatedly in V.1.4.R of a conformity of divine intellect to things in the world, emphasizing that there is only one such conformity. Different states of affairs might conform with divine intellect in different ways, he says, but there is only one conformity in the opposite direction. This appears to have dire consequences for Aquinas' notion of First Truth. Either (a) its conformity with things is different from that of created truths, or (b) First Truth itself is true in some sense inherently different from conformity. To escape (a), an alternative relation of conformity would be needed, something not forthcoming in *De Veritate*. To escape (b), an alternative sense of truth would be needed that does not involve conformity, which again is not provided in this treatise dedicated specifically to truth.

The treatise *De Veritate* is not the only writing in which Aquinas encounters problems stemming from simplicity of the divine intellect. In the surprisingly short Article 14 of Question 14 of Part 1 of *Summa Theologica*, he addresses the query "whether God knows enuncible things (*enuntiabilium*)?" The term *enuniatio*, it was noted above, is often used in place of *propositione* (proposition). As a *propositione* is something declared or proposed, so an *enuntiatio* is something asserted; and what is asserted is a certain relation between subject and predicate. By very nature, an *enuntiatio* involves a complex of distinguishable parts. It is not clear how a completely simple divine intellect can know complex propositions.

Article 14 of Question 14 of *Summa Theologica* is addressed to this very issue. Aquinas' discussion of Article 14 begins with two objections, purportedly leading to a negative answer. The first is premised on the affirmation that "to know enuncible things belongs to our intellect insofar as it composes and divides. But there is no composition in the divine intellect" (*Cognoscere . . . enuntiabilia convenit intellectui nostro, secundum quod componit et dividit. Sed in intellectu divino nulla est compositio*). Premises of the second objection are: "every kind of knowledge is made through some likeness. But in God there is no likeness of enuncible things, since he is entirely simple" (*omnis cognitio fit per aliquam similitudiem. Sed in Deo nulla est similitudo enuntiabilium, cum sit omnino simplex*). Phrasing aside, this objection is tantamount to the second problem raised above.

Aquinas' reply to these objections is based on a previously argued premise to the effect that "God knows whatever is in his own power or in that of creatures" (*Deus . . . scit quidquid est in potentia sua vel creaturae*). His reasoning invokes the essence of God, which is understood as containing all perfections found in the essences of all other things (see the argument of Question 14, Article 6). Among these latter perfections are those of knowing assertions of divisions and compositions. In relevant upshot, by knowing his own essence, God knows enunciable things.

With this understanding of God's essence at hand, Aquinas has quick answers to the two initial objections. To the first, he responds that the objection would hold "if God knew enunciable things after the manner of enunciable things" (*si Deus cognosceret enuntiabilia per modum enuntiabilium*). This is the extent of his response to the first. His response to the second is no less cursory, to the effect that "God by his existence, which is his essence, is the likeness of all those things that are signified by enunciation" (*Deus per suum esse, quod est eius essentia, est similitudo omnium eorum quae per enuntiabilia signiificantur*). The reader is left to mull over how the "entirely simple" (*omnino simplex*) Creator in the first objection could be the likeness of complex created things. Aquinas' quick answers are less than satisfactory.

Our present concern, of course, is not with the perfunctory character of Aquinas' response, but with the nature of First Truth as it resides in the divine intellect. Being entirely simple, the divine intellect cannot entertain distinct subject and predicate terms that are essential to the makeup of created truth. As noted above, this means either (a) that conformity of intellect with things in the case of First Truth is inherently different from that of created truth, or (b) that First Truth is inherently different from created truth in not being based on conformity in the first place. In either case, First Truth and created truth are inherently different in makeup. As far as I can determine, there are no resources in St. Thomas' writings for making them mesh.

4.2.4

Unless First Truth can be synchronized with ordinary truth, however, there are several roles Aquinas assigns to First Truth that appear unintelligible. One such is that of providing the measure by which things are deemed true. This role is intimated in a descriptive phrase attributed to Anselm in V.1.6.R, namely: "the First Truth according to which all things are said to be true as by an extrinsic measure" (*veritate prima, prout secundum eam omnia dicuntur vera quasi mensura extrinseca*). A direct affirmation of First Truth's relation to true things in this role is found in the same response, in the words "created things change in their participation in First Truth; yet First Truth itself, according to which they are said to be true, does not change in any way" (Latin above). If First Truth differs from created truth in either respect (a) or (b) specified above, they are sufficiently different to make it unclear how they could be related by participation. (Beautiful things, analogously, cannot participate in Plato's universal Beauty if they inherently differ from the latter in character.)

Another respect in which created truth is taken to be divine in origin pertains to its alleged dependency upon the divine intellect. As stated in V.1.4.R. "Truth is primarily in a thing because of its relation to the divine intellect, inasmuch as it is related to the divine intellect as its cause" (*prius... inest rei veritas in comparatione ad intellectum divinum ... cum ad intellectum divinum comparetur sicut ad causam*). Accordingly, the passage continues, "something is said to be true primarily because of its order to the truth of the divine intellect" (*res aliqua principalius dicitur vera in ordine ad veritatem intellectus divini*). Another reference to the divine source of created truth is found in V.1.5.R, which affirms that "all things receive the name true from First Truth" (*denominantur omnes res verae a prima veritate*). If the truth of true things is inherently different from that of First Truth, however, there is no apparent rationale for naming the former after the latter.

Problems stemming from the simplicity of the divine intellect, and that of its residual First Truth, extend to even deeper levels of the account in *De Veritate*. Quoting Augustine in V.1.4.R, Aquinas writes that "the truth of the divine intellect is one alone, and from it are drawn the many truths of the human intellect" (*Veritas... intellectus divini est una tantum, a qua in intellectu humano derivantur plures veritates*). Truth predicated of things in relation to the human intellect, however, "is accidental to those things" (*est rebus... accidentalis*); for "supposing that the human intellect did not or could not exist, things themselves would still remain essentially the same" (*posito quod intellectus humanus non esset nec esse posset, adhuc res in sua essentia permaneret*). This is a statement affirming the independence of things in the world from human existence. Even if human intellect were not present in the world, other things would remain unchanged.

This statement in V.1.4.R is a radical affirmation of anti-relativism, which is to say a statement of radical realism. Things (other than human) are what they are, independently of human involvement. The way things are follows from the unchanging character of First Truth in the divine intellect. Essentially the same claim is made in V.1.2.R, where again it is expressed in hypothetical form: "Even if there were no human intellects, things would be said to be true because of their relation to the divine intellect" (*etiam si intellectus humanus non esset, adhuc res verae dicerentur in ordine ad intellectum divinum*). Realism of this rigid sort is a hallmark of Thomistic metaphysics. But insofar as it is based on a radically simple First Truth, this realism suffers from inherent unintelligibility.

Another consequence of a radically simple First Truth has to do with the infallibility attributed to Christian faith. In V.14.8.R, Aquinas states unequivocally that "the essential object of faith is First Truth" (*per se obiectum fidei veritas prima est*). In V.14.4.R, he also asserts that "faith is a divinely infused habit" (*est habitus fidei divinitus infusus*) in "the speculative understanding" (*intellectu speculativo*). The habit of faith, moreover, is a virtue of the understanding. And as affirmed in V.14.5.R, "it is impossible for a habit existing in the understanding to be a virtue, unless it is such that by it one infallibly speaks the truth" (*intellectu existens virtus esse non possit, nisi sit talis quo infallibiliter verum dicatur*).

Faith must derive this infallibility, Aquinas goes on to say, "from its adherence to some testimony in which truth is infallibly found" (*ex hoc quod adhaeret alicui testimonio, in quo infallibiliter veritas invenitur*). Since "all created truth is liable to fail save insofar as regulated by uncreated truth" (*omnis creata veritas defectibilis est, nisi quatenus per veritatem increatam rectificatur*), the virtue of faith must "embrace the truth which is in divine knowledge" (*adhaerere . . . veritati quae in divina cognitione consistit*). In upshot, "a person of faith is freed from the instability of manifold error through the simple and never-changing truth" (*fidelis per simplicem et semper eodem modo se habentem veritatem liberatur ab instabili erroris varietate*).

In this line of reasoning, "simple and never-changing truth" (First Truth) is understood as the basis of infallible faith. This freedom from error is a precursor of the infallibility that figures prominently in later Thomistic-based theology. Attribution of infallibility to First Truth itself, however, remains inherently unclear. Truth beyond error is no more perspicuous than truth itself. And how something entirely simple might be true remains unexplained, despite the considerable length of Aquinas's discussion in *De Veritate*.

## 4.3 Aquinas on Belief

There are many passages in relevant texts suggesting that Aquinas, like Augustine, considered faith to be equivalent to belief. One such is the response in V.14.1.R, where he says "the import of belief is the act of faith" (*Credere . . . actum fidei importat*). Another is V.14.2.R, where he quotes Augustine (favorably) as saying "faith is the virtue by which what is not seen is believed" (*fides est virtus qua creduntur quae non videntur*). Subsequently in V.14.7.R he affirms that "to believe [the word of] God is an act of faith" (*actus fidei . . . credere Deo*). As part of a difficulty raised in the article following, moreover, it is pointed out that "belief in God is a means of faith" (*medium fidei est . . . credit Deo*; see also V.14.8.R).

In due course, we will examine reasons to think that Aquinas in fact did not consider belief and faith to be equivalent. The relation between them, however, is sufficiently complex to warrant a careful explication of belief by way of preparation. We turn accordingly to an examination of passages that disclose the nature of belief as St. Thomas conceived it.

Aquinas launches his inquiry in Question 14 of *De Veritate* with a definition of belief taken from Augustine, namely: "to believe is to think with assent" (*credere est cum assensione cogitare*). Expanding on the definition in V.14.1.R, Aquinas asserts "we do not assent to a given thing unless we hold it as true" (*non . . . assentire nisi quando inhaeremus ei quasi veo*). The basic definition is completed in V.14.3.R, with the remark that the element of assent is added to a given belief by "the command of the will" (*ex imperio voluntatis*).

This definition is elaborated by series of remarks on the relation between will and belief, found both in the *Summa Theologica* and in *De Veritate*. The basic connection is affirmed in Article 2 of the former specified above, with Aquinas' remark that belief occurs when "the will moves the intellect to assent" (*ad intellectum pertineat . . . voluntate motus ad assentiendum*). Not only does the will "extend" (*pertineat*) the intellect in this fashion, it also focuses the intellect on a single object. As Aquinas puts it in the preceding Article 1 of the *Summa*, "the intellect of the believer is limited to one object by the will" (*intellectus credentis determinatur ad unum . . . per voluntatem*).

Turning next to *De Veritate*, we find an affirmation of the connection between will and belief in V.14.3.R. As he puts it here, "assent of belief comes only by command of the will" (*Credere autem . . . non habet assensum nisi ex imperio voluntatis*). Because of this connection,

Aquinas says, the merit of a belief depends on the merit of the volitional assent that produces it. In his words, "it is for this reason that belief can be meritorious" (*inde est quod ipsum credere potest esse meritorium*). In the case of belief, as in other matters Aquinas discusses, merit of assent depends on the extent to which the will itself has achieved perfection. And "insofar as the will is perfected by charity" (*ita cum caritas sit perfectio voluntatis*, V.14.5.R), merit of assent depends upon the extent to which it is motivated by charity. The conclusion established by this line of reasoning is stated in V.14.6.R: insofar as "believing depends on the will, an act [of believing] cannot be perfect unless the will is made perfect by charity" (*credere dependeat et ex . . . voluntate . . . talis actus perfectus, nisi et voluntas sit perfecta per caritatem*).

In contexts treated previously in the present study (Augustine, the NT), believing *that* was distinguished from believing *in*, and the latter further divided into believing (i) in persons, (ii) in (Christian) doctrine, and (iii) in information sources. Instances of each can be found in the texts from Aquinas now being considered.

Belief (i) in Jesus Christ is exemplified in V.14.2.R, where Aquinas translates part of John 6:40 as "everyone who sees the Son, and believes in him, may have everlasting life" (*omnis qui videt filium et credit in eum, habet vitam aeternam*). In another example from V.14.7.R, Aquinas says that "belief on (the word of] God" (*credere Deo*) and "belief in God" (*credere in Deum*) are the same act of virtue exercised in different circumstance. The "belief on God's word" mentioned in this passage should also count as an instance of belief (iii) in information sources. More explicit examples of (iii) are found in V.14.1.R and V.14.8.R. The former goes to the heart of the matter in proclaiming "we are moved to believe in what God says, because we are promised eternal life as a reward if we believe" (*movemur ad credendum dictis Dei, inquantum nobis repromittitur, si crediderimus, praemium aeternae vitae*). With reference to all the truths of the Creed referred to previously, the latter passage goes on to say "we must believe everything because of divine testimony" (*quod quamvis divino testimonio sit de omnibus credendum*).

A passing reference to belief (ii) occurs in the first objection in Article 6 of Question 2 under the Second Part of the Second Part of the *Summa*. Included in the objection is reference to certain things "necessary for salvation that must be believed explicitly" (*explicatio credendorum est de necessitate salutis*). The author's response to the objection leaves this reference intact. It is plausible to understand the things necessary for salvation as doctrines designated by the Church as being conducive toward that end. These are doctrines instituted by the Church, that is to say, belief in which provides a pathway to eternal life.

There are numerous passages in the documents under consideration that mention belief *that* something is the case. One such is *De Veritate* V.14.9.R, containing the observation that one might "believe that God exists" (*credere Deum esse*) before actually "believing in God" (*credat Deum*). Others include V.14.8.R and V.14.12.R. In addition to providing an example of believing *that*, V.14.12.R illustrates a sense of believing *in* that extends beyond senses (i), (ii), and (iii) above. In this passage, the author is discussing time-differences among people who believe that the resurrection of Christ has occurred. For these people, he observes, belief that it occurred goes hand-in-hand with belief in the resurrection itself. He explains the general connection between these forms of belief in the following words: "the sense of 'I believe in the resurrection' is 'I believe that the resurrection is, was, or will be'" (*sensus . . . credo resurrectionem, id est credo resurrectionem esse, vel fuisse, vel futuram esse*). The resurrection, of course, is an event in the Christian story, quite distinct from a person, a doctrine, or a source of information. This puts it in a separate category of believing *in*. Believing in (iv) Christ's resurrection is the counterpart of having faith in that event.

With this examination of belief as a background, let us address the question of the relation between faith and belief as Aquinas conceived them.

## 4.4 Aquinas on Faith

In V.14.2.R, Aquinas offers what he calls a "scientifically based definition" (*definitionem . . . artificialiter formare*) of faith. The definition reads: "faith is a mental habit, by which eternal life originates in us, and which makes our understanding assent to things that do not appear" (*fides est habitus mentis, qua inchoatur vita aeterna in nobis, faciens intellectum non apparentibus assentire*). The final phrase is taken from his translation of Heb 11:1 in the initial lines of Article 2, which says that faith is "the substance of things hoped for, the evidence of things that do not appear" (*substantia rerum sperandarum, argumentum non apparentium*). Aquinas' translation, of course, comes from the Latin Vulgate, and is untouched by subtleties (and difficulties) of the original Greek discussed in chapter 2 of the present study. In keeping with the Vulgate Latin, the term *argumentum* here probably should be understood in the sense of warrant or witness rather than of epistemic justification. In the context of Aquinas' definition, faith is the witness on which assent to unseen things is based.

Aquinas' definition portrays faith as the origin of eternal life, meaning that it initiates a believer's journey along the way to that end. In V.14.10.R, the "way of faith" (*via fidei*) is mentioned explicitly as providing a "ready access to salvation" (*facilis aditus ad salutem*) that is available to people generally regardless of their cognitive circumstances. The habit mentioned in the definition is further described in V.14.4.R as a "divinely infused habit of faith" (*habitus fidei divinitus infusus*). Its purpose, as described here, is to enable "the understanding to follow promptly the commands of the will" (*intellectus prompte sequatur imperium voluntatis*). Like the assent of belief cited previously, the assent of faith is due to an "act of the will" (*actus voluntatas*). A further similarity with belief is that the will commanding an act of faith is also perfected by charity. As Aquinas observes in formulating objections preliminary to his definition in V.14.2.R, "faith is increased to perfection by charity" (*fides magis perficitur per caritatem*).

Considered in their spiritual context, Aquinas depicts faith and belief as playing similar roles in the several respects mentioned. He finds a fundamental difference between them, however, having to do with the objects toward which they are directed. Acts of belief are directed toward circumstances or states of affairs. Examples are available in V.14.8.R of *De Veritate*. One such is the "belief that God suffered" (*credimus Deum passum*), which is directed toward the state of affairs of God's suffering. Another is the "belief that this took place through divine power" (*credimus divina virtute fieri*), which is directed toward the circumstance of this suffering being brought about by divine agency. In this particular context, as elsewhere, belief is an attitude entertained toward things that happen (or might happen) in the world.

Acts of faith, on the other hand, are directed toward spiritually significant entities. Aquinas puts the point succinctly in V.14.8.R, with the affirmation: "faith is principally about God" (*fides principaliter (est) de Deo*). Equally straightforward is his statement in V.14.7.R, which affirms that "First Truth is the proper object of faith" (*veritas . . . prima est proprium obiectum fidei*). Any appearance of conflict between these two pronouncements is dispelled by numerous passages in *De Veritate*

that indicate an identify between First Truth and God. One such indication is found in V.14.4.R, where Augustine is cited as saying that "faith
is the illumination of the mind with respect to the First Truth" (*fides est
illuminatio mentis ad primam veritatem*). Another occurs in V.14.7.R,
with the observation that well-formed faith (*Fides . . . formata*) "assents
to First Truth with a perfect will" (*perfecta voluntate assentit primae veritati*). Also relevant is V.14.2.R, where Aquinas observes that faith "finds
completion in the will" (*habet complementum in voluntate*), insofar as its
"proper object is truth" (*proprium obiectum . . . est verum*).

Acts of belief are directed toward states of affairs, while acts of
faith are directed toward the truth that is God. First Truth clearly is not
something that happens in the world, which means that it is not a state
of affairs. This basic difference in object enhances the importance of
the question of how exactly these two acts of the intellect are related in
Aquinas'treatment. We now turn to that question.

In V.14.1.R, Aquinas says that "the import of belief is the act of faith"
(*Credere . . . actum fidei importat*), as quoted previously. The apparent
meaning of this assertion is that belief constitutes an act of faith, which is
to say that faith acts through belief. No matter how the object of faith is
characterized (God, First Truth, etc.), it must be believable. Support for
this requirement is found in Aquinas' formulation of a "friendly" objection to Article 8 of Question 14: "Just as the visible is the object of sight,
so the credible is the object of faith" (*sicut visibile est obiectum visus, ita
credibile est obiectum fidei*).

In the preliminary remarks of article 4 of question 14, Augustine is
said to have interpreted 1 Cor 4:7 as referring to "the faith that is in the
wills of those who believe" (*fidem quae in credentium voluntate*). This
reference to Augustine pertains to the role of faith in providing direction
to the wills of believers. It is because of faith that believers are motivated
to fix their attention on God. This is the case for believers generally, past,
present, and future. As Aquinas notes in V.14.11.R, "there are some matters of faith that everyone is bound to believe in every age" (*aliquid est
in fide ad quod omnes et omni tempore . . . credendum tenentur*). In temporal succession, matters of faith have precedence, followed by assent of
individual believers. As remarked in V.14.2.R, "the faith of our fathers
is a means leading us to believe [subsequently]" (*fides patrum est nobis
medium inducens nos ad credendum*).

Apart from professions of faith, a given person's faith might be in-
vested either in divine persons or in events of Christ's life that remain

mysterious. In Article 7 of Question 2 of the Second Part of the Second Part of the *Summa Theologica*, for an example of the first, Aquinas surmises that "the gentiles had neither explicit nor implicit faith in Christ" (*gentiles non habuerunt fidem de Christo nec expliucitam nec implicitam*). Faith in divine mysteries is illustrated in article 8 of the same question. Along with "faith in the Trinity" (*fide Trinitatis*), Aquinas says, there is "the mystery of Christ" (*mysterium Christi*) in which the Trinity is implicated. In effect, the Trinity and the mystery of Christ are universal requirements of personal faith.

Apart from being directed toward different objects, faith and belief are concurrent occupants of the individual person's intellect. The nature of that co-occupancy is an important factor in understanding Aquinas' teaching regarding the role of faith in religious life. The life of a genuine believer is marked by repeated acts of faith. By considering what this amounts to specifically, we may gain further insight into his views about how faith and belief are related.

### 4.4.1

There are grammatical peculiarities that call the nomenclature "act of faith" into question. The infinitive "to act" in English designates something an agent does. We might expect an act of faith, accordingly, to involve an activity undertaken by an agent. But there is no word in coherent English (such as "to faith") for such an activity. In the vocabulary of faith alone, accordingly, there is no way of designating a genuine activity that would constitute an act of faith.

English grammar aside, the same problem arises with the Latin noun *fides*. Apart from the translation "faith" peculiar to theology, the Latin term is commonly translated "confidence," "loyalty," or maybe "fidelity." As with the absence of a deviant verb like "to faith" in English, there is no Latin verb corresponding to *fides* in any of these specific senses. There is another standard nontheological use, however, in which Latin *fides* is equivalent to the English term "trust." And "trust" can mean either the activity of trusting (as in "I trust my personal physician") or the trust conveyed by the act of trusting (as in "he enjoys my trust"). The Latin equivalent of "to trust" is the active verb *fidere*.

Outside of a theological context, in brief, the standard meaning of *fidere* is confined to that of "to trust" or near equivalent. Importing the term into a theological context does not result in a verb referring to an activity that might properly be called "faithing." This accords with the fact that in the writings of St. Thomas we have been considering, there is no use of the verb *fidere*. There is occasional reference to "having faith," such as *fidem non habeat* in the opening paragraphs of article 4 in *De Veritate*, question 14. But having faith is an activity of having rather than of "faithing." Having faith is no more an action of faith than having a heavy heart is an action of the heart.

There are many references in these writings, however, to faith having an active influence on other things. In V.14.4.R, an "act of faith" (*actus fidei*) is said to "produce an act of charity" (*generat . . . caritatis actum*). In V.14.11.R, habitual faith is said to "prevent one from assent to certain articles that one knows only implicitly "(*retardatur ne assentiat contrariis articulorum, quos etiam solum implicite novit*). Speaking generally in V.14.3.R, Aquinas claims that "everyone posits that faith is a virtue" (*fides ab omnibus ponitur esse virtus*), and that "virtue by its very name means the completion of an active power" (*virtus ex sui impositione nominis significat complementum activae potentiae*). How could the referent of a noun to which no active verb corresponds function as an active power subject to completion?

The answer lies in the relation between faith and belief, and constitutes one of the main differences between them. Faith is an attribute imparted by divine grace (Question 14, Article 9). Being thus imparted, faith is a gift. And like all gifts, faith is passively received. In and by itself, faith is passive rather than active. Faith is so related to belief, however, that it finds expression in the activity of believing. An act of faith is tantamount to the act (or acts) of belief in which it is expressed. A paradigmatic illustration is given by St. Thomas himself, in his response to the objections raised under Article 2 of Question 2 of the Second Part of the Second Part of the *Summa Theologica*: "an act of faith is to believe in God" (*actus fidei credere in Deum*).

The activity of faith, in effect, is tantamount to the activity resulting from the beliefs by which the life of a faithful Christian is shaped. In the association of faith and belief that figures so prominently in the works of Aquinas, faith is passive but belief is active. Generalizing the foregoing observation by St. Thomas in the *Summa*, we may say that exercise of an active belief constitutes an act of passive faith.

This is the answer to the previous question of how faith can function as a power subject to completion. What completion means here is perfection of the power in question. And what perfection amounts to in the case of faith is explained in V.14.5.R of *De Veritate*, with the observation that "what there is of perfection in faith is derived from charity (*quod est perfectionis in fide, a caritate deducitur*). In the Latin Vulgate, St. Thomas's Bible, the term *agapē* is translated "charity" rather than "love." More faithfully translated, V.14.5.R says that faith is perfected in love.

Having resolved this immediate problem, however, we should return to the main project of the present study. This study aims at coming to terms with the twentieth-century papal encyclical *Fides et Ratio*, which opens with the evocative pronouncement: "Faith and reason are like two wings on which the human spirit rises to the contemplation of truth" (Latin above). The method of this study is to trace the evolution of the concepts of truth, faith, and reason, from the NT up to the twentieth century. Next in order is what St. Thomas had to say about *ratio* (reason). The primary text for this part of the study is Question 15 of *De Veritate*, entitled "Higher and Lower Reason."

## 4.5 Aquinas on Reason

The term *logos* had a wide range of meanings in classical Greek, many having to do with language (word, speech, discourse, conversation, etc.). Plato occasionally used it to designate reason, as in *Republic* 401D1 and *Timaeus* 29A7. When Aristotle says at *Politics* 1253a that man is the only animal with the gift of *logos*, however, he is referring to language rather than to reason. Despite not uncommon claims to the contrary, Aristotle did not define man as an animal with reason.

Among roughly three hundred occurrences of the term *logos* in the NT, common meanings are those of "speech," "saying," and of course "word" itself. In the opening passages of the Gospel John, Jesus and God are both designated *logos*, and the *logos* that is Jesus is said to have taken on flesh. There are no uses of the term to mean (the power of) reason in the NT. Not only is reason never mentioned in the NT, but moreover it contains no distinct cases of reasoning in the form of demonstrative arguments. Use of reason in this form would have counted as doing theology. And the NT authors were intent on recounting their personal connections with Jesus, with no incentive to engage in theological speculation.

In his role of theologian, Augustine was preceded by Tertullian and Origen, who both wrote primarily in Greek. From Augustine through the Middle Ages, however, Christian theology in the western Church was conducted in Latin. The Latin term for reason, of course, is *ratio*, which can convey a range of meanings comparable to that of the Greek *logos*. As we have seen, several distinct meanings are represented in the theological writings of Augustine. In a sense he treated as basic, Augustine tied the operation of reason to that of the bodily senses. The connection is spelled out in VII.xvii.23 of the *Confessions*. Bodily sensations are conveyed to an inner faculty of representation (imagination), images of which then are referred to the reasoning faculty where they are judged for accuracy and significance. For Augustine, in contrast with Aristotle, a human being is distinguished from other animals by his or her faculty of reason.

Inasmuch as reason is tied basically to the senses, entities without bodies lack basic reason. Relative to this basic sense, the eternal reason Augustine attributes to God must be figurative rather than literal. Given its lack of bodily involvement, however, eternal (divine) reason can dwell within the mind, where it provides a criterion by which the mind's other contents can be judged for veracity. Eternal reason also provides an internal light by which such judgment can take place. Augustine's so-called "illumination theory" is discussed at length above, along with other of his theological doctrines concerning reason.

Augustine relies heavily on reason himself in developing these theological doctrines. On the basis of his own reasoning, he concludes that God is identical to Truth, that God has desires (e.g., to be believed in), and that unaided reason is too weak to discover God's Truth. But nowhere in the works we have considered does Augustine pause to reflect on the nature of the reason he employs to establish such conclusions. Nowhere does he consider whether indeed such conclusions are within reach of human reason in the first place. To posit a divine power that guarantees the reliability of theological reasoning is an exercise of theological reasoning itself. And it is not self-evident that the rational discipline of theology is capable of establishing its own reliability.

St. Thomas is more forthcoming than previous theologians in this regard. There are several Questions in *De Veritate* alone that address the nature of reason and its imputed powers. Most explicit in its treatment of these issues is Question 15, pertaining to Higher and Lower Reason and the relation between them. We turn now to Question 15, along with other relevant writings of St. Thomas.

4.5.1

The main term for reason in *De Veritate* is *ratio*, which is used an average of more than four times per standard-sized page in the relatively short discussion of Question 15. Less frequently used in this discussion are *ratiocinatio*, for reasoning, and *rationalis*, for rational. The term *ratione* is occasionally used for reason in the specific sense of cause; and *rationem* is used for (substantial) nature in a few isolated cases. Another less frequently used term for reasoning is *discursus* (discourse, V.15.1.R), apparently a shortened form of *rationis discursus* (movement of reason, V.15.1.R).

Reason is explicitly defined in V.15.1.R as "a transition from one thing to another by which the human mind reaches or arrives at knowledge of something else" (*discursum . . . quo ex uno in aliud cognoscendum anima humana pertingit vel pervenit*). In contrast with Augustine, it should be noted, reason for Aquinas is not essentially tied to the senses. This leaves it free it to operate on the level of intellect itself.

Also noteworthy is that reason is characterized as a kind of motion. Earlier in V.15.1.R, Aquinas compares the way angels receive knowledge with the way of human beings. "Higher spiritual substances" (*substantiae spirituales superiores*), he says, "receive knowledge of truth by an initially sudden and simple reception, without any motion or discursion" (*sine aliquo motu vel discursu statim in prima et subita sive simplici acceptione cognitionem obtinent veritatis*). "Lower [spiritual substances]" (*inferiores*), however, "arrive a perfect knowledge of truth only through a certain movement, in which they go from one thing to another" (*ad cognitionem veritatis perfectam pervenire non possunt nisi per quemdam motum, quo ab uno in aliud discurrunt*). This part of his discussion ends with the observation that the reasoning process is aimed at "reaching knowledge of things unknown through what is known" (*ex cognitis in incognitorum notitiam perveniant*).

Angels receive knowledge immediately through a kind of "simple reception," whereas human knowledge is gained by reasoning from things known previously. Not surprisingly, this description of human reasoning fits what today is known as syllogistic (or Aristotelian) logic. If the premises of a valid syllogism are true, then the conclusion must be true as well. And according to the Aristotelian tradition, knowledge that a proposition is true can be gained by deducing it syllogistically from other propositions known to be true previously. For Aquinas, such reasoning leads to what he calls "science" (*scientia*). As he puts it in V.14.9.R, "it is by reason that science is made perfect" (*scientia per rationem perficitur*).

The perfection of scientific knowledge is also referred to as its "term" (*terminus*). Citing Aristotle's *Physics* (no specific reference) as authority, Aquinas remarks in V.15.1.R that "as motion is related to rest as its source and its term, so reason is related to understanding, as also is generation related to existence" (*sic motus comparatur ad quietem et ut ad principium et ut ad terminum, ita etiam et ratio comparatur ad intellectum . . . et ut generatio ad esse*). As motion generally starts with rest, this passage says, so the motion of reason in particular must begin with something already understood. The passage quoted continues with an explanation of this requirement. The motion of reason must "begin with some simple acceptance of truth" (*ab aliqua simplici acceptione veritatis inciperet*), where "what is accepted is an understanding of principles [beginnings, starting points]" (*quidem acceptio est intellectus principiorum*).

This discursive movement of reason, Aquinas says, proceeds "to first principles" (*ad principia prima*), "in which [the process of] reason is resolved" (*in quae ratio resolvit*). As far as reason in general is concerned, the upshot is (a) that "understanding is the source of reasoning in the course of discovery" (*intellectus inveniatur rationis principium quantum ad viam inveniendi*), and (b) that reason "issues in judgment as its proper term" (*terminus vero quantum ad viam iudicandi*).

As a consequence, "although knowledge proper to the human mind takes place by way of reasoning" (*quamvis cognitio humanae animae proprie sit per viam rationis*), "it participates to some extent in the simple knowledge which occurs in higher substances" (*in ea aliqua participatio illius simplicis cognitionis quae in superioribus substantiis*). This section concludes with a quote from Dionysius, to the effect that "the lower nature at its highest point reaches something of what is lower in the higher nature" (*inferior natura in sui summo attingit ad aliquid infimum superioris naturae*).

4.5.2

Aquinas opens his response in Question 15, Article 1, of *De Veritate*, by agreeing with Augustine that "spiritual substances" (*substantias spirituales*) are ordered by higher and lower. Part of the superiority of angels in the spiritual order is that they receive knowledge of truth without the discursive process of reasoning. Human beings are lower because they come to know truth only by "moving from one thing to another" (*ab uno in aliud discurrunt*), and "gain knowledge of things unknown through those that are known" (*ex cognitis in incognitorum notitiam perveniant*).

Later in this response he also follows Augustine in listing the several stages through which the human mind advances in knowledge. In stage (1), the mind "knows forms in matter through the senses" (*per sensum cognoscat formas in materia*). Next, in stage (2), "[it knows] accidental forms without matter though the imagination" (*per imaginationem formas accidentales, tamen sine materia*). Stage (3) is "[knowledge of] the essential form of material things by reason, without individual matter" (*per rationem ipsam essentialem formam rerum materialium sine individuali materia*). Then in stage (4), it "rises higher in the knowledge of created spirits" (*ulterius consurgit . . . cognitionem de spiritibus creatis*) to the level of "understanding" (*intellectum*), which consists of "prior knowledge of inward substances that exist entirely without matter (*substantias penitus sine materia existentes per prius cognoscunt*). With mind thus elevated, the final stage (5) arrives when it "extends even further to some [kind of] knowledge of God himself" (*ulterius pertingit in aliquam cognitionem ipsius Dei*), and thus "is said to have intelligence" (*dicitur intelligentiam habere*).

With respect to faculties involved, this progression follows the order of (1) sensation, (2) imagination, (3) reason, (4) understanding, and then (5) intelligence. Each faculty is spoken of (explicitly or by implication) as a form of *cognitio* (thinking, understanding, perceiving), which like *contemplatio* (observing, contemplating, considering) is a general term for mental awareness. For Augustine, as argued above, reason extended beyond the sensory realm is figurative rather than literal. But for Aquinas, reason occupies a stage in the progression of human knowledge that leads beyond the sensory to a marginal awareness of divinity.

The progression from sensation (1) to intelligence (5) provides a context in which higher and lower reason can be defined and related. Aquinas begins his response in Article 2 by observing that higher and lower reason are not different "powers of mind" (*potentiae animae*), but rather the same power "serving tandem functions" (*per officia geminamus*). A power (*potentia*) functions by becoming active, which generates a corresponding act (*actus*). Drawing on Aristotle, Aquinas observes further that mental acts "are specified by their terms" (*comparetur ad actum sicut terminus*), which is to say by the objects toward which they are directed. In effect, he concludes, "acts are distinguished according to their objects" (*actus penes obiecta distinguantur*). As far as powers of the mind are concerned, "diversity of objects brings about diversity regarding powers" (*obiectorum diversitas, potentiarum diversitatem inducit*).

As his next step toward distinguishing higher and lower reason, Aquinas observes that the rational mind relates in different ways to different stages in the progression (1) through (5). Being capable of higher things, reason looks down on objects of stages (1) and (2) (objects of sensation and imagination). Being involved as it is with physical objects, on the other hand, reason looks up to objects of stages (4) and (5) (objects of understanding and intelligence). Higher reason is that of stage (3) looking upward, whereas lower reason is that of stage (3) looking downward.

In Aquinas's own terms, stage (3) is called higher reason "in its reference to higher natures, either as contemplating their nature and truth in themselves" (*Secundum enim quod ad superiores nauras . . . sive ut earum veritatem et naturam absolute contemplans*), or "as taking them as a model for activity" (*quasi exemplar operandi accipiens*). The reason of stage (3) "is called lower reason" (*inferior ratio nominatur*), in turn, "insofar as it is directed toward lower [things], either to perceive them through contemplation or to manage them in action" (*Secundum vero quod ad inferiora convertitur vel conspicienda per contemplationem, vel per actionem disponenda*).

So much for the higher and lower reason of Question 15. On balance, as we shall see, Aquinas's treatment of reason is far more disciplined that that of John Paul II in *Fides et Ratio*.

## 4.6 Critique of Reason in Aquinas

There are two reasons implicated in Aquinas's account, which he does not distinguish explicitly. One is the reason that is the subject of the account (reason(subj)), the reason about which the account is written. The other is the reason employed by Aquinas in constructing the account, which is to say the author's reason (reason(auth)). The account of reason(subj) has been constructed by reason(auth). But the account does not apply to the reason(auth) by which it was constructed.

Whether reason(auth) or otherwise, Aquinas's reason(subj) is not a reason actively at work in real life. No actual reason served as a model after which reason(subj) was fashioned. Reason(subj) instead is a theoretical construct, fabricated to meet certain requirements. Reason(subj), that is to say, was constructed to play a preconceived theoretical role.

Let us review features of Aquinas's reason(subj) that reflect its de facto theoretical role. In V.15.1.R, reason is characterized as "a transition from one thing to another by which the human mind arrives at knowledge of something else" (Latin above). The transition alluded to is from knowing particular premises to knowing a conclusion with content that goes beyond the content of the premises.

Such a transition, however, is logically invalid, for reasons that can illustrated by Venn diagrams. Consider the syllogistic inference: If all S is M, and all M is P, then all S is P. In Venn diagrammatic form, the inference consists of three intersecting circles, corresponding to S, M, and P, respectively, showing that no S exists outside of M and no M exists outside of P (the two premises), and furthermore that no S exists outside of P (the conclusion). If the inference is valid, diagramming the premises results in diagramming the conclusion as well. In the case of an invalid inference, however, diagramming the premises would not result in diagramming the conclusion. If diagramming the purported conclusion requires more than diagramming the premises, then the conclusion goes beyond the premises and the inference is invalid.

In non-syllogistic inference, as argued previously, the requirement is the same. If the content of the conclusion goes beyond that of the premises, the inference is invalid. The quotation from Aquinas's V.15.1.R characterizes an invalid inference. His reason(subj) is a theoretical construct that in application would violate the laws of logic. Valid (deductive) reasoning cannot extend knowledge beyond what is already known.

Another problematic thesis of V.15.1.R compares the knowledge of angels with that of human beings. Angels are said to be higher than humans in the spiritual order because they receive knowledge of truth without use of reasoning. Humans are inferior because their access to truth is discursive, "moving from one thing to another" (Latin above). As previously noted, however, Aquinas thought that human reason is able to "gain knowledge of things unknown through those that are known" (Latin above). And among things initially unknown are things in the spiritual domain that angels know without reason. Human access to such things, Aquinas maintains, is facilitated by what he refers to as "higher reason."

Higher reason is distinguished from lower reason in V.15.1.R. The distinction has to do with the objects toward which the two modes of reason are directed. Lower reason is directed toward objects of sensation and imagination. Higher reason, by contrast, is directed toward "higher natures, either as contemplating their nature and truth in themselves" (Latin above), or in patterning its own activity with them as exemplars. Higher reason prepares the human mind for "knowledge of created spirits" (Latin above). It serves as a "springboard," so to speak, for understanding higher things.

Higher reason is a theoretical construct, which is to say a form of reason(subj). It cannot credibly belong to reason(auth), since this would amount to Aquinas's own reasoning assigning features to itself. But reason(auth) by itself cannot alter its own nature. A person training to be a weather-forecaster cannot increase his or her skills at prediction just by predicting increased skills at the end of training. No more can a person manipulate his or her powers of reason just by applying reason in making theories about them.

Aquinas's reason(subj) is a theoretical construct devised to meet certain preconceived requirements. These requirements, it appears in retrospect, were primarily theological in nature. First and foremost, his reason(subj) was required to produce knowledge of "things unknown" by inference from "things known." Among things initially unknown are spiritual beings such as angels, eternal truths that serve as prototypes of created truths, and the unique Truth that is God himself. Endowed with such capacities, Aquinas's reason(subj) provides a precedent for the reason built into John Paul II's *Faith and Reason*. But neither Aquinas's reason(subj) nor that of John Paul II's encyclical, as we shall see, produces inferences that are logically valid.

Aquinas's reason(subj) is faulty in that it purports to extend knowledge without empirical support. As argued in chapter 1, knowledge is a mental state directed to states of affairs (SOAs) as objects. And reasoning by itself cannot shift the mind's focus from one SOA to another. What reason can do in this regard is specify circumstance under which additional SOAs might be presented to the mind open for verification by experience. Additional knowledge is gained when these further SOAs are empirically verified. Whatever means of verification are employed, empirical verification is necessary for the extension of genuine knowledge. Aquinas's V.15.1.R falls short in its depiction of a kind of knowledge that is accessible by reason alone, without benefit of further verification.

## 4.7 Summary of Chapter

The foregoing investigation has focused on Thomas Aquinas's views of truth, of faith, and of reason. A brief review of its main results is in order. In the review that follows, attention will be limited to the views themselves, without regard to the (often complex) arguments by which the author supports them. Text citations will be avoided, as will reference to distinctive formats in which his views are presented.

Unlike Augustine, Aquinas had a systematic account of propositional truth. For Aquinas, a proposition consists of a subject and a predicate, mentally related in ways provided by syllogistic logic. Corresponding to propositions are complex events in the world. A proposition is true just in case its parts are arranged in the same way as are parts of the corresponding events. The relation between propositions and the events that render them true is referred to as "adequation" (conformity). Given their truth-making role, Aquinas extends the term "true" to conforming events themselves. Both truths in the mind and truths in the world are "created truths," stemming from "uncreated Truth" in the mind of God.

Aquinas's preferred label for uncreated (changeless, eternal) Truth is "First Truth." Among its many roles, First Truth not only is the source of created truths but also supports the human mind in its awareness of truth. First Truth both enables the mind to grasp created truth (as in Augustine's illumination theory), and provides a criterion by which the veracity of created truth can be assessed. The eternality of First Truth makes it a key component of religious faith, pertaining to the ultimate goal of eternal life.

Thus conceived, this unchanging First Truth supports a radical realism regarding created truths. Aquinas's view on the matter is that contents of the created world would not change even if human beings did not exist. First Truth is responsible for the way things are, which makes the way things are independent of the human intellect. In Aquinas's own words, "supposing that the human intellect did not or could not exist, things themselves would still remain essentially the same."

An apparent difficulty with this concept of Eternal Truth has to do with its incomposite character. If First Truth were composite, it would not be eternal because its parts could separate. Without parts, however, it would lack the composite structure that enables created truths to conform with events in the world. Either First Truth is true in some manner not involving conformity, or it conforms in a way Aquinas seemingly did not try to clarify. In either case, it is unclear how incomposite First Truth could be the source of composite created truth.

Next comes Aquinas's understanding of faith. According to his "scientifically formulated" definition, faith is a mental habit that (1) begins our journey to eternal life, and (2) produces assent to things that are not perceived. In role (1), faith is further described as divinely inspired and as involving an act of will perfected by charity (love). Role (2) is taken directly from his translation of Heb 11:1. Since the things to which understanding assents are unseen, assent here cannot be based on empirical evidence. Faith itself is divinely infused, and itself provides witness to divine things that are not seen.

As with Augustine, faith for Aquinas is closely related to belief. Following Augustine, Aquinas defines belief as thinking with assent. To assent, he says, is to hold the concerned thought as true. A thought is true, as before, just in case it conforms with the way things stand in the world. Assent is forthcoming when the mind judges that the thought (proposition) in question conforms in this manner. We believe what we find true, and disbelieve what we find false. A belief itself is true, of course, only when the mind assents to a thought (affirmative or negative) that actually is true. When it assents to a false thought, the resulting belief itself is false. A relevant implication of Aquinas's analysis is that the truth-status of a belief can change with changes in the world at large.

Unlike Augustine, Aquinas emphases respects in which faith differs from belief. A major difference has to do with their respective objects. Acts of belief are directed toward events in the world, whereas acts of faith are directed toward divine entities (God, under one or another description). This goes hand in hand with the variable character of belief, previously noted, in contrast with the unchangeable character of religious faith. A related difference stems from Aquinas's definition of faith, which portrays it as assent to things that cannot be seen. Belief pertains primarily to things in the perceptible world, whereas faith pertains to imperceptible things.

The most telling difference, however, has to do with the manner in which faith is expressed by acts of belief. As a gift of God, faith is passive (something received) rather than active. This means that faith cannot act on its own. Yet Aquinas frequently mentions acts of faith, which he says are expressed in the acts of belief that represent them. Within the range of human activity, faith is manifest in personal acts of belief. An illustration is provided in the *Summa Theologica*, where Aquinas affirms that "an act of faith is to believe in God." Faith in God, in other words, is expressed in the beliefs about God that a faithful person lives by. In sum, faith is immutable in being directed toward an immutable object, but is expressed in beliefs that vary with changing circumstances.

We turn finally to a summary of Aquinas's understanding of reason. According to his explicit definition, reason is a faculty by which the human mind extends its knowledge from a given thing to something else. Exercise of reason (i.e., reasoning) is a transition from one state of knowledge to another. A paradigm for Aquinas is syllogistic reasoning, in which knowledge of premises is extended to knowledge of conclusions. According to his analysis, reason begins with fixed premises, moves through various stages of inference, and terminates with fixed conclusions that can be used as premises in other inferences. In scientific reasoning specifically, Aquinas remarks, its motion (the inference) is related to its rest (the conclusion), as (a) reason itself is related to the understanding it produces, and more abstractly as (b) generation is related to existence.

A distinctive feature of Aquinas's account is his multi-leveled ordering of mental states. Part of this account is a distinction between higher and lower reason. The ordering progresses from (1) sensation to (2) imagination, to (3) reason, to (4) understanding, and then to (5) intelligence. In its intermediate role, reason can deal both with lower (1) and (2) (the sensible world) and upper (4) and (5) (the intelligible world). Reasoning not only moves the mind logically from premise to conclusion; it also guides the mind in its progression upward from (sensory-based) conjecture to higher truth.

The mental progression from sensation to intelligence corresponds to an ontological progression from lower to higher being. Highest in being is God, who exists essentially. Beneath God comes the angels. Lower yet are living animals with various nutritive and perceptual faculties. Given their distinctive faculty of discursive reason, human beings are highest among living creatures.

This sets the stage for Aquinas's distinction between higher and lower reason. In its intermediate position, reason can deal with lower levels of being than that of humanity itself. In this capacity, Aquinas describes it as lower reason. Reason can also deal with intelligible beings higher than itself, in which role it is described as higher reason. This is the reason employed in exploring the nature of immaterial angels and in characterizing the attributes of God.

As noted in the previous section, however, Aquinas's theoretical account of reason is faulty. It errs in assuming that reason can extend knowledge into domains where empirical verification is not possible. Faith has access to such domains, but cannot be augmented by knowledge gained by reason independently of empirical support.

Thomas Aquinas had a powerful mind, and was a thinker of exemplary intellectual integrity. It was not his lot to mount a critique of either the credibility of his reason(subj) or the soundness of his own reason(auth) by which that construct was created. The anomalies we have been considering in his reason(subj), however, make it clear that critiques of both are much to be desired.

It is a matter of some significance, in this regard, that the Transcendental Thomists intervened between Thomas Aquinas and John Paul II. The Transcendental Thomists were heavily influenced by Immanuel Kant's *Critique of Pure Reason*.

# CHAPTER 5

# Transcendental Thomism

## 5.1 Background to Kant

St. Thomas was not alone in taking the power of his own discursive reason for granted. So also did Augustine, Tertullian and Origen, and indeed Aristotle himself. Aristotle, of course, had well-developed theories about various functions of the mind (e.g., in *De Anima*), as well as a systematic account of scientific reasoning. But theories about the mind and its modes of reasoning do not constitute an inquiry into the rational powers by which such theories are produced. What Aristotle, Augustine, and Aquinas all lack is an analysis of the powers and limits of human reason itself.

In point of fact, the same may be said for dominant philosophers of the modern period. The legendary method of Descartes was to search out a starting point he could not doubt (the "Cogito"), and then to construct a comprehensive overview of the world on this indubitable basis. But Descartes's overview may have exceeded what sound reason can accomplish. And as far as his method itself is concerned, the limits of reason cannot be probed by attempting to doubt them.

The skepticism of Hume extends doubt in an opposite direction, attempting to undermine established beliefs rather than to provide an indubitable basis for human knowledge. Hume's is a skeptical doubt, bent on demolition rather than construction. But like Descartes, Hume does not explore possible limits of his own use of doubt as a philosophic method. It remains possible that there are some things that can be doubted privately but not publicly. And philosophy, by nature, is a public discipline. Despite their different aims in employing doubt as part of their respective philosophic projects, neither Hume nor Descartes addresses the question of whether there are limits to the employment of doubt as a theoretical method.

Across the range of western philosophy from Aristotle to Hume, there is recurrent need for an explicit examination of the powers and limits of human reason. What is needed is what we are led to expect by the title of Kant's epoch-making *Critique of Pure Reason*. Pure reason for Kant is reasoning that does not involve ongoing sense experience, in contrast with empirically-based reason dealing with practical affairs. Pure reason includes the theoretical reasoning of mathematicians, philosophers, and theologians. With the reasoning of Augustine and Aquinas primarily in mind, let us turn to Kant's examination of the powers and limits of theoretical reason.

## 5.2 Kant's *Critique of Pure Reason*

Kant's intent in writing the *Critique* is stated in the Preface to the First Edition, published in 1781. What he intended to accomplish, Kant says, is

> a critique of the faculty of reason in general, in respect of all knowledge after which it may strive *independently of all experience*. It will therefore decide as to the possibility or impossibility of metaphysics in general, and determine its sources, its extent, and its limits. (Norman Kemp Smith's 1929 translation, italics included; German text will not be given, inasmuch as the translation is usually more accessible than the original text).

By way of anticipation, it should be noted that Kant's critique yielded a comprehensive overview of his own making, but one constructed within the limits revealed by that critique.

The briefer *Prolegomena to Any Future Metaphysics* was published in 1783, before the expanded Second Edition of the *Critique* in 1787. Kant's famous remark about being stirred from his "dogmatic slumber" is found in his introduction to the *Prolegomena*, namely:

> I openly confess my recollection of David Hume was the very thing which many years ago first interrupted my dogmatic slumber and gave my Investigations in the field of speculative

philosophy a quite new direction" (P. 8, translated in 1950 by L. W. Beck; as above, there is no point in repeating the original text).

What Kant found so disturbing was Hume's analysis of the relation between cause and effect, which for Hume was mere sequence short of necessity.

The *Critique* begins with an examination of space and time, which Kant designates forms of intuition (sensibility). Space is the form of external sensibility. All representations of outer origin occur in space, which underlies all external relations (like cause and effect). Time is the form of internal sensibility. Contents of the mind are presented in temporal sequence. External events also occur in time, every event both following and preceding other events (as cause precedes effect). Space and time apply only to sensible representations (*phenomena*), not to so-called "things in themselves" (*noumena*) they might be taken to represent.

The forms of space and time are *a priori*, in the sense of existing before (prior to) and apart from the experiences they characterize. Geometry is the study of things structured in space, and yields judgments which themselves are *a priori*. Being thus prior in origin, judgments of geometry are apodictic (necessary). Such judgments constitute knowledge of things in space prior to their occurrence. Arithmetic is the study of things in necessary sequence (n before n+1, etc.). Judgments pertaining to numerical relations also are apodictic. Along with geometry, arithmetic yields *a priori* judgments that represent structures displayed by empirical phenomena.

Judgments not certifiable in advance are termed "*a posteriori.*" Such judgments are made after (posterior to) the experiences to which they apply. The truth of such judgments cannot be known in advance. Practical affairs, by and large, are conducted on the basis of *a posteriori* judgments. When reasoning is involved in practical affairs, it employs forms of reason that are not apodictic, such as induction, supposition, and experimentation. Kant's first *Critique* has little to say about practical forms of reason.

Kant also distinguishes between analytic and synthetic judgments. Analytic judgments are those in which the concept of the predicate is contained in the concept of the subject. In this case, the predicate can be grasped by analyzing the subject. Synthetic judgments are those in which the predicate lies outside the subject. To bring subject and predicate together is to combine them synthetically. In thus conjoining them, content from the predicate is added to the subject, which is to say that the subject is amplified by the predicate. For this reason, Kant also refers to synthetic judgments as ampliative.

From these definitions, it is apparent that analytic judgments are *a priori* and that *a posteriori* judgments are synthetic. But the definitions allow that some judgments might be both synthetic and *a priori*. Kant was convinced that mathematical judgments possess both characteristics. Although *a priori* and apodictic, judgments about the disposition of objects in space are not analytic. The property of containing angles totaling 360 degrees is not included in the concept of a triangle (otherwise non-Euclidean geometry would not be possible). Judgments of geometry, accordingly, are synthetic *a priori*. In like fashion, the property of being a member of an unending series is not included in the concept of a (natural) number. The judgment of arithmetic that every number has a successor, accordingly, is likewise synthetic *a priori*.

Arithmetic and geometry are synthetic *a priori* sciences. In Kant's estimation, however, metaphysics falls short of this status. Driven by questions it cannot address scientifically, human reason is naturally disposed to seek metaphysical answers. While such answers might disclose limits to rational inquiry (their regulative role), however, they do not themselves constitute apodictic knowledge (that is, they lack a constitutive role). Pursued (fruitlessly) as an avenue to genuine knowledge, metaphysics admits only dogmatic employment.

The *Prolegomena to Any Future Metaphysics* goes further in analyzing the predicament of this would-be science. In the final section "How Is Metaphysics Possible as Science?" the title-question receives an evasive answer. Briefly paraphrased, the answer is that this possibility hangs on its being able to produce convincing examples of synthetic *a priori* knowledge. Reflecting on the metaphysics of his time, Kant thinks that this possibility is remote. In relation to his critique and its requirements, metaphysics is to genuine knowledge as alchemy is to chemistry, or astrology to astronomy. The scientific credentials of metaphysics, he remarks, have not improved since the time of Aristotle.

Not only is metaphysics unable to produce genuine knowledge, it is also defective in its relation to possible experience. In the section "How is Metaphysics in general Possible?" Kant charges that metaphysics can blunder in various ways "without any fear of being detected in falsehood." The "purely fictitious propositions" it generates "cannot be refuted by experience." Neither, for the same reason, can they be verified. Generally speaking, metaphysics is so removed from "objective reality" that it produces "assertions whose truth or falsity cannot be . . . confirmed by any experience."

## 5.3 The Neo-Thomistic Response to Modernity

Catholic thought was slow to react to the Kantian critique, but when it came the reaction was hostile. Its animus was not directed against Kant specifically, but rather against his influence on modern thought. Kant was viewed as the harbinger of what the Church termed "Modernity," a cultural mind-set attacked vigorously by a series of unbending popes. Notably first in the sequence was Pius IX, who convened the First Vatican Council (1869–70) and declared *ex cathedra* the Immaculate Conception of the Virgin Mary. Pius IX issued a "Syllabus of Errors" (*Syllabus Errorum*) in 1864, consisting of eighty modernist theses he deemed heretical. The eightieth and last of these alleged errors is that the Roman pontiff should reconcile himself with progress, liberalism, and modern civilization. Pius IX himself was intent on avoiding that heresy.

Papal infallibility was proclaimed in *Pastor Aeternis* (Eternal Shepard), issued by the First Vatican Council over Pius IX's signature. This dogma, described as "divinely revealed," affirms that "the Roman pontiff is possessed of that infallibility with which the Divine Redeemer willed that his Church should be endowed in defining doctrines regarding faith and morals." Within months after being proclaimed infallible, Pius IX defined the doctrine of the Immaculate Conception.

Leo XIII was known for his opposition to the "modern" (Darwinian) view that the human species evolved, and for his authorship of the encyclical *Aeterni Patris* (Eternal Father). The subtitle of the encyclical is *On the Restoration of Christian Philosophy in Catholic Schools in the Spirit of the Angelic Doctor, St. Thomas Aquinas*. Catholic schools include seminaries, colleges, and research universities. The philosophy of St. Thomas, the encyclical states, should guide the pursuit not only of philosophy but of other disciplines, explicitly including the liberal arts and the physical sciences.

Of particular concern is the relation prescribed by *Aeterni Patris* between philosophy and theology. Although a discipline of enquiry itself, philosophy is subject to guidance by divine truth in the province of theology. As the encyclical puts it (section 8), philosophy is the "handmaid and attendant" (*ancillae et pedisequae*) of faith. To aid in this regard, Leo XIII sponsored a new edition of St. Thomas' works, which came to be known as the "Leonine" edition. It is worth noting, in anticipation of later developments, that section 31 of the encyclical states explicitly that the works of St. Thomas are to be studied themselves, rather than being taught in manual form that might contain errors. This instruction soon was to be contravened.

Pius X, like Pius IX before him, attacked modernity directly. Two strongly worded attacks bearing his name were issued in 1907. One, titled *Lamentibili Sane Exitu* (Truly Lamentable Departure), was prepared for his signature by that part of the Roman Curia soon to be renamed "Supreme Sacred Congregation of the Holy Office" (previously the Inquisition). This wordy and stylistically awkward document contains sixty-five tenets, which it roundly condemns, that were considered to be typical of modern thought. Modernity is explicitly mentioned in the subtitle of the second, the full title of which is *Pascendi Dominici Gregis: De Modernistram Doctrinis* (Feeding the Lord's Flock: On the Doctrines of the Modernists).

The encyclical *Pascendi Dominici Gregis* contains some remarkable passages. In section 46, the author states that every science and art should serve theology actively as "handmaid and attendant" (*ancilliarum . . . famulentur*). In Aeterni Patris, philosophy alone had been assigned to that role. After *Pascendi Dominici Gregis,* all arts and sciences are deemed servants of theology. As far as philosophy specifically is concerned, all its professors are warned in section 45 that they are in peril if they set St. Thomas aside. In section 39, tenets of modernity are described generally as a "summary of all heresies" (*omnium haereseon conlectum*). Pius X prescribes two strategies for guarding against heresy. One is to require all clergy to take an "anti-modernist oath." The other is to keep them away from heretical literature. To this latter end, he made mandatory the practice of bishops giving their *imprimatur* to innocuous books, accompanied by a *nihil obstat* and the name of the bishop who issued it.

As just noted, Pius X's *Pascendi Dominici Gregis* requires that professors of philosophy adhere to the metaphysical teachings of St. Thomas. Included in that document is a list of twenty-four theses selected from these teachings (drawn mostly from the *Summa Contra Gentiles*) that philosophers should accept as basic for their work. When Pope Benedict XV (Pius X's successor) published *Codex Iuris Canonici* (Code of Canon Law) in 1917, he ordered that these twenty-four theses be instituted for that purpose. The key requirement of the *Codex* is that the doctrines, methods, and principles of St. Thomas be used in teaching philosophy and theology. (This document apparently was never published in its original Latin.)

The call in *Aeterni Patris* to make the teaching of St. Thomas basic to instruction in Catholic seminaries and universities was given specific content in terms of these twenty-four theses. While all are drawn from the writings of St. Thomas, however, it is worth noting that these theses derive in large part from his reading of Aristotle. Approximately half are Christian adaptations of basic Aristotelian concepts (substance and accident, act and potency, etc.), and a few have no apparent connection with Aristotle. The remainder, however, are straight Aristotle without Christian embellishment. In effect, the popes' mandate that Catholic thought be based on St. Thomas is a requirement that it remain anchored in the Aristotelian tradition. By papal intent, at least, a Catholic philosopher is an Aristotelian.

What the popes mandated has come to be known as Neo-Scholasticism or Neo-Thomism. In effect, the Scholasticism that flourished freely in the thirteenth and fourteenth centuries was forcibly reinstated half a millennium later. Implementation of this Thomistic mandate was left to philosophers who specialized in writing textbooks. Inasmuch as the purpose of these textbooks was to instruct students in the rudiments of Thomistic thought, they became known as manuals (handbooks), corresponding to the instruction manuals one receives with a new machine or appliance. There were manuals pertaining to various facets of Catholic thought, including ontology, metaphysics, and philosophy of nature (science), along with psychology, ethics, and logic. (A onetime colleague of mine wrote a logic manual that contained exercise pages to be torn from the back, thus depriving the book of resale value.)

Needless to say, these instruction manuals had little scholarly value. People composing them were expected to remain faithful to previously existing texts, carefully guarding against the introduction of new thoughts of their own. And people read them without gaining scholarly skills that might be employed in advancing the frontiers of knowledge. The stultifying effect of manual instruction contributed to the progressive decline of Neo-Thomism in the period leading up to the Second Vatican Council. Catholic philosophy required the fresh air of Vatican II to gain the new vigor it showed later in the twentieth century.

## 5.4 The Emergence of Transcendental Thomism

The anti-modernity movement in the Church was a response to its perception of the nemesis posed by the influence of Kant. Underway during roughly the same time was another movement in the Church that viewed the influence of Kant more positively. This other movement was not a defense of modernity, but rather an attempt to extend Kant's critique in a direction favorable to Christian spirituality. Reflecting Kant's view of the self as transcendental, this other movement is commonly designated "Transcendental Thomism."

The movement consisted primarily of a group of Jesuit theologians. All wrote in languages other than Latin, and all were opposed to Neo-Thomism. First among them chronologically were Pierre Rousselot (1878–1915) and Joseph Maréchal (1878–1944). Following these two, both in time and influence, were Karl Rahner (1904–84) and Bernard Lonergan (1904–84). Rousselot and Maréchal wrote in French, Rahner in German, and Lonergan in English.

Looking ahead to John Paul II's *Fides et Ratio*, we should note that John Paul II regarded the Jesuit order with suspicion. Early in his pontificate, he took steps to neutralize its liberal influence. Wary relations between Pope and Jesuits were described in the *New York Times* of October 24, 1981, under the title "Pope Puts Jesuits Under Closer Rein." The Pope's main grievance was that the Jesuits were hard to govern. None of the four Jesuits above is mentioned in *Fides et Ratio*. To help delineate the perspective from which that encyclical was written, we should consider what these "suspicious" theologians had to say.

## 5.5 Rousselot and Maréchal

Pierre Rousselot's major written work was *L'intellectualisme de saint Thomas*, published in 1908. The book is both a reaction to Neo-Thomist scholasticism and a development of the author's own views inspired by St. Thomas. Among the faults he finds in Neo-Thomism is its reliance on discursive reason in expounding theological doctrine. The life of the spirit, he argues, is not well served by a form of reasoning based on logical inference. A closely related flaw is Neo-Thomism's tendency to understand reality in terms of propositional descriptions. Propositions are creations of the human intellect, unsuited for description of religious experience. Fixation on propositions, Rousselot charges, is a form of idolatry, amounting to worship of a human creation.

Rousselot's own views were an outcome of his attempt to expand Kant's conception of the noumenal self into the dimension of spirit. Kant's critique dismissed the noumenal self as unintelligible. Rousselot's response was based on the reality of intelligence itself. Intelligence, for Rousselot, is an ontological principle with manifestations on various levels of being. God, by nature, is Infinite Intelligence. Human intelligence is manifest in human understanding, which is occupied with material events in space and time. In between is the intelligence of angels, approaching but subordinate to that of God. The goal of the human spirit is to become one with divine Intelligence, a condition described by mystics as a beatific vision.

Divine Intelligence, being perfect, is all comprehensive, which entails that it comprehends itself. God's intelligence thus is self-comprehension, which amounts to its being an object of its own activity. The being of God is pure intellect with itself as object. Human intelligence is ordered to progress stagewise toward self-comprehension, a progression that Rousselot views as sacramental in character. This leads to a description of his worldview as a "sacramental ontology." Every step taken in this ritual-laden progression is an affirmation of the divine Intelligence toward which it is directed. Such affirmation renders logical proofs of God's existence extraneous baggage, an impediment in the spirit's journey of self-comprehension.

Although Rousselot is sometimes described as a Transcendental Thomist, his main contribution to that school was his influence on Karl Rahner. He died in battle at age thirty-seven.

## 5.5.1

Joseph Maréchal was ordained a Jesuit priest in 1908. In addition to his novitiate training, he earned a degree in natural science from Leuven in 1905. He is said to have considered this scientific training a barrier against what he termed "auto-suggestive metaphysics," bespeaking his specific interest in experimental psychology. After a brief stay with Wilhelm Wundt in Munich, and several years in England during WWI, he returned to Leuven in 1919, where he taught the history of philosophy and psychology in the Jesuit scholasticate. During the following two decades, he published *Etudes sur la Psychologie des Mystique* and four volumes of his magnum opus *Le Point de Depart de la Metaphysique* (another volume was published posthumously). He stopped teaching and writing in 1939, due in part to ill health and (some say) in part to a feeling that his work had not been duly recognized.

According to Maréchal's reading of Kant, the noumenal domain of the first *Critique* is linked with the transcendental unity of apperception in ways that Kant had failed to appreciate. Whereas for Kant the formation of objects under the categories is static (like the imprint of a cookie cutter), Maréchal thought that the form-giving process should be understood as dynamic instead. In structuring the phenomenal world, the self (as subject of apperception) plays an active rather than a static role. Along with the intellectual dynamism of the subject, moreover, Maréchal purported to find a finality (end) that is foreign to Kant's analysis. His interpretation of this finality was in line with his understanding of Catholic teaching.

While extensively influenced by Kant, Maréchal thought of St. Thomas as his primary mentor. His rendition of the finality motivating the intellectual subject was based on a passage found in Aquinas' *De Veritate* (Question 22, Article 1): "All knowing beings implicitly know God in everything they know" (*omnia cognoscentia implicite cognoscunt Deum in quodlibet cognito*). According to Maréchal's interpretation of this passage, God himself is the complete Unity of being, and the intellectual self's urge for intelligibility can be satisfied only by assimilation with this absolute Unity. This driving force is an underlying constituent of the process by which the human intellect gains knowledge. In terms germane to Kant, the ultimate end of intellectual activity is to discover the unconditional ground of the conditional world of human experience. Maréchal was the first Catholic scholar to be commonly designated a Transcendental Thomist.

## 5.6 Karl Rahner

Karl Rahner was born in Freiburg (1904), entered the Society of Jesus in 1922, and was ordained in 1932. He began doctoral work in philosophy at Freiburg in 1934, only to have his thesis rejected in 1936. Among various grounds that have been suggested for its rejection, the "official" reason seems to have been its deviation from orthodox Neo-Thomism. He then moved to Innsbruck, where he quickly completed a doctorate in theology in 1937 and began teaching the same year. The rejected Freiburg dissertation was subsequently published as a book in 1941, under the title *Geist in Weld* (Spirit in the World).

Karl's elder brother, Hugo (1900–1968), was also a Jesuit teacher and scholar. Hugo entered the order in 1919, received his doctorate from Bonn in 1934, and began teaching in Innsbruck two years before Karl arrived. When the theology faculty was shut down by the Nazis in 1938, Hugo went to Switzerland and Karl went to Vienna. In 1945, Hugo returned to Innsbruck in the role of dean, and subsequently became rector. Hugo's main scholarly work was a biography of Ignatius of Loyola, published in 1956.

Karl himself, after almost a decade of pastoral work in Vienna, returned to Innsbruck to teach courses on the Eucharist and Mariology. Then without warning, in 1962, his superiors in Rome informed him that he could no longer teach or publish without advance permission. His views, apparently, were considered too unorthodox, particularly those on the Eucharist which rejected transubstantiation. In 1964, he was transferred to Munich, having been assigned a chair vacated by an ailing Romano Guardini. This apparent return to grace was due to his involvement in Vatican II, to which we turn presently. Karl left Munich for Münster in 1967, staying there until 1981, when he retired to spend his last years in Innsbruck. He continued writing until the end, and was said to have died from exhaustion.

Karl Rahner was an extraordinarily prolific writer. In the roughly 45 years between *Geist und Welt* and his death, he published over 3,500 titles in some dozen languages. Articles have been written surveying his publications. Additional books of his own authorship include *Worte ins Schweigen* (1938), *Hörer des Wortes* (1941), and *Gruntkurs des Glaubens* (1976). Most of his work, however, was in the form of journal articles and edited volumes. Edited works include the *Lexikon für Theologie und Kirche* (1957–65), the sixteen-volume *Schriften zur Theologie* (1954–84), and the six-volume *Sacramentum Mundi* (co-edited, 1968). A collection of his essays, *Prayers and Meditations: An Anthology of the Spiritual Writings by Karl Rahner*, was published by the author in 1980.

5.6.1

Like most German intellectuals of his time, Rahner was acquainted with
Kant as part of his academic background. He also attended Heidegger's
seminar on Kant in 1936. The focus of the seminar, however, was on the
*Critique of Judgment* rather than the *Critique of Pure Reason.* It seems unlikely that he had either opportunity or incentive to undertake a detailed
study of Kant's first *Critique,* with the consequence that his acquaintance
with this work was largely secondhand. According to his own report, the
Kant that influenced Rahner was learned mainly from Maréchal.

As commonly understood today, the title "Transcendental Thomist"
designates scholars who read St. Thomas in a Kantian light. Maréchal was
the first to be generally known as a Transcendental Thomist. Like Kant's
influence itself, Rahner's claim to this title is derivative from Maréchal.
In effect, the Kantian light in which Rahner viewed St. Thomas was filtered through a lens of Maréchal's making. We turn presently to specific
aspects of Rahner's view that reflect this influence.

While working for a philosophy degree in Freiburg, Rahner was
one of several young Jesuits who attended lectures and seminars given by
Martin Heidegger (1889–1976). Others in the group were Johannes Lotz,
Fernando Polanco, and Gustav Slewertz. Heidegger was on friendly terms
with these men, and (by his own account) frequently entertained them in
his house. Rahner himself attended eight of Heidegger's courses during
four semesters of 1934–36. While attending these lectures and seminars,
Rahner surely was aware of his mentor's political involvement. In June
1933, Heidegger had been appointed rector of Freiburg, but resigned
the next year under pressure for policies reflecting his membership in
the Nazi party. This seems not to have hindered his friendship with the
young Jesuits. When Rahner's philosophy thesis was turned down in
1936, however, although the "official" reason may have been conflict with
Neo-Thomism, another reason must have been disapproval of its obvious
dependence on the thought of Heidegger.

Heidegger had a reason for cultivating friendship with the young
Jesuits in his entourage. Early in his academic career, Heidegger himself
was preparing to enter the priesthood. He was dissuaded, at least in part,
by the failure of his efforts to gain appointment to Freiburg's chair of
Catholic philosophy. After this disappointment, his religious orientation
began to shift. In 1917, he married Elfride Petri (a Lutheran), a marriage
that persisted until his death in 1976. He considered himself an atheist

throughout his late career, maintaining that philosophy necessarily is an atheistic calling. Despite this, there have been numerous studies in recent years of religious themes embedded in his *Sein und Zeit*.

Rahner himself wrote a brief appreciation of Heidegger's religious significance in the form of a preface to *Karl Rahner: The Philosophical Foundations* (by Thomas Sheehan, 1987). Obviously written shortly before his death, this short piece is given over to praise of his old teacher. At the end of his life, Rahner still thought of Heidegger as the main source of inspiration in his career. He describes himself in this Preface as a "student of Martin Heidegger," and goes on to say "although I had many good professors in the classroom, there is only one I can revere as my teacher, and he is Martin Heidegger." By way of assessing Heidegger's religious importance, Rahner writes: "Catholic theology, as it is today, can no longer be thought of without Martin Heidegger, because even those who hope to go beyond him and ask questions different from his, nonetheless owe their origin to him." Many people, looking back on Heidegger today, view him as an unrepentant member of the Nazi party. In remarkable contrast, Rahner viewed him as the source of a new departure in Christian thought.

## 5.6.2

Rahner's participation in Vatican II is a matter of controversy. Some view it as vindication of an unjustly maligned theologian, others as a power play by a fortuitously situated opportunist. The story begins in 1962, the year Rahner was prohibited from teaching or publishing without advance approval from Rome.

The central theme of Vatican II was *aggiornamento* (bringing up to date). In words attributed to its convener, Pope John XXIII, the intent was "to throw open the windows of the Church so that we can see out and the people can see in." Before he died in 1963, John XXIII appointed Rahner as *peritus* (expert consultant) to the council. As one of its most prolific theologians, Rahner had gained reputation as an advocate of a less reclusive Church. Months after being muzzled by his Jesuit superiors, Rahner moved to Rome as an advisor to a reform-minded pope.

Other expert consultants at Vatican II were Yves Congar (1904–95), John Courtney Murray (1904–67), and Joseph Ratzinger (1927-). Congar was a French Dominican, whose teaching and publishing were restricted from 1954 to 1956 for his support of France's worker-priest program, who wrote several works on the Holy Spirit, and who was named cardinal by John Paul II in 1994. Murray was an American Jesuit known as an advocate of open cooperation between Catholicism and other religions, who in 1954 was prohibited from publishing his views by his superiors in Rome, and who was the chief author of Vatican II's *Dignitatis Humanae* (On the Dignity of the Human Person). Ratzinger, during the years of Vatican II, was known as a liberal theologian. In the course of his more conservative later years, he was made cardinal by Pope Paul VI, appointed by John Paul II as Prefect of the Congregation for the Doctrine of the Faith, and succeeded John Paul II as Pope Benedict XVI in 2005. In 2013, he resigned the papacy to adopt the title "Pope Emeritus."

Rahner's influence on Vatican II was extensive, but in ways not always easy to sort out. As with other *periti*, there were topics in which he had special interests. Rahner's interests tended to be pastoral in character. He advocated increased autonomy of the local church, along with collegiality among different faiths in pursuit of their common pastoral missions. But *periti* typically were not given administrative responsibilities that focused their attention on specific tasks. This means that the influence of an individual *peritus* is often hard to distinguish clearly. A notable exception is the collaborative effort of Rahner and Ratzinger, undertaken at the behest of several European bishops. This effort resulted in the document "*De Revelatione Dei et Hominis in Jesu Christo Facta*," which explored the relation between the Church and Holy Scripture.

There was one topic of general concern to the council, however, that was associated with Rahner explicitly. The topic was striking enough in its significance to become known by a distinctive label, which is "anonymous Christian." Rahner accepted the teaching that salvation comes through Christ, but could not accept that people who had never heard of Christ were for that reason condemned. Salvation is within reach, he argued, by following one's own conscience, provided one's conscience by grace of God is informed unknowingly by Christian principles, and provided also that one has not knowingly rejected Christ. A Buddhist monk (Rahner's example), accordingly, might be an anonymous Christian, but a person who deliberately has left the Church could not.

Rahner's concept of the anonymous Christian found its way into *Lumen Gentium*, Vatican II's Dogmatic Constitution on the Church. Quoted in part, this document says:

Those also can attain to everlasting salvation who through no fault of their own do not know the gospel of Christ or his Church, yet sincerely seek God and, moved by grace, strive by their deeds to do his will as it is known to them through the dictates of conscience" (section 16, in translation; a roughly equivalent statement appears in Vatican II's Constitution *Gaudium et Spes*)

The Latin phrasing of *Lumen Gentium* found its way into the 1994 *Catechism of the Catholic Church* (article 847): *Qui enim Evangelium Christi Eiusque Ecclesiam sine culpa ignorantes, Deum tamen sincero corde quaerunt, Eiusque voluntatem per conscientiae dictamen agnitam operibus adimplere, sub gratiae influxu, conantur, aeternam salutem consequi possunt* (Those who, through no fault of their own, do not know the Gospel of Christ or his Church, but who nevertheless seek God with a sincere heart, and, moved by grace, try in their actions to do his will as they know it through the dictates of their conscience—those too may achieve eternal salvation). Rahner's vision of the anonymous Christian is now among the official teachings of the Catholic Church.

## 5.6.3

Maréchal, we recall, read St. Thomas from a perspective conditioned by Kant's *Critique of Pure Reason*. But there were aspects of the *Critique* which he considered inadequate. One such had to do with the dynamism of the self's role in shaping experience, another with the teleological character of that form-making process. Against Kant, Maréchal argued that the self's role in that process is active rather than passive. More fundamentally, he argued that the ultimate end of human intellectual activity is to discover the unconditional (transcendental) ground of the conditions imposed by the self on the phenomenal world. Rahner agreed with Maréchal in both respects. These views earned for Maréchal the title "Transcendental Thomist," which Rahner inherited by adopting these particular views.

As Maréchal provided the context in which Rahner read St. Thomas, so Heidegger provided the context in which he read Maréchal. Among many other respects in which he was influenced by his old teacher, Rahner was indebted to Heidegger both for certain philosophic tenets and for the terminology in which they were expressed. In Rahner's *Geist und Welt* (the failed doctoral thesis published in 1941), the world (*Welt*) is Heidegger's *Dasein*. Rahner referred to it with the neologism *Bei-sich-sein* (being-present-to-itself). The *Geist* (spirit) of the title, in turn, is the active intellect that shapes the world of experience. Rahner designated this intellect *Vorgriff* (roughly "prior grasp") and its activity *Woauf* (a neologism meaning roughly "where toward"). In this terminology, the *esse* (being) of St. Thomas becomes the *Woauf* of the *Vorgriff*.

The *Vorgriff*, for Rahner, is the precondition of knowing generally, which Itself is unconditioned. The *Woauf* of the *Vorgriff* is directed toward Absolute Being, which is God. The dynamic of the *Vorgriff* is such that it enables the human intellect to tend ever closer to Absolute Being in its activity. One avenue of approximation (tending toward) has to do with communication. God communicates with his human subjects through grace, who in turn are free to accept God's grace and to communicate it among themselves. Responding to the gift of grace by human intercommunication is one way of approximating Absolute Being.

Another means of approximation is the pursuit of understanding itself. Rousselot held that understanding something is an affirmation (positive acknowledgement) of that thing's intelligibility. Since God is pure intelligibility, understanding itself is an affirmation of God. Accepting essentially the same view, Maréchal extended it with the statement that every act of knowing is an implicit affirmation of the absolute Truth that is God. Rahner accepted both of these tenets. As an affirmation of God, Rahner held, understanding is an acknowledgement of God's existence. In his reading, this is the meaning of St. Thomas's *De Veritate* Question 22, Article 1: "All knowing beings implicitly know God in everything they know" (*Omnia cognoscentia implicite cognoscunt Deum in quodlibet cognito*).

Given this inherent awareness of God in human knowing, logical proofs of God's existence are extraneous and inappropriate. Logical proofs are inappropriate, Rahner thought, because they are based on propositions, and God's being cannot be captured in propositions. The Neo-Scholasticism of the Counter-Reformation was formulated in propositional language, which for Rahner was equivalent to relinquishing the choice of weapons to one's opponent. Pre-Vatican II Neo-Thomism was subject to the same criticism. Rahner considered himself a staunch defender of orthodoxy, but rejected formulations of the Church's traditional teachings in Neo-Thomistic terms. In a *New York Times* article published shortly before his death (Thomas Sheehan, "The Dream of Karl Rahner," February 4, 1982), Rahner described Neo-Thomistic philosophy as "dead." Be that as it may, Rahner considered logical proofs of God's existence to be superfluous, given the awareness of God that is inherent in one's knowledge of the world.

A person comes to know the world by asking questions about it. Insofar as knowing is an avenue to God, accordingly, asking questions provides an auxiliary path. In *Geist und Weld*, the fact that being is questionable (*Fragbarkeit*, from Heidegger) is identified as a foundational factor in God's relation to human beings. Being is open to questioning; and asking questions about it is essential to being human. In Rahner's own terms (translated from *Geist und Weld*), "Man questions. This is something final and irreducible. . . . Man questions necessarily." A man exists, he goes on to say, "only insofar as he asks about being." So basic is humanity's involvement with questioning that a person's existential status itself is "a question about being." The wonderment of human existence is the ultimate (unanswerable) question, in that it admits no answer that does not lead to another question.

## 5.6.4

According to the *New York Times* article cited above, Rahner learned from Aquinas "that man, for all his spirituality, is inescapably material . . . even in so-called afterlife." Rahner's source for this in Aquinas was *Summa Theologica*, First Part, Question 84, Article 7. In considering this article in context, we should bear in mind that Rahner read Aquinas through Maréchal, that he read Maréchal through Heidegger, and that for Heidegger *Dasein* (being-in-the-world) is neither material nor immaterial. *Dasein* rather is a mode of being that encompasses things commonly termed "consciousness," "world," "subject," "object," etc., but itself is not subdivided into pre-established categories.

The question posed in Article 7 is whether the intellect can understand through its intelligible species (thoughts) without recourse to phantasms (images of sensible things). Aquinas' case for a negative answer has two main parts. One consists of a quotation from Aristotle's *De Anima*, saying "The soul understands nothing without a phantasm." The other is a brief argument to the effect that knowledge is a proportionality between intellect and object known, and that the proper object of an embodied intellect is corporeal by nature. Aquinas' discussion in Article 7 clearly pertains to embodied intellect, leaving open the further question of disembodied intelligence (e.g., in angels). In his reading of this article, however, Rahner apparently overlooked its accommodation of incorporeal intelligences. He apparently read it instead as support for his Heideggerian conception of intellect as one facet of *Dasein*. Such an intellect could function as either material or immaterial, depending on its role in particular circumstances.

This reading might help make sense of certain other views advanced by Rahner that on the surface seem unintelligible. One such concerns the body and immortality. Contrary to the standard Christian view that soul is freed from body at death and issues into an immaterial afterlife, Rahner maintained that immortality itself is a bodily state. This accords both with his reading of the *Summa*, Article 7, and with the Heideggerian tenet that soul and body are facets of *Dasein* in which they do not exist apart from each other. The embodied soul has a capacity for immortality, a capacity that is enhanced by spiritual growth. Viewed from Rahner's Heideggerian perspective, immortality is a bodily state, achieved through grace, in which the divine Word is maximally present. In Rahner's view, accordingly, spiritual growth reflects the progressive entry of the divine Word into the spiritually endowed body.

Heidegger's *Dasein* excludes fixed substance of any sort. In particular, it excludes the transformation of one substance into another which is implicated in the Catholic doctrine of transubstantiation. Although Rahner celebrated the Eucharist as a Catholic priest, he chose to emphasize the end or purpose of the sacrament rather than what the priest effects at consecration. Rahner thus proposed that what happens during consecration be named "transfinalization" rather than "transubstantiation." Pope Paul VI explicitly rejected Rahner's proposal in his encyclical *Mysterium Fidei* (1965), insisting on the traditional "transubstantiation." The pope further distanced himself from Rahner's view by reaffirming the doctrine of the Eucharist as a change in substance, referring his faithful readers back to the Council of Trent.

## 5.6.5

Heidegger's *Sein und Zeit* has radical things to say about time (*Zeit*). A brief survey of his views on time will throw light on Rahner's radical interpretation of Christ's resurrection. Heidegger rejected the conception of time as a linear and unending sequence of "nows," a conception that traces back to Aristotle's *Physics*. He also rejected the Augustinian conception of past-present, present-present, and future-present, which he thought gives undue priority to the present. And he rejected Augustine's Christian-inspired distinction between time and eternity. For Heidegger, the primary phenomenon of time is what he termed *Sein-zum-Tode* (being-toward-death). Projection toward impending death is Dasein's equivalent of "having-been-ness" (*Gewesenheit*), which treats the present as an opportunity, in a "moment of vision" (*Augenblick*), to freely redeem what it will become.

The futurity of *Sein-zum-Tode* has to do with significance, as distinct from actual temporal measurement. Like others of his era, Heidegger measured actual time with clocks and wristwatches. The significance of *Sein-zum-Tode*, however, is the redemptive opportunity it presents to the person undergoing it.

Heidegger was intent on gaining redemption in a manner not dependent on divine intervention. Rahner adopted this conception of redemption in being-toward-death, but retained God as a contributing factor. For Rahner, the narrative of redemption is the narrative of Christ's death and resurrection, the two of which he viewed as inseparable both in occurrence and in significance. Rahner's views in this regard are recorded in his *Grundkurs des Glaubens* (*Foundations of Christian Faith*, 1978).

For Rahner, to repeat, spirit and matter (the world) are indissolubly united. The world of matter (an aspect of *Dasein*) consists of events in space and time. Christ's death on the cross occurred in a particular place and at a particular time. Christ's resurrection, however, was not another such event. His crucifixion and his resurrection were tied together, in a way that precludes their separate existence. It is obvious that Christ must have died to be raised from the dead. But it is not obvious, apart from his mission, that he must rise as a condition of his death on the cross. Christ's earthly mission, as Rahner portrays it, is what ties death and resurrection inseparably together.

As Rahner portrays it, Christ's mission was to accomplish the redemption of those who followed him by his unblemished sacrifice on the cross. That was the purpose for which the Father incarnated his Son in human form. This purpose was accomplished with the sacrifice of the unblemished victim. But God had yet to authenticate the mission as duly accomplished. God had yet to "sign off," so to speak, on the completion of Christ's earthly mission. God's sign that the mission had been accomplished was to present a vision of the risen Christ to a few preselected apostles (Acts 10:41). Put otherwise, the resurrection was the Father's way of authenticating that his Son's mission had been flawlessly completed.

According to Rahner, by way of upshot, Christ's resurrection was not a return to the earthly realm of space and time. It rather was the Father's seal on what his Son had accomplished during his earthly mission. As Rahner puts it in *Foundations of Christian Faith* (p. 279), "By the resurrection . . . Jesus is vindicated as the absolute savior" by God.

### 5.6.6

The designation "Transcendental Thomist," which Rahner inherited from Maréchal, has misleading connotations. The "Transcendental" part suggests compliance with Kant's transcendentally situated critique of metaphysical reasoning. It suggests a theoretical orientation that accepts Kant's restrictions on what he perceived as the excesses of traditional metaphysics, including those of Neo-Scholasticism. With this connotation at hand, one is led to think of Transcendental Thomism as an approach to St. Thomas that abides by the limits on metaphysics set by the *Critique of Pure Reason*.

Neither the approach of Maréchal nor that of Rahner abides by such limits. Maréchal was indebted to Kant not for a regimen but for a problem. As Maréchal understood Kant, there was a problem accounting for the involvement of the self in the application of the categories. Maréchal viewed that involvement in terms of an active principle oriented toward an end, a metaphysical view itself at odds with Kant's critique. Rahner entertained a similar view, albeit couched in Heideggerian language. The worldview of *Sein und Zeit*, which Rahner for the most part accepted, is far beyond the pale from a Kantian perspective.

The "Thomism" part of "Transcendental Thomism" can also be misleading. In other contexts, a Thomist is someone who is conversant with St. Thomas' work, who is preoccupied with his teachings, and who accepts his authority in ecclesiastical matters. As Jesuit priests, both Maréchal and Rahner became acquainted with Aquinas' teachings through the distorting lens of Neo-Thomism. In their dissatisfaction with this approach, neither made Aquinas' writings the main focus of his scholarship, or deferred to Aquinas' authority in theological disputes. Doing work relevant to the interpretation of St. Thomas does not earn one the status of being a Thomist.

So, while Maréchal and Rahner are known as standard-bearers of Transcendental Thomism, that label does not serve as a characterization of their actual views. The label rather signifies a cluster of views, with the common feature of reading St. Thomas in the light of a Kantian critique. Another prominent theologian identified by that label is Bernard Lonergan, whose views we will turn to examine shortly.

## 5.6.7

The 1982 *New York Times* article by Thomas Sheehan, cited previously, opens with the author's compelling observation: "Karl Rahner . . . is, I think, the most brilliant Catholic theologian since Thomas Aquinas." In an earlier *New York Times* article (September 23, 1979), Eugene Kennedy quoted theologian Martin Marty as saying: "Compared to Karl Rahner, most other contemporary Christian theologians are scrub-oak." Marty goes on to mention the results of a 1978 poll in which 554 North American theologians from seventy-one denominations estimated that Rahner followed only St. Thomas and Paul Tillich as major influences in their work, ahead of Martin Luther and St. Augustine. The author adds his own appreciative observation, to the effect that the "liberal reflections of German theologian Karl Rahner may have a far greater impact on the future of Catholicism than the charisma of Pope John Paul II." From the perspective of more than four decades later, this prediction appears erroneous.

## 5.7 Bernard Lonergan

Bernard Lonergan was born in Buckingham, Quebec, in 1904, and joined the Jesuit order at age seventeen. He studied philosophy at Heythrop College, London, during which stay he acquired external degrees in mathematics and classics from the University of London. His instructors at Heythrop were devotees of Suarez, founder of an unusually conservative branch of Neo-Thomism. Lonergan left Heythrop thoroughly dissatisfied with that brand of philosophy.

During the Great Depression, he became preoccupied with the history of its economic origins, and began reading Toynbee, Marx, and other thinkers who dealt with such issues. He also studied the Catholic historian Christopher Dawson. In the process, he became concerned about the failure of the Church to make available a Christian account of history to counter atheistic accounts like that of Marx. Lonergan asked his superiors for an assignment that would enable him to develop such an account, but was refused. His superiors ordered him to continue studies in the Gregorian leading to a doctorate in dogmatic theology, in preparation for joining the faculty there.

The topic of Lonergan's doctorate was the theology of grace in Thomas Aquinas. His doctoral studies were interrupted by WWII, at which point he returned to the Jesuit seminary in Montreal. This gave him opportunity to study Aquinas in close detail, resulting in his becoming a Thomist in a sense far removed from the Neo-Thomism that had repelled him during his earlier training. He received his doctorate from the Gregorian in absentia, having defended his thesis in 1946 before a specially convened board of colleagues in Montreal.

Lonergan began thinking on topics pertaining to insight in 1946. Most of the book *Insight: A Study in Human Understanding*, published in 1957, was written between 1949 and 1953. A major interruption in his scholarly life occurred in 1964, when he went to the United States to undergo treatment for lung cancer (he previously smoked tobacco "in moderation"). His two other major works are *Verbum: Word and Idea in Aquinas* (1967), and *Method in Theology* (1972). He also wrote several textbooks, notably on Trinitarian theology and Christology. Two scholarly books on economic topics were published posthumously: *For a New Political Economy*, and *Microeconomic Dynamics: An Essay in Circulation Dynamics.*

Bernard Lonergan was a consummate member of the Society of Jesus, educated in Jesuit seminaries, serving on Jesuit faculties, and impeccably obedient to his Jesuit superiors. Even the Gregorian where he studied is historically a Jesuit institution, founded in 1551 by Ignatius Loyola. The only non-Jesuit institution to occupy a substantial portion of his time was Harvard University, where he served as Charles Chauncey Stillman Professor of Roman Catholic Theological Studies in 1971–72. From 1975 to 1983, Lonergan was Distinguished Visiting Professor at Boston College. Other honors include induction as Companion of the Order of Canada (1971) and a substantial number of honorary degrees (mostly from Catholic institutions).

Lonergan was featured in the Religion section of the April 20, 1970, issue of *Time* magazine. The story focused on a meeting celebrating his thought held in Florida a week or two earlier. Attendees included mathematicians, scientists, and politicians from several countries, as well as various philosophers and theologians. Among the latter were several who had studied under him at the Gregorian. Lonergan himself was present, and seemed delighted at the interaction his work had stimulated.

Cross-disciplinary interaction like this is a central theme of the vision of human knowledge developed in *Insight*. This vision displays a stage-wise progression in the achievement of knowledge generally, described as (1) experience, (2) understanding, and (3) judgment. Lonergan's view was that all disciplines share in such a progression, theology included, and that theology could learn from the methods successfully applied in mathematics and experimental science. His *Method in Theology* was a sustained attempt to demonstrate how scientific method might play out in theology. From the perspective of the sixty-six-year-old Lonergan, the conversation among theologians and scientists at the Florida conference must have been a replay of the interaction among kindred disciplines to which his scholarly life had been committed.

Referring to Lonergan's "grasp of the understanding that underlies every science," one voice in the conference described him as "the 20th century counterpart of a Renaissance Man." More specific praise is contained in the first sentence of the *Time* article in question, which is: "Canadian Jesuit Bernard J. F. Lonergan is considered by many intellectuals to be the finest philosophic thinker of the 20th century."

## 5.7.1

What is truly distinctive about Lonergan is not his rank among twentieth century philosophers (dozens surely rank higher), but rather his opposition to the methods of theology then-current in many Catholic schools. Such methods begin with first principles, from which consequences are deduced regarding the topic at issue. When the topic is reason or understanding, for instance, the first principles probably would include the principle of non-contradiction (namely, that the assertion and the denial of a given proposition cannot both be true). Other possible candidates are the principle of causation (everything has a cause) and the principle of finality (all agency is directed toward an end). An approach that begins with first principles is commonly known as a metaphysical approach.

Lonergan's alternative method, on the other hand, follows the model of empirical science by beginning with the gathering of relevant data. With regard to states of mind involved in the process, inquiry begins with the emergence of topical questions, proceeds by the formation of hypotheses in response to these questions, and moves on to judgments about the adequacy of these hypotheses. Even inquiry in abstract disciplines like mathematics follows this general pattern, with the mathematician seeking insight by reviewing previously established theorems on related topics. What is emphatically novel is Lonergan's conviction that this method applies in theology as well. Rejecting the standard metaphysical method, Lonergan advocated that theology proceed by the method of inquiry.

There is a generic sense in which "inquiry" means an investigation of one sort or another. A metaphysically-inclined theologian, for instance, might find occasion to investigate the logical consistency of a given set of general principles. But this would not amount to inquiry in Lonergan's sense. For Lonergan, one distinctive feature of inquiry is its stagewise progression. It begins with limited understanding and progresses to understanding that is increasingly comprehensive, with each stage building on previous stages. Inquiry at each stage is self-corrective, in a sense illustrated by the methods of experimental science. If one experiment fails, corrections are made in experiment-design or in the way its variables are tested. This leads to a further experimental effort to achieve the goals at which the project is aimed. A specific example might be the ongoing attempt to discover a cure for cancer, which has gone through several experimental stages. Abstracting from any specific case, Lonergan argued that the goal of inquiry in general is understanding. Since he often spoke of understanding as a form of insight, it might also be said that Lonergan considered insight to be the goal of inquiry in general.

For purposes of comparison, the dominant feature of Lonergan's method is its dynamism. The method is dynamic both in context and in application. Its application involves experimentation, self-correction, and trial-and-error, all procedures incorporating progressive activity. The context in which inquiry occurs also is dynamic, involving alterations often beyond immediate human control. As may be recalled, Lonergan once asked his superiors for permission to work on a Christian account of history to counter the atheistic account of Marx. Although the request was declined, Lonergan remained convinced that history is a determining factor in human affairs generally. At any given stage of human development, the progressive course of history sets the context in which human inquiry takes place. The method of inquiry, accordingly, is dynamic, both in the context of its application and in the way it is applied.

The method of classical theology is metaphysical. It is also static in being based on immutable first principles. Beginning with these fixed principles, the method features a "top-down" derivation of theological doctrine by logical inference. Lonergan's method of theological inquiry, on the other hand, is dynamic rather than static. As just noted, it is dynamic both in application and in context of application. Lonergan's method features a "bottom-up" development of creative insight, which he views as leading to an enhanced understanding of the human condition and of humanity's dependence on a beneficent God.

## 5.7.2

Western philosophy may plausibly be divided into a tradition tracing back to Plato and a tradition tracing back to Aristotle. One useful basis of division is the relative priority these traditions assign to metaphysics and to epistemology (theory of knowledge). For purposes of comparison, metaphysics should be understood broadly as an account of the nature of things that exist, augmented by a study of being itself (ontology). Epistemology should be understood, in turn, as a study of the knowledge of things that exist, addressing issues both of what can be known and of how knowledge can be achieved. At stake in the comparison is whether the study of knowledge (1) precedes the account of the nature of things, or rather (2) ensues within the confines of a pre-established metaphysical account.

Aristotle was the precursor of philosophic systems (including Neo-Thomism) founded on metaphysical principles. While Aristotle clearly had views about the character of human knowledge, mainly in his *De Anima* and *Posterior Analytics*, these views were shaped to fit in with his overall metaphysics. In none of his surviving works, at least, does metaphysics yield precedence to theory of knowledge.

Plato was the world's first great epistemologist. One of his dialogues (the *Theaetetus*) is devoted primarily to the topic, and several others (the *Republic*, the *Sophist*, and the *Statesman*) make major contributions. In the transition from middle to late dialogues, Plato's metaphysics changes along with his epistemology. In the *Republic*, a typical middle dialogue, knowledge is confined to the eternal Forms, and is precluded from the realm of sensible objects. Whereas in the *Philebus*, among later dialogues, knowledge amounts to precise awareness of divisions along continua of sensible opposites (hotter/colder, drier/wetter). In both cases, the method of knowing is coordinated with, but not determined by, the nature of what is known. In both cases, that is to say, metaphysics yields priority to considerations of epistemology.

This distinction between Platonic and Aristotelian traditions elucidates the difference between the approaches to theology by Lonergan and by the metaphysical theologians. Lonergan clearly belongs to the Platonic tradition. Indications of this allegiance come in various forms. On one hand, biographical sources agree in mentioning Plato as a primary influence on Lonergan's early work. And in later collections of his earlier writings, Lonergan himself acknowledged Plato's influence. While these sources indicate an early interest in Plato, however, they leave open questions about relative priority of epistemology and metaphysics in Lonergan's theology.

Later sources, however, contain specific indications of Lonergan's epistemological orientation. An article in the October 11, 2004, issue of *America: The Jesuit Review* (entitled "The Mystery of Lonergan"), for instance, connects Lonergan's empirical method with his interest in Plato. According to the author (Richard M. Liddy), the book *Plato's Doctrine of Ideas*, by J. A. Stewart, led Lonergan "to understand Plato, not as a proponent of forms in the sky [*sic*], but rather as a methodologist asking questions that promote understanding." The method in question gives priority to considerations affecting the acquisition of knowledge. If the goal is to understand a given domain of human interest (such as the nature of friendship), questions are formulated to help explore that domain. In the tradition of Plato's emphasis on epistemology, Lonergan's theological method gives priority to the formulation of questions that provide insight into the topic under investigation.

In stark contrast with Lonergan's Platonism, the approach of metaphysical theology sits firmly in the tradition tracing back to Aristotle. This is the tradition giving metaphysics priority over theory of knowledge. This theology begins with first principles, from which it proceeds to deduce consequences relevant to the topic at hand. This approach does not accommodate an epistemological investigation regarding the suitability of the rational procedures it puts to such use. An approach giving priority to reasoning from first principles provides no platform for a critical examination of the reasoning involved.

5.7.3

Lonergan was a seasoned scholar of St. Thomas, and followed his lead more often than not. There are certain basic issues, however, on which he differed radically from St. Thomas' views. One such is the issue of realism. Let us review the realism of St. Thomas's *De Veritate*, as a preliminary to examining Lonergan's version.

St. Thomas's realism is based on his conception of First Truth, which he also designates the truth of the divine intellect. In V.1.4.R, as observed previously, Thomas states that the truth of the divine intellect is unique, and that the many truths of the human intellect are derived from it. He goes on to assert that even if there were no human intellects, "Things themselves would still remain essentially the same." First Truth is the source of things being what they are, in complete independence from human involvement. Essentially the same claim is made in V.1.2.R, where he says that even if there were no human intellects, "things would be said to be true because of their relation to the divine intellect." This is realism in its most extreme form. According to Aquinas, the things that pass before our minds as we encounter the world owe nothing whatsoever to our encountering them.

Lonergan's realism not only diverges from St. Thomas's, it also is more sophisticated. As noted previously, Lonergan's general method of inquiry applies to disciplines ranging from mathematics and experimental science to philosophy and theology. He called it his Generalized Empirical Method, GEM for short. Lonergan described GEM as a "critical realism," likening it to the correspondence theory of truth he found in Aristotle. The "realism" part of the description responds to the fact that true statements are about things that exist in the actual world. The "critical" part is a studied allusion to the critical bearing of Kant's *Critique*.

In the sense pertaining to GEM, a critical judgment is one guided by criteria. The criteria in question operate at several levels in the process of inquiry. At the initial level, that of experience, the criterion calls for due attention to established patterns of perception (e.g., entering a library, we expect to see books on the shelves). At the level of understanding, the criterion requires a plausible answer to questions of cause, purpose, and so forth (e.g., books are kept in libraries for purposes of storage and preservation). At the third level, that of judgment, the criterion to be satisfied is that the understanding reached on the second level accords with the perceptions of the first (e.g., the purpose of preservation adequately explains the perceived collection of books). The fourth level is one of evaluation or value-judgment, at which point the inquirer is held to the criterion of taking responsibility for the outcome of inquiry overall (e.g., by openly attesting that the question of why all the books are stacked together has been satisfactorily answered).

To each of these levels corresponds certain intellectual qualities the inquirer brings to bear in attempting to abide by the relevant criteria. At the level of experience, the inquirer needs to be attentive. In striving for understanding, he or she needs to be intelligent. Judgment, in turn, requires being reasonable, and decisions regarding value require responsibility. The criteria of inquiry, and the intellectual qualities that go with them, are the ingredients of objectivity. And objectivity is the sum and substance of Lonergan's realism.

In Lonergan's terminology, an objective judgment is one reached in the course of inquiry guided by such criteria. Objectivity is a composite state comprising judgments that are individually objective. Objectivity on the part of a given inquirer is tantamount to a course of inquiry that is progressively more attentive, more intelligent, more reasonable, and more responsible. As these desired features become enhanced and augmented, the world view entertained by the inquirer becomes progressively more objective.

Objectivity in general is an amalgam of objective states reached on the individual level. Individual projects of inquiry are aimed at results intended ultimately as contributions to the constitution of objectivity in general. One aspect of objectivity in general is a composite judgment reflecting the agreement of particular judgments reached by individual inquirers. Lonergan's realism pertains to the relation between this composite judgment and circumstances in the world toward which that judgment is directed.

According to Lonergan, there is a structural parallel between the composite judgment and the corresponding set of circumstances. As he understood it, this is the parallel between judgment and world described by Aristotle's correspondence theory of truth. The correspondence theory is Aristotle's counterpart of the relation between the First Truth of St. Thomas and things that exist in the created world. As discussed above, the realism of St. Thomas consists in his view that the structural correspondence between true judgments and things in the world is grounded in First Truth, and would remain the same even if human beings did not exist. In effect, the realism of St. Thomas removes human beings from the truth-making relation between First Truth and reality. Lonergan's realism, in stark contrast, makes human involvement an essential part of the truth-making relation.

Lonergan's realism affirms a truth-making correspondence between objectivity in general and the actual world. Objectivity in general, to repeat, encompasses individual judgments arrived at objectively by individual members of the community of inquiry. Judgments by individual inquirers are essential to the correspondence affirmed by Lonergan's realism. The worldview based on this correspondence is a perspective shared by individuals given to objectively inclined inquiry.

### 5.7.4

Lonergan described his Generalized Empirical Method as a "critical realism," intending by "critical" an association with Kant's first *Critique*. He may or may not have been aware of ongoing discussions of critical realism occupying other philosophers of the time. Particularly noteworthy in this regard is the book *Critical Realism* by Roy Wood Sellars, published in 1916. Then in 1920 a collection entitled *Essays in Critical Realism: A Cooperative Study of the Problem of Knowledge* was published by George Santayana, C. A. Strong, Durant Drake, et al. Philosophers other than the authors represented in this collection include R. W. Sellars and A. O. Lovejoy. Many articles on the topic appeared subsequently, including a critical evaluation "What Is Realism?" (*Journal of Philosophy* 44 1947) by John Wild of Harvard.

In this broader context, critical realism is a response to crude forms of naïve realism. According to naïve realism, phenomena such as shapes, colors, and sounds presented to the mind in its perception of external objects are actual properties of the objects themselves. Critical realism typically eliminates certain phenomena from that status, but retains others. Shape is retained, along with size, hardness, and motion (traditional primary qualities), while color, sound, odor, taste, and the like (traditional secondary qualities) are generally eliminated. An earlier version of critical realism is that of John Locke, who held that both primary and secondary qualities in the mind are caused by external objects, but that only primary and not secondary qualities resemble properties of objects that cause them.

Another version of critical realism, under development when Lonergan was writing, is that of Roy Wood Sellars. Its basic tenet is that we perceive real external objects, rather than intermediaries of some sort between perceiver and object. Sellars' view is based on a firm distinction between the content of perception and its object. The content of perception is dependent on characteristics of the perceiving organism, such as alertness and visual acuity. In a normal instance, however, the object of perception is some facet of the external world. What is present *to* perceptual awareness (the external object) is not the same as what is present *in* awareness (sense impressions, etc.). The "realism" part of Sellars' account is the independence of the objects we perceive from the circumstances of perception. The "critical" part is its avoidance of naïve realism.

For a better understanding of his views by future readers, it would have been helpful if Lonergan had said more about his critical realism in relation to these other views. This would have been helpful as well in assessing the realism maintained in John Paul II's *Fides et Ratio*, to which we turn in the following chapter.

CHAPTER 6

# John Paul II and *Fides et Ratio*

## 6.1 His Life, His Death, and His Physical Stamina

THE FUNERAL OF JOHN Paul II, held on April 8, 2005, attracted an estimated four million people to the Holy City of Rome. Among them were four kings, five queens, as many as seventy presidents and prime ministers, and fourteen leaders of other religions. This pope unquestionably was one of the most loved and most respected human beings living in the final quarter of the twentieth century.

Even apart from his reception as pope, Karl Josef Wojtyła (1920–2005) was an unusually gifted individual. He had a genius for language. By his early twenties, he had learned a dozen or so languages, several of which he continued using as pope. He had scholarly talents as well. After completing studies leading to his ordination in 1946, he earned a doctorate in philosophy in 1948 from the Angelicum in Rome. Named for the "Angelic Doctor," St. Thomas, the Angelicum was a major center of Neo-Scholastic philosophy. He then returned to Jagiellonian University in Krakow, where he had studied language and philology previously, to receive a doctoral degree in theology in 1954. Among his scholarly publications that followed, perhaps the most notable is *The Acting Person: A Contribution to Phenomenological Anthropology* (English translation 1979). In this work, he develops a view he called "Phenomenological Thomism," a hybrid of traditional Thomism and the personalism of Max Scheler.

During his early years in Krakow, Wojtyła was active as a playwright and poet. Seven plays from this period have been preserved, but probably would not have survived if written by a less prominent author. The two books of poetry he composed in Krakow, however, contained several pieces of genuine artistic merit. John Paul II continued to write poetry during his years in the Vatican. Selections from this later work have been collected under the title (in translation) *The Roman Triptych: Meditations*. The first section of the triptych is called "The Stream." Its main theme is that one's life passes like a running stream, and that this passage of life has meaning. The second part is called "Meditations on the Book of Genesis at the threshold of the Sistine Chapel." Its main theme is that Michelangelo's rendition of Genesis in color should inspire the cardinals when they pick out the next successor of Peter. The third section of the triptych is named "A Hill in the Land of Moria(h)." Its main theme is that God, unlike Abraham, brought the sacrifice of his only Son to completion on the alter. Whatever its pontifical intent, *The Roman Triptych* is a compelling work of art.


6.1.1

As a youth, Karol Wojtyła lived through the Nazi occupation of Poland (1939–45), and spent much of that time in forced labor. In 1940, he was struck by a tram and suffered a fractured skull. Later the same year he was hit by a lorry in a quarry, which left him slightly hunched over with misaligned shoulders. Then in 1944 he was hit by a German military truck, this time suffering a severe concussion. On this occasion, his recovery was aided by attention from German paramedics. These events solidified his intention to enter the priesthood, to which he was ordained in 1946. At the time he was made pope in 1978, his physical health at age fifty-eight was comparable to that of the young seminarian some forty years earlier. Although slightly hunched over, he ran regularly in the Vatican gardens, lifted weights, and went hiking or skiing when opportunities arose. His favorite ski run was in the Tatra mountains of Poland, known for precipitous trails that had proved fatal to less experienced skiers.

John Paul II's physical stamina undoubtedly helped him survive the assassination attempt in 1981. On that occasion, two pistol bullets fired by Turkish mercenary Mehmet Ali Akra struck the pope and caused extensive bleeding. His condition was soon stabilized in the hospital, from which he was discharged in good health several weeks later. John Paul II visited his would-be assassin in jail the following year and forgave him personally. Ali Akra was released in 2000 and sent back to further imprisonment in Turkey, during which later confinement he converted to Catholicism. Another attempt on John Paul II's life was made in 1982, this time by a disgruntled priest. In this case the pontiff was not injured.

John Paul II's overall good health began to decline in the 1990s. He suffered a fall in 1993 that dislocated his right shoulder, and another in 1994 that resulted in a broken femur. On Christmas day of 1995 he had a dizzy spell that led to cancellation of his scheduled *Urbi et Orbi* address. These mishaps were probably indications of incipient Parkinson's disease. In 1996, a Vatican spokesman announced that the pope was suffering from extrapyramidal syndrome, a condition with Parkinson-like symptoms. Although severely stooped and generally seated in public appearances, the pope retained his mental clarity. He continued regularly to travel abroad and to participate actively in world affairs.

Then a news release from Rome, dated January 3, 2001 (Sarah Delaney, "Doctor Confirms Pope John Paul Has Parkinson's," *Washington Post*), informed the world of the pope's declining health. To quote, "the pontiff looked especially frail and tired at this year's Christmas ceremonies at the Vatican." The news release also noted that "the pope's tremulous left hand, rigid facial expressions and shuffling gait have become increasingly evident over the past several years." Relative to the date of the news release, those past several years include the time during which *Fides et Ratio* (made public in 1998) presumably was being written.

John Paul II's last public appearance was on Palm Sunday, March 4, 2005. He appeared briefly at the window overlooking St. Peter's Square, waved a palm frond before the crowd, and moved away without speaking. St. Peter's Square was also filled with people on April 2, 2005, when the much-beloved pope died in his quarters above.

## 6.2 His Charisma

One of the most charismatic world leaders of his time, Pope John Paul II was the very opposite of a demagogue. He inspired people with love and hope, rather than inflaming them with hate and fear. Although there is no way of being sure, he probably drew the largest crowds in papal history. He traveled more than any previous pope to spend time in person with his people. When he stood before them with outspread arms, the gesture was expansive. They were his flock, and he their good shepherd. These features of his papacy were commemorated by Pope Francis in his tribute to John Paul II on May 28, 2020, the one-hundredth anniversary of his birth. As reported by the *Catholic News Agency* (Carol Clatz, God 'Visited His People' in John Paul II"), Francis referred to St. John Paul as a shepherd who "was close to the people, going out, traveling across the world to find them and to be close to them."

The expansive character of John Paul's papacy was epitomized in various other ways. For years before 1988, the number of cardinals in the Church held steady at 120. By 1998, under John Paul II, it had expanded to 127, and by 2001 to 135. The College of Cardinals, of course, includes electors of future popes, always chosen from among their own numbers. (The College of Cardinals can be stacked like the US Supreme Court.)

Another upsurge brought about by John Paul II was in the number of saints canonized during his pontificate. On average, the preceding five popes of the twentieth century had canonized roughly two saints per year. John Paul II canonized 482 in his twenty-six years as pope, which comes close to ten times the previous average. When he joined their company in 2013, one might like to think, St. John Paul was welcomed by a large number of previous beneficiaries.

All in all, Karol Wojtyła was remarkable in many respects. Athlete, playwright, poet, pope; orator, globetrotter, shepherd, saint. In each respect he was marked by an expansive character. It is time now to address his historic encyclical, which begins, true to form, with an expansive flourish.

## 6.3 The Encyclical

The prefatory statement of *Fides et Ratio* is both eloquent and inspiring. It is expressed in figurative language that evokes a vision of the human spirit's innate desire to know God and to dwell in his presence. This desire is illustrated by citations from the Old and the New Testaments. Exodus 33:18 depicts Moses, in the presence of God, beseeching God with the words "Please show me your face." In Ps 27:8, David cries out to God in his heart "Your face, Lord, do I seek." In Ps 63:2–3, the psalmist praises God, after having beheld God's "power and glory" in the sanctuary. John 14:8 records Philip's request to Jesus: "Lord, show us the Father, and it is enough for us." And 1 John 3:2 anticipates the time when God appears and "we shall see him like he is." John Paul II's choice of these passages makes it clear that his opening statement is intended to direct the reader's thoughts to his or her personal relation to God.

In keeping with its evocative imagery, the opening statement itself has a figurative dimension. The "human spirit" (*hominis . . . animus*) is lifted "to the contemplation of truth" (*veritatis ad contemplationem*) on the "wings of faith and reason" (*FIDES ET RATIO . . . pennae*). The truth in question is "God himself" (*Deus . . . ipse*). And the great benefit to be gained is that, "by knowing and loving Him" (*cognoscentes Eum diligentesque*), human individuals "may come to the fullness of truth about themselves' (*ad plenam . . . de se ipsis pertingere possint veritatem*). Figuratively speaking, that is to say, faith and reason lift the human spirit to a state of knowing and loving God that reveals its essential humanity. Echoing 1 John 3:2, the message is that when we see God as he is, we will understand respects in which we are like him.

The opening statement, however, has a literal dimension as well. And read literally, the statement's content is more difficult to grasp. Faith and reason cooperate in conveying the human mind (*animus*; intellect, spirit) to a contemplation of truth. The wing-part is figurative, but the faith, reason, and truth in question are all to be taken literally. And the part about understanding respects in which we are like God has a literal cast as well. This literal orientation carries over into the body of the encyclical, which opens with a statement of de facto intent. Its purpose, at least in part, is "to trace a journey which has led humanity all the way through the centuries to meet and to distinguish truth more and more deeply" (*plaga, iter quoddam dignoscatur quod, progredientibus saeculis eo usque hominum genus perduxerit ut cum veritate paulatim congrediatur seque cum illa componat*).

## 6.4 Truth in the Encyclical

The term *veritate* (truth) occurs in the first sentence of the encyclical proper, following three occurrences in the brief preface. Forms of *veritas* also occurs roughly 250 times in the 108 sections of the encyclical overall. An informative comparison in this regard can be made with uses of the term *alētheia* in the NT. *Fides et Ratio*, of course, is a much shorter document; yet it has more than twice the occurrences of the relevant term. Approximate word counts of the two texts indicate that *veritas* occurs over ten times more frequently in *Fides et Ratio* per thousand words than *alētheia* does in the NT. John Paul II's use of *veritas* in the encyclical is an expansive gesture in itself, like so many other expansive aspects of his pontificate. For whatever reason, the author of *Fides et Ratio* had a singular preoccupation with truth. As Spinoza came to be known as a "God-intoxicated" philosopher, so the author of the encyclical might be characterized as "truth-intoxicated" pontiff. It is appropriate to begin our examination of *Fides et Ratio* with a careful look at what it has to say about truth.

Of the approximately 250 occurrences of the noun *veritas* in *Fides et Ratio*, roughly one-third are used in a generic (other than specifically religious) sense. An illustrative generic use is found in section 5 (abbreviated as #5), with reference to people of false modesty who are content with "partial and provisional truths" (*veritatibus ex parte et ad tempus*). The remaining two-thirds are used in one or another obviously religious sense. Several of the more important of these senses are distinguished below. Cognate terms inviting adjectival (true) and adverbial (truly) translations will not be considered in this study. Our concern is limited to the noun *veritas*.

The category of religious truth is dominated by truths pertaining to God. These truths are characterized in more than a dozen different ways. One characterization is that of revealed truth. In #9, for instance, there is reference to a "revealed truth" (*Revelationis veritatem*) that is not a product of human reason. Another instance is found in #35, in its reference to the relation "between revealed truth and philosophy" (*inter veritatem revelatam et philosophiam*). Another common characterization is that of divine truth, as in #44, where faith is distinguished from divinely bestowed wisdom by pointing out that "faith accepts divine truth as it is" (*fides assentit veritati divinae . . . seipsam*). Divine truth is also mentioned in #66, which refers to the "divine Truth" (*divinam Veritatem*) proposed in Sacred Scripture. Yet another characterization, that of full truth, is mentioned twice in #34 by the expressions *plenitudo veritatis* (quoted in Latin) and *veritatis plenitudinem*.

Other characterizations occur only once, including (a) "principal truth" (*principales veritates*, #5), (b) "transcendent truth itself" (*veritatem se transendentem*, #5), (c) universal truth" (*veritatem universalem*, #27), (d) "ultimate truth" (*veritatis ultimae*, #56), (e) "immutable truth of God" (*immutabilem Dei veritatem*, #71), (f) "total and definitive truth" (*totam ultimamque . . . veritatem,* #82), (g) "complete truth" (*integram veritatem,* #92), and (h) "God's own truth" (*Deo veritatem . . . ipso,* #94).

A notable exclusion from terms in this category is *veritate prima* (First Truth), an expression that occurs frequently in Aquinas's *De Veritate.* For Aquinas, of course, First Truth is the truth identical with God himself. To be sure, God is identified with Truth in #92, but under a different description: namely, "the Truth that is the living God" (*Veritas, Deus vivus*). It is interesting that Jesus Christ also in identified with truth earlier in the encyclical. In #33 we read of the ultimate appeal to humanity which is "Jesus Christ, who is the very Truth" (*Christo Iesu, qui est ipsa Veritas*).

The truth associated with Jesus Christ in #33 is another category of truth, with instances designated by various expressions other than in this particular section. In #30 there is mention of "the truth revealed in Christ Jesus" (*veritatem in Christo Iesu revelatam*). Another expression is "the truth of Christ" (*Christi veritatis*) in #104. A closely related category is that represented by "Christian truth" (*christiana veritas*) in #38, and by "truth of the Christian faith" (*christianae fidei veritas*) in #40. Another category of interest is the "catholic truth" (*catholicae veritatis*) of #6, said by John Paul II to be the responsibility of bishops such as himself.

With respect to cases included, however, the largest category of religious truths in the encyclical is probably that of statements or affirmations with overtly religious reference. Addressing Catholic philosophers and theologians in #54, the author distinguishes between "sacred and human truth" (*divinam humanamque veritatem*). The category of religious truth in question is what this passage designates as sacred, a designation we will adopt for present purposes. What is meant by sacred truth here can be further specified by contrasting it with so-called human truth.

As a first approximation, human truth can be characterized as that of statements the truth-value of which depends upon how things stand in the natural world. The status of these statements as either true or false can be determined, so to speak, only "after the facts" on which that status depends. To borrow a term from Kant, such statements could be characterized as *a posteriori.* They assert (rightly or wrongly) what is the case in the world as it is, which cannot be ascertained prior to the relevant facts.

Human truth is exemplified in #30 of the encyclical, in its reference to a "mode of truth proper to everyday life and to scientific research" (*veritates cotidianam vitam scientificamque pervestigationem respiciunt*). Another clear reference to human truth occurs in #75, which addresses "truth within the natural order" (*veritatem intra naturalem provinciam*).

Yet another can be found in #25, which describes the human being (Homo) as the only creature interested "in the real truth of things he perceives" (*authenticae veritati rerum quae illi obsersantur*).

There are frequent references in the encyclical to sacred truth as well. In #15 the author quotes John 8:32, where Jesus says "You will know the truth, and the truth will set you free" (*Cognoscetis veritatem, et veritas liberabit vos*). In the same section there is mention of "the truth made known to us by Revelation" (*nobis Revelatio cognoscere permittit veritas*), subsequently referred to as "this revealed truth" (*Haec veritas revelata*). In #47, "instrumental reason" ("*rationes instrumentales*") is contrasted with reason "directed toward the contemplation of truth and the search for the ultimate goal and meaning of life" (*Pro veritatis contemplatione atque finis ultimi sensusque vitae inquisitione*). And as the encyclical draws to a close, its author calls upon Christian philosophers to assist those "who do not yet grasp the full truth which divine Revelation makes manifest" (*qui nondum omnem veritatem capiunt quam divina Revelatio ostendit*, #104).

These several passages illustrate the differences between sacred truth and its worldly counterpart. Human truth is encountered or discovered by observation, often as a result of deliberate inquiry. Sacred truth, by contrast, is disclosed or revealed, sometimes without initiative on the part of the recipient. Moreover, what is discovered in the former case is some aspect of the spatial-temporal world, whereas sacred truth has neither spatial nor temporal dimensions. A particularly significant feature of sacred truth is that it constitutes a fixed end in itself to be attained. Human truth is a fact of the world as it is, and facts of the world are not fixed goals in and by themselves. But sacred truth is an abiding goal to be achieved, which brings fulfillment to those who achieve it.

In most respects, sacred truth transcends the limits of space and time. One temporal aspect of sacred truth, however, is that it takes time to achieve it. Rather than occurring suddenly, like a flash of mental insight, attainment of sacred truth sometimes requires a lifetime of preparation. To be sure, there are times when a person might be closer to achieving it than at others. But proximity here is measured by degrees of fulfillment, rather than by yardsticks or chronometers. "Full truth" (*plenam . . . veritatem*), according to #2, "will appear with the final revelation of God" (*ultima in Dei revelatione ostendetur*). This prognosis is accompanied by a quotation from 1 Cor 13:10–12, which says (in part) that "when truth in full" (*plenam . . . veritatem*) is made apparent, we shall see "face to face" (*facie ad faciem*).

It was noted above that the designation translated "First Truth," which appears frequently in Aquinas, is not used in *Fides et Ratio*. In Aquinas, First Truth serves as a criterion by which created truths are authenticated. A similar role, however, is played by the "Word of Wisdom" (*Verbum Sapientiae*) in the encyclical, described in #23 as "the standard of both truth and salvation" (*veritatis regulam simulque salutis*). Employing different terminology for a similar role, #71 describes the Gospel as "the most immediate standard of truth regarding God's revelation" (*norma veritatis novissima pro Dei revelatione*).

As a final observation on the topic, however, it should be noted that sacred truth may be subject to the same deep-seated difficulty that affects the First Truth of St. Thomas. In the account of St. Thomas, First Truth is the ultimate source of created truth. And created truth acquires its status as such by adequation (conformity) with the way things stand in the world. Adequation, however, consists in a correspondence in structure between the factors involved, which in turn requires that the factors involved be complex in make-up. The difficulty in question lies in the nature of First Truth, which (being essentially one) lacks complexity in all respects. But a unity that yields complexity shares in the complexity of its product. A consequence is that (simple) First Truth cannot be the source of (complex) created truths, as Aquinas claims.

Whether the difficulty carries over to the sacred truth of the encyclical depends on the reading of a phrase in #82. The role of Sacred Scripture in a person's life, the author says here, assumes that the individual can "know and grasp the clear and simple truth" (*cognoscere . . . et comprehendere perlucidam semplicemque veritatem*) it contains. According to one reading, this is a literal description of the Gospel's truth as "clear and simple." Apparent support for a literal reading can be found in #73, which refers to "Truth revealed" (*Veritatem revelatam*) as "simple truth" (*simpliciter . . . veritatem*). If the Gospel's truth is to be understood as simple in a literal sense, however, it would lack the complexity required to match any truth-giving fact.

According to an alternative reading, "clear and simple" is an idiom roughly equivalent to "easily understood." If the description were to be read as idiomatic, the anomaly above could be avoided. But there is nothing in the encyclical to suggest that its author would speak in other than a literal manner when addressing issues of such importance. The likely upshot is that the simple Truth of the encyclical suffers from the same basic incoherence as the First Truth of St. Thomas' *De Veritate*.

## 6.5 Faith in the Encyclical

There are several respects in which the treatment of faith in *Fides et Ratio* is on shaky grounds. One problem is with its treatment of the intellectual state of faith as capable of action. Agents in a given state might act, but this is different from the state acting itself. Another problem is its conflation of faith with the state of belief. As observed previously, these problems can be at least partially remedied by careful attention to the analysis of faith by St. Thomas in *De Veritate*. Other issues regarding faith in the encyclical, however, cannot be resolved so conveniently. As a preliminary to dealing with these issues, let us review certain aspects of how faith is treated by earlier writers.

In English translations of the NT, the noun *pistis* is uniformly rendered "faith," and the verb *pisteuō* "to believe." There is no verb form of *pistis* inviting a translation like "to faith," and no noun form of *pisteuō* to be translated simply "belief." Faith (the noun) is a state of mind or intellect, and believing (the verb) is something the mind does. Given this grammatical difference, there should be little temptation to conflate believing with faith. If "believing" were substituted for "faith" in the frequently cited definition of faith at Heb 11:1, the result would border on nonsense.

Augustine's *Confessions* was written in Latin, employing the noun *fides* for faith instead of *pistis,* and the verb *credere* for believing instead of *pisteuō*. In our foregoing discussion of section XIII.xxi.29, this passage was read as one of several in which Augustine appears to conflate the state of faith with the activity of believing. If this reading is correct, the *Confessions* foreshadows the assimilation of faith to believing that poses problems for *Fides et Ratio*.

In Question 14 of his *De Veritate*, Thomas Aquinas subjects the relation between faith and believing to careful analysis, and shows clearly why the two should be kept distinct. Although both are integral to Christian life, they differ essentially in the objects toward which they are directed. Acts of believing are directed toward states of affairs (facts). An example given in V.14.8.R is believing that God suffered, which is directed toward the fact of God suffering with his Son on the cross. Acts of faith, on the other hand, are directed toward spiritual entities, an example of which is the assertion in V.14.7.R that "First Truth is the proper object of faith." First Truth obviously is not a state of affairs, but rather an entity existing apart from the world of spatial-temporal facts.

Although distinct, the state of faith and the activity of believing are intimately related in *De Veritate*. The sense of so-called acts of faith lies in this relation. Being a state of intellect, faith is inactive, meaning that it cannot act in and by itself. A comparable state of intellect is integrity; although a person might act with integrity, the state of integrity is incapable of action itself. Faith engages in action by proxy instead. The state of faith is so related to believing that an act of faith is tantamount to the act of believing by which that state is expressed. An example of this relation is given in Article 2 of Question 2 of the Second Part of the Second Part of the *Summa Theologica*, which says "it is an act of faith to believe in God." Actions that express a person's belief in God express that person's faith in God as well. This way of understanding acts of faith, of course, depends on a distinction being made between the inactive state of faith and the activity of believing.

In *Fides et Ratio*, however, there are passages suggesting that faith and belief are assumed to be equivalent. In #79, for instance, the author quotes with approval Augustine's assertion regarding believers that "in believing they think, and in thinking they believe; if faith does not think, it is nothing" (*et credendo cogitat, et cogitando credit . . . fide si non cogitatur nulla est*). Augustine conflated faith and belief, and it appears that John Paul II has followed suit.

Other passages to the same apparent effect are found in #98 and #106. In his advice to moral theologians and philosophers at #98, the author considers it urgent that they return to the point where "the understanding of faith pertains to the moral life of believers" (*intellegatur fides ad credentium vitam . . . spectans*). Similar advice to "believers among philosophers" (*Credentibus . . . in philosophica*) is put forward in #106, instructing them (as believers) to exercise reason "which has received assistance from faith" (*adiumentum quod fides ministrat*). While the case for an equivalence of faith and belief in *Fides et Ratio* is not ironclad, it apparently was persuasive enough to lead the Paulist translators of the document to render *fideles* (person of faith) as "believer" on numerous occasions (e.g., #39, #71, #75, et al.). If the encyclical does not distinguish between faith and belief, however, it cannot rely on Aquinas' analysis in the *Summa Theologica* of a so-called "act of faith." The encyclical remains burdened with the incoherence of attributing activity to the inactive state of faith.

6.5.1

Thomas Aquinas, as we have seen, provides valuable insight into how faith and belief are related. Beyond their being directed toward different objects, however, *De Veritate* is less informative than one might wish about the characters of faith and belief themselves. And what it says is more a matter of theological embellishment than an elucidation of faith and belief in the lives of individual Christian people. This is the case with the encyclical *Fides et Ratio* as well. Further study of this latter document will proceed more smoothly with accounts of faith and belief in ordinary circumstances immediately at hand.

As St. Thomas noted, faith typically is directed toward persons (God, Jesus Christ), or perhaps toward something representing them (God's word, the Gospel), whereas belief is directed toward states of affairs (that of Mary being a virgin, or of Christ being crucified). Satan presumably might believe that Christ was crucified, but certainly would not have faith in this event. For a secular example of this difference, someone might believe that democracy is the best form of government, but harbor little faith in the democratic system. Being convinced (believing) that the system ideally is superior to others does not produce faith in its ability to excel in practice. Conversely, one might reside faith in a candidate for political office while withholding belief that he or she will prevail in the election. To show faith by supporting his or her candidacy "through thick and thin" is compatible with not believing that success will be forthcoming at the polls.

Further differences can be found relating specifically to religion. Consider the matter of God's existence. One might come to believe that God exists on the basis of a proof to that effect. But belief that God exists is not the same as faith in God. A follower of Satan might believe that God exists but maintain faith in the devil instead. Consider also one's engagement with the religion one is committed to follow. Followers of Jesus practice their faith in Jesus, but do not practice the beliefs their faith incorporates. While one might engage in a practice (e.g., venerating the cross) founded on what one believes (that Christ died on the cross), beliefs themselves are not practiced. The exhortation "keep the faith" is a call to continue in the practice of keeping the faith, whereas "keep the belief" has no apparent meaning.

The practice one maintains in keeping the faith is a matter of complying with or abiding by that religious commitment. The term "practice" here serves as a verb, inasmuch as complying with certain dictates is something one does. There is another use, however, in which "practice" functions as a noun. In this use, it is roughly synonymous with "vocation" or "walk of life." A lawyer, for example, is someone engaged in the practice of law, and a physician someone occupied in the practice of medicine. Law and medicine are practices to which these practitioners are committed.

The noun "practice" also admits a verbal use distinctly different from that above. In the previous sense, the verb "to practice" means to abide by or to comply with. To practice courtesy is to abide by the norms of civil behavior, which themselves are not practices. In the relevant further sense, by contrast, "to practice" (verb) means "to engage in a practice" (noun). Accordingly, the physician practices medicine and the lawyer practices law. Thus also, a Christian is committed to practicing certain forms of comportment identified specifically with the Christian faith. Let us consider further the concept of "practice" as something one does in its application to Christianity in particular.

The concept of a practice is clearly delineated in Alasdair MacIntyre's *After Virtue* (1981). A practice involves a community of people committed to the achievement of goals from which the community at large will benefit. Achievement within the community is non-zero-sum, meaning that some can benefit without others suffering. In the particular case of the Christian community, the practice of faith incorporates the goal of becoming worthy of eternal life. Success achieved by saintly members of the group enhances, rather than hinders, the chances of success by others in the group as well.

Practices involve the participation of both masters and neophytes, which is to say both teachers and learners. In the practice of law, students learn from their professors in law school. In the practice of faith, catechumens learn from their instructors. After catechesis, younger members learn from older members of the faith. In versions of Christianity that incorporate a magisterium, lay people generally are instructed by assemblies of authorities, such as bishops. There is a sense, moreover, in which current members of the faith are instructed by earlier members. As portrayed in *After Virtue*, another feature of practices is their incorporation of traditions. Current members learn from the traditions of their faith.

With regard to faith, a crucial aspect of practices is that they inculcate adherence to certain moral virtues. One such virtue is that of honesty. Members of the community of faith are held accountable if they engage in false witness (Exod 20:16). Another moral virtue is that of justice. A maxim of the Christian faith is the Golden Rule, phrased in Matt 7:12 as "treat people the same way you want them to treat you" (*thelēte . . . poiōsin . . . hoi anthrōpoi, houtōs kai humeis poieite autois*). The virtue of abiding with moral values in the practice of Christianity is stressed in *Fides et Ratio* #25, which points out that "there exists a serious moral obligation to seek the truth and to adhere to it once it is known" (*est . . . perquirendae veritatis gravis moralis obligatio eidemque cognitae adhaerescendi*).

A paramount virtue in the Christian faith is that of courage. In a society given to injustice, treating one's neighbor justly can often be hazardous. Lives were lost in America's civil rights movement, and similar examples abound in the histories of other societies. While the practice of Christianity was gaining a foothold in its early stages, countless people were martyred for their adherence to the faith. And practicing Christianity takes courage even today, especially in authoritarian societies which view that practice as a political threat. Demonstrations advocating the Christian value of racial justice in mid-2020 America resulted in extensive loss of life, including lives of many demonstrating in behalf of justice.

For present purposes, thinking of faith as a practice helps heighten the contrast between faith and belief. As suggested above, there is no clear sense in which entertaining one or another belief constitutes participation in a practice. Consider further the profession involved in reciting a creed. The Apostles's Creed, of course, begins with *Credo* (I believe), followed by a profession of what one purports to believe. In reciting this creed, one professes belief in the Holy Spirit. But believing in the Holy Spirit is not itself a practice. It is not something a neophyte learns from a master, not something subject to standards of excellence, and not something conditioned by tradition. Believing in the Holy Spirit is just something one does. For another example, consider John 11:27, where Martha tells Jesus she believes that he is the Christ, the Son of God. But believing this about Jesus is not a practice in which Martha participates. Taken by themselves, beliefs such as these have roles to play in the Christian faith, but are not communal practices to which believers are committed.

Secular beliefs are no different in this respect. In the course of practicing law, lawyers entertain beliefs about the reliability of certain witnesses and the availability of certain documents. But to entertain such beliefs is not to engage in a practice. In their practice of medicine, similarly, doctors arrive at beliefs about the accuracy of diagnostic tests and about the significance of certain symptoms. But apart from their place in the practice of medicine, such beliefs themselves do not constitute practices.

## 6.5.2

A further difference between faith and belief is that belief, unlike faith, typically admits truth-values. Beliefs, that is to say, are either true or false. A given belief shares the truth-value of its propositional object. The belief that Indiana is south of Michigan is true because it is directed toward a true proposition. And the proposition that Indiana is east of Illinois is true because it refers to an actual state of affairs. Conversely, the belief that the earth is cubical is false because the proposition that the earth is cubical fails to correspond to an aspect of the actual world.

Since Christian faith is directed toward divine Persons, however, and since persons do not admit truth-values, Christian faith itself cannot be true in the sense that beliefs might be true. Yet there are passages in *Fides et Ratio* that refer explicitly to truth(s) of faith in this sense. In explaining the intent of the encyclical, for instance, the author remarks that a duty assigned him by Vatican II was "to corroborate the truth of faith" (*Fidei veritatem confirmantes*, #6). In #44, he affirms that wisdom presupposes faith, and "the truth of faith itself" (*veritate ipsius fidei*) is the basis of its right judgment. As part of his advice to philosophers in #77, he tells them that "the truths of faith (*fidei . . . veritatibus*) make demands that must be followed when they contribute to theology. Other explicit references to truths of faith are found in #97 and #105.

These passages are phrased to speak of a definite property attributed to faith (the truth of faith) specifically. The sense cannot be that of "genuine faith," possibly borne by the expression "true faith." An example of "true" used in the sense of "genuine" is "true God from true God" in the Nicene creed. What this means in the creed is that both the Father and the Son are really God, real in the sense of really being God. This is a use of "true" as an adjective. A corresponding adverb would be "truly," as in the affirmation that both Father and Son are "truly God." But when "truth" appears in the expression "truth of faith" of the encyclical, it clearly is being used as a noun.

The encyclical speaks of faith as being true in the sense that beliefs can be true. But Christian faith is directed toward Persons of the Godhead, whether Father, Son, or Holy Spirit. And like less exalted persons, divine Persons are not states of affairs in the actual world. Beliefs are rendered true by actual states of affairs. By its very nature, faith cannot be true in this sense.

The reference to truths of faith in the passages from *Fides et Ratio* cited above remains anomalous. As seen above, faith itself cannot meaningfully be assigned a truth-value. The faith one resides in the Persons of the Godhead, accordingly, is neither true nor false in any standard sense Furthermore, to refer to such faith as true is not merely to characterize it as genuine rather than specious, as in "true God from true God." The relation of Christian faith toward its object cannot be one that involves activity of any sort. This precludes its being analogous to plighting one's troth, which involves an active commitment to another person.

The upshot of these considerations is that the references to truths of faith in the encyclical remain anomalous. There is no coherent sense in which Christian faith can be characterized as true. There may indeed be truths of various sorts that are illuminated by faith. But faith is not a bearer of truth itself.

## 6.5.3

An intriguing aspect of the encyclical is the variety of things its author says are illuminated by the light of faith. One such is the "Church's Magisterium" (*Ecclesiae . . . Magisterium*), in its "critical judgment by the light of faith" (*sub fidei lumine suum iudicium criticum*) of philosophies that "contend with Christian doctrine" (*cum doctrina chistiana contendunt,* #50). In #51, the author insists that the "need for keen judgment in the light of faith" (*sub fidei lumine acumen iudicii deposcitur*) becomes more urgent with the current "proliferation of philosophic conjectures and arguments" (*opinationes ac argumenta philosophica . . . multiplicentur*). Needless to say, these are not words of encouragement for philosophers who contribute to this proliferation. Suspicion of deviant philosophy continues in #99, with regard to instruction in the faith: "catechesis has important philosophic implications" (*catechesis* [italicized in text] . . . *complectitur philosophica aliqua consectaria*), the author observes, that "must be investigated in the light of faith" (*fidei sub lumine vestiganda*).

Other roles assigned to the light of faith seem driven by less contentious interests. One positive role has to do with the "full and ultimate meaning of life" (*complexivum ultimumque vitae sensum*), which "traditionally has been the goal of philosophy" (*translaticia philosophia quaesivit,* #56). Here the author, acting "in the light of faith which finds this ultimate meaning in Jesus Christ" (*sub lumine fidei quae in Christo Iesu hunc ultimum sensum agnoscit*), encourages philosophers, "be they Christian or not" (*christianos vel non christianos*), to "trust in the power of human reason" (*rationis humanae facultati confidant*) and not to set goals for themselves that are "overly modest" (*nimis mediocres*). What the author means by this is elucidated in #43. "Faith does not fear reason" (*Fides . . . rationem non metuit*), he assures his readers; rather "faith builds on and completes reason" (*fides supponit et perficit rationem*). "Illumined by the light of faith" (*fidei lumine illustrata*), reason is freed "from the fragility and weakness" (*a fragilitate et a limitatione*) it suffers "from commission of sin" (*ex peccati commissione*).

This allusion to the weakness of reason due to sin, we may note in passing, ties in with a conception of original sin that affects John Paul II's treatment of reason, a conception that prevails throughout the encyclical. According to Genesis, Adam and Eve disobeyed God's command to avoid eating from "the tree of the knowledge of good and evil," and suffered dire consequences from that original sin. Beyond consequences explicitly described in the biblical account, the author of *Fides et Ratio* speaks as if human reason itself was adversely affected. This "initial disobedience" (*prima inoboeditione*), he says in #22, "so wounded human reason that henceforth its progress toward full truth would be impeded" (*atque rationi humanae vulnera intulerunt quae progressionem illius ad plenam veritatem erant impeditura*). Described in words from Rom 1:21, the effect was that men and women "became futile in their thinking" (*eorum ratiocinationes detortae*). Unless otherwise augmented, the reason disabled by original sin is incapable of reaching the full truth regarding life's meaning. According to #43 of *Fides et Ratio,* the additional power it needs to arrive at full truth comes when reason is illuminated by the light of faith.

Other ways in which faith supports reason, according to the encyclical, are mentioned in #56 and #76. According to the former, "faith is a dependable and persuasive advocate of reason" (*Fides . . . rationis fit certus atque suadens advocatus*). According to the latter, "faith purifies reason" (*fides purificat rationem*) and "liberates reason from excessive self-confidence" (*rationem a nimia confidentia exsolvit*). Conversely, faith is said in #48 to benefit from reason as well. "Deprived of reason" (*ratione carens*), "faith runs the risk of no longer being universal in scope"

(*Fides . . . in periculo versatur ne amplius sit universalis oblatio*). Without robust reason, faith "is gravely at risk of devolving into myth or superstition" (*in grave periculum incidit ne in fabulam ac superstitionem evadat*). As artisans who employ reason as a tool, philosophers might take heart at being assigned the role of applying reason to preserve faith from myth and superstition.

## 6.5.4

Setting the relation between faith and philosophy aside for now, let us take stock of how faith overall is treated in *Fides et Ratio*. The noun *fides* appears roughly twelve dozen times in the encyclical, not counting the adjective *fideles* (often used in the sense of "faithful person"). In most uses, it designates either (a) an individual's state of faith, or (b) faith as a unified set of teachings. Faith of the first sort is personal, of the second institutional.

Personal faith itself falls under three categories. There is (a.i) faith as an intellectual state of an individual person. An example is the state of assent mentioned in #75, where the "assent of faith" (*fidei assensus*) is said "to involve the intellect and will" (*tum intellectum tum voluntatem obstringit*). Then there is (a.ii) a person's faith directed toward a divine entity, illustrated in #44 by the observation that "faith accepts divine truth as it is in itself" (*fides assentit veritati divinae secundum seipsam*). The former (a.i) is faith as a state of acceptance, the latter (a.ii) faith focused on a specific object. Category (a.ii) also includes faith in divine mysteries, as with the remark in #14 that the human mind can comprehend "the mystery of life" (*vitae comprehendendum mysterium*) only insofar as this mystery is "embraced by faith" (*in fide complecti*).

Distinctly different from these is (a.iii) the faith constituted by a person's participation in a communal practice of faith. Although the encyclical does not mention the practice of faith explicitly, an equivalent of participating in the practice is cited in #71, where the author notes that "cultural context" (*cultura . . . illius loci*) "permeates the living of Christian faith" (*Christiani . . . fidem experiuntur . . . imbuitur*). Whereas faith (a.i) is a mode of acceptance and faith (a.ii) an attitude directed toward a divine object, faith (a.iii) is participation in a way of life.

Institutional faith (b) can be identified either (i) by its contents as a body of teachings or (ii) by its public designation as such a body. Relevant to (b.i), #45 refers to "philosophy separate from the truths of faith" (*philosophiam seiunctam . . . ad fidei veritates*). In this reference, the truths separate from philosophy clearly are the constituent tenets of the Christian faith. An illustration of (b.ii) is evident in #40, with its account of St. Augustine's conversion when "the truth of Christian faith became apparent" (*chrisianae fidei veritas apparuit*) to him. What became apparent to Augustine was the authenticity of that faith as a recognized body of teachings. Faith in sense (b.i) is the institution identified by a particular set of tenets, whereas faith in sense (b.ii) is an institution identified by its reputation.

Despite these various aspects, faith in the encyclical retains an overall unity. Section 101 speaks of "many different forms of learning and culture" (*multiformitate sapientiae et culturarum*), sustained "within the unity of faith" (*in fide unitate*). And in #45, the author laments the modern schism of rational knowledge from faith, a faith that "in Patristic doctrine and Medieval teaching" (*doctrina Patrum doctorumque Medii Aevi*) "amounted to a profound unity both theoretically and practically" (*cogitaverat atque exsecuta erat . . . profundam unitatem*).

Problems remain with the location of the agency involved in faith (a). Faith (a.i) is a person's state of assent. Assent here is something the person does. The agent of assent is the person involved, not the state of assent itself. Assent per se is not capable of doing things on its own. Faith (a.ii) involves focusing a person's attention on a specific object. Focusing one's attention on an object, likewise, is something a person does. The attention thusly focused, however, is not an agent capable of doing something on its own. Faith (a.iii), in turn, is participation in a communal practice. Participating in a practice is an activity pursued by a person. The person involved is the agent performing that activity. The activity itself, however, is not an agent capable of yet other activities. In each case, the faith involved is the upshot of something the faithful person does, but in no sense something capable of doing things itself.

Faith as an act of mind is not itself capable of action. Yet the encyclical *Fides et Ratio* casts faith in numerous active roles. Several of these have to do with reason or understanding. In #20, the document says "faith liberates reason" (*rationem fides liberat*). In #76, "faith purifies reason" (*fides purificat rationem*). And in #67, faith is proclaimed able "to show fully the path to reason in a sincere search for the truth" (*iter plene demonstrare rationi illi, quae sincere veritatem requirit,* quoted in Latin text). There is a sense, moreover, the author claims (#43), in which faith (*Fides*) is an "exercise of thought (*exercitium cogitationis,* quoted in Latin text). An even more robust activity is attributed to faith in #92, where the author refers to the "vigorous dynamism found in faith itself" (*vim dynamicam, quae in ipsa fide* inest, quoted in Latin text).

The culmination of this inventory of activities assigned to faith comes in #66, where John Paul II propounds the theological concept of *intellectus fidei* (faith's understanding). To this understanding he assigns the task of "expounding clearly" (*clarius recludit*) the "divine Truth 'proposed to us in Sacred Scripture understood according to Church teaching'" (*divinam Veritatem "propositam nobis in Scripturis Sacris secundum doctrinam Ecclesiae intellectis"*). This requires not only comprehending "the propositions in which the Church's teaching is laid out" (*enuntiationum quibus Ecclesiae doctrina componitur*), but also "acclaiming the salvific meaning of those propositions' (*salutis sensum extollens quam tales enuntiationes*). In this short series of sentences, faith is assigned a lion's share of the intellectual tasks usually divided between philosophy and theology.

It is hard to imagine, however, how tasks so daunting could be performed by a personal faith (a) which is not itself capable of action. And it is inconceivable that they be performed by institutional faith (b), which is a set of doctrines that can be acted on but cannot itself perform actions. In upshot, #66 appears marginally intelligible at best.

Aquinas had a way of avoiding impasses like this. His way involved a distinction between faith and belief. For Aquinas, inactive states of faith are expressed by active beliefs. Believing that Christ is the Son of God produces actions expressing one's faith in God. In its role as active proxy, belief evinces acts of faith. But *Fides et Ratio* does not distinguish between faith and belief, which makes Aquinas' solution unavailable.

Other difficulties follow from equating faith with belief, beyond that of coping with acts of faith. One is that of retaining credible readings of key passages in the NT. In Heb 11:1, we recall, faith is defined as "the assurance of things hoped for, the conviction of things not seen" (Greek above). This is far afield from any plausible definition of belief, inasmuch as belief itself is not assurance of anything, and emphatically is not limited to invisible things. And in 1 Cor 13:13, St. Paul concludes an impassioned acclamation of love with "for now, faith, hope, and love remain, these three; but the greatest of these is love" (*nuni de menei pistis, elpis, agapē, ta tria tauta· meizōn de toutōn hē agapē*). To my ear, at least, substituting "belief" for "faith" in the translation of this passage would demean Paul's acclamation.

In like manner, substituting *credere* for *fides* in the opening statement of *Fides et Ratio* surely would alter its intended meaning. The human spirit is not elevated to contemplation of the truth in question by the synchronized wings of belief and reason. Reason cooperates with belief in the pursuit of empirical knowledge, both in science and in the course of daily life. But truth in the sense the encyclical intends is not accessible to reason paired with belief instead of faith. The encyclical is addressed to the role of faith in Christian life, which is quite different from the role of mere belief. If it had been called *Credere et Ratio*, instead of *Fides et Ratio*, the title of the encyclical would not match its actual contents.

## 6.6 Reason in the Encyclical

The approach to reason in *Fides et Ratio* is not entirely unique, insofar as it shares key themes with both *Dei Filius* and *Aeterni Patris* of the First Vatican Council. But in the history of western thought generally, the reason of the encyclical is decidedly idiosyncratic. The encyclical's portrayal of reason is dictated by theological considerations, with little attention to how reason functions outside a theologically committed context. To set the stage for an examination of reason in the context of the encyclical, let us briefly reconsider a few historically noteworthy treatments of reason examined in more detail above.

Aristotle contributed to our understanding of reason in two major respects. The most enduring of these was his development of the syllogism in the *Prior Analytics*. Earlier thinkers had employed syllogistic reasoning, but Aristotle was to first to establish it on a formal basis. Aristotle's second major contribution was his theory of scientific inference. Inquiry begins with empirical observation, from which general principles are derived by induction. Deductions from these principles then lead to further observations by which the principles can be refined and corrected. Aristotle himself employed this method, primarily in his study of biological phenomena. Aristotle's treatment of reason was rooted in practice, with no evident tinge of doctrinal preconditions to be satisfied.

Kant's contribution was to set limits on the speculative use of reason. Unlike Aristotle, Kant did not advance the use of reason in expanding human knowledge. He rather exposed the hazards of reason used to reach conclusions not grounded in human experience. While posed as a response to Hume's skepticism, his first *Critique* also purported to disqualify the use of reason in the service of metaphysics (consider the title of his shorter *Prolegomena to Any Future Metaphysics*). In chapter 3 of the Transcendental Dialectic, Kant argues in particular that reason is not capable of proving the existence of a supreme being. Arguments purporting to do so generally conclude by attributing existence to God as a necessary property. As Kant maintains in the Transcendental Doctrine of Method, however, this is not intelligible because "existence is not a predicate."

The movement known as "Transcendental Thomism" was an attempt to reconcile Kant's critique with the dominant philosophy of the Catholic Church. As such, it was a major part of the Church's nineteenth century reaction against Neo-Scholasticism. For the most part, its attempted reconciliation involved an acceptance of Kant's main arguments against the metaphysical use of reason. Represented by Pierre Rousselot and Joseph Maréchal, and to some extent Karl Rahner (all Jesuits), Transcendental Thomism lost momentum in the early twentieth century. Later in that century, Bernard Lonergan (another Jesuit) took over as the main critic of Neo-Scholasticism. It is noteworthy that none of these Jesuit theologians is even mentioned in *Fides et Ratio*.

Another approach to reason touched upon above is that of philosophy of science. Among topics treated by this discipline is the nature of knowledge produced by successful scientific inquiry. Although methods vary from field to field, some sort of rational inference is invariably involved. Among such are induction, deduction, mathematical modeling, and statistical analysis. While empirical science is at least mentioned in *Fides et Ratio*, its treatment there yields no insight into possible similarities between the use of reason in science and its use in the theology of that document.

The use of reasoning in scientific enquiry, nonetheless, is a third distinctive treatment with which the treatment of reason in *Fides et Ratio* can be contrasted and compared. Regarding the first of the three, Aristotle contributed substantially to the methods by which reason advances human knowledge, as well as to the range of knowledge achieved by human reason. The treatment of reason in the encyclical, however, makes no genuine contribution to that effect. Kant, in turn, critically examined the use of reason in speculative metaphysics. The encyclical not only disregards Kant's critique, but employs reason in a manner to which that critique explicitly objects. Regarding the third comparison, experimental science deploys reason to arrive at new facts about the empirical world.

But the reasoning employed in *Fides et Ratio* reveals few if any new facts about the world we actually experience.

We return presently to give that document a chance to speak for itself. Before returning, however, there is one more thing to note. None of the illustrative cases of reason above illuminates the reason employed by the relevant authors in producing the illustrations in question. Aristotle's account does not apply to Aristotle's reasoning in producing that account itself. Kant's treatment does not throw light on the reasoning (often opaque) employed in developing it. And philosophy of science has provided scant information about the faculty of reason employed by scientists in pursuing their practice.

*Fides et Ratio*, likewise, provides no insight whatever into the thought processes engaged by the author in preparing it for promulgation. That noted, we return for a detailed examination of the reason portrayed in John Paul II's document.

### 6.6.1

As commonly conceived, reason is a mental faculty of a human agent. Another such faculty is memory. The faculty of memory is exercised when the agent remembers something, and the faculty of reason is exercised when the agent engages in reasoning. The faculty of reason itself is not an agent, and does not itself engage in reasonable activities. A rational person employs his or her faculty of reason in making rational inferences, but the faculty of reason itself does not make inferences. To speak of the faculty of reason as itself a rational agent is analogous to speaking of the ability to move as itself in motion.

As treated in *Fides et Ratio*, however, reason itself functions in the role of an agent. Rational accomplishments are attributed to reason itself, as distinct from rational human agents. Like memory, the capacity to reason is an attribute of a substantial entity, namely of a human person. To think of an attribute of a substance as a substance itself is a form of what philosophers sometimes call hypostatization. Its hypostatization of reason is one respect in which the encyclical's treatment of reason is idiosyncratic.

Among things reason is said to do in the encyclical are included various acts of intellect. In #8, a complaint is lodged against views that deny "reason's natural capacities" (*rationis naturalium potestatum*) for gaining knowledge. Section 42 affirms that "reason's function (*munus rationis*) is "to discover meaning" (*invenire sensum*), and "to disclose explanations" (*detegere causas*) that will allow everyone "to understand the doctrines of faith" (*fidei doctrinam intellegendam*). Another task, alluded to in #84, is that "human reason [should] disclose the essence of reality" (*rationis humanae . . . rerum essentia detegatur*). The fact that reason's ability to accomplish this task is currently being questioned, the author says, confirms "our crisis of confidence in the powers of human reason" (*illius discriminis fiduciae . . . de rationis humanae potestate*). In these passages, the hypostatization of reason is extended to the assignment of capacities to the capacity of reason itself.

Reason is also depicted as being receptive to movement by outside influences. It is capable not only of acting, but of being acted upon (passively) by other agents. Section 33 warns that "reason needs to be sustained by trusting dialogue and sincere friendship" (*rationem . . . fidenti dialogo et authentica amicitia esse sustentandam*). Section 51 refers to consequences of "human reason originally sluggish and wounded by sin" (*ratione humana propter peccatum sauciata et hebetata oriantur*). Section 84, in turn, alludes to scholarly positions that "obscure the doctrines of faith" (*fidei doctrinam obscurant*) in a manner that "humiliates reason" (*rationem demittunt*). Being sustained, being wounded, and being humiliated are various ways in which the encyclical asserts that reason can be passively affected.

Another passive characteristic of reason, according to the encyclical, is that of being subject to natural limits. In #28, the author observes that "the natural limitation of reason" (*Naturalis limitatio rationis*), coupled with an inconstant spirit, "obscure and forestall" (*obumbrant saepeque avertunt*) a person's search for truth. Another reference to reason's "inherent limitations" (*finibus constitutivis*) occurs in #51, with the remark that these limitations make the "inalienable capacities of reason" (*non alienabiles facultates rationis*) difficult to discern.

According to #22, however, God intervenes by granting "human reason a capacity that seems to surpass its natural limits" (*Hominis rationi . . . facultas quae excedere videtur ipsos eius naturae limites*). Later in the same section, this capacity is identified as "the human power of metaphysics" (*potestatem hominis metaphysicam*). The power of metaphysics, the author claims, allows human reason seemingly to surpass its natural limits.

Divine help is also acknowledged in #80. The "mystery of the Incarnation" (*Incarnationis mysterium*) poses challenges that "carry philosophy to its limits" (*extremae fiunt philosophiae*). In its radical response to these challenges, "human reason is called upon to create its own logical method" (*incitatur ratio humana ut suam efficiat logicam viam*) that circumvents those initial limits. In the words of the encyclical, this revision in logic amounts to "demolishing the walls by which it [human reason] risks being confined" (*deruendos muros quibus periculum est ne ipsa circumdetur*). On the part of reason, this is a revision that itself must be steeped in mystery. Only "in the mystery of the Incarnate Word" (in Verbi Incarnati mysterio), the author avers, will "the innermost essence of God and humanity to be rendered intelligible" (*Intima . . . Dei hominisque essentia intellegibilis redditur*). In its natural form, reason falls short of grasping the mystery of the Incarnation. To bring this mystery within reach, reason is told to change the logic by which it proceeds.

John Paul II's view of reason in #80 is astonishing. Reason is the instrument of philosophy. As long as its commonly recognized limitations (so-called "confining walls") remain in place, reason will be unable to support philosophy in its attempt to deal with "the mystery of the Incarnation." To meet the challenge, reason is called upon to alter the way it proceeds (its *logicum viam*). In effect, reason is called upon to make up its own rules.

Section 22 brings God to bear as enabler of reason's project of reinventing itself. The power of metaphysics is a result of this project. With a potent metaphysics at its command, philosophy can deal with the mystery of the Incarnation, which will render intelligible the essence of humanity. All this, the author tells us, is dependent on reason changing the logic by which it operates. With all this at stake, philosophy must comply with this call for change.

Other requirements to be met by a compliant philosophy are announced in #66. One pertains to the role of philosophy in support of theology: "speculative dogmatic theology" (*theologia dogmatica speculativa*) relies on a "philosophy of the human being, the world, and more importantly of 'being' itself, which in fact is based on objective truth" (*philosophiam hominis, mundi atque, altius, ipsius "esse," quae quidem in obiectiva veritate innititur*) (The term *esse* is always enclosed by quotation marks in the Latin of the encyclical. Whether these should be interpreted as "scare quotes," indicating an unusual usage, is unclear.)

This claim is repeated and embellished in #97, where "the *understanding of faith* demands the acquisition of a philosophy of being which primarily enables *dogmatic theology* to perform its functions properly" (*intellectus fidei postulat ut philosophia essendi partes quae in primis sinant ut theologia dogmatica consentaneo modo expleat sua munia*; italics in Latin text). More follows in this section on the philosophy of being. It is "an active, dynamic, philosophy which views reality in its ontological, causal, and unifying structures" (*philosophia actuosa seu dynamica quae ipsis in suis ontologicis, causalibus et communicativis structuris praebet veritatem*). And it endures because it "is based on the act of 'being' itself" (*actu ipso "essendi" sustentatur*).

The philosophy of being is linked to objective truth in #90, where the author takes issue with "the common perspectives of many philosophies that have rejected the meaningfulness of being" (*communem multarum philosophiarum prospectum quae iam a sensu essendi recesserunt*). These obdurate philosophies entail "the negation of all objective truth" (*omnis . . . veritatis obiectivae negationem*). The point is repeated a few lines later, with the caution not to forget that "the neglect of 'being' itself inevitably leads to losing touch with objective truth" (*neglectum ipsius "esse" necessario secum etiam longinquitatem adferre ab obiectiva veritate*).

The close association of "being" and objective truth in these passages bespeaks adherence to the realism articulated by St. Thomas. In *De Veritate* (V.1.2.R), we may recall, Aquinas affirmed that the truth of things derives from the divine intellect, and would persist even if human intellect did not exist. Realism based on divine intellect (First Truth) became a hallmark of Thomistic metaphysics, as noted previously. *Fides et Ratio* acknowledges this source in #82. An adequate Christian philosophy, the author says, must be addressed not only "to particular and subordinate aspects of things themselves" (*ad elementa peculiaria et relativa . . . rerum ipsarum*), but also "to the very essence of things known" (*ad essentiam ipsam obiectorum cognitionis*). It must "confirm the human capacity to reach *knowledge of the truth*" (*hominis comprobetur facultas adipiscendae veritatis cognitionis*, italics in Latin text), by means of "that *adequation of thing and intellect* to which teachers of Scholastic learning referred" (*illam adaequationem rei et intellectus quam Scholasticae disciplinae doctores appellaverunt*, italics in Latin text). St. Thomas is listed first among these teachers in footnote 99 to #82.

There are other passages in which Thomistic realism is characterized with reference to "objective truth." In #66, John Paul II declares that it is necessary (*Necesse*) that "the reason of the believer" (*fidelis ratio*) obtain "a real knowledge of created things, which also are treated by divine revelation" (*veram . . . cognitionem de rebus creatis . . . quas res etiam revelatio divina tractat*). This enables the reason of the believer to serve "speculative dogmatic theology" (*theologia dogmatica speculativa*), which depends on a "philosophy of 'being' that is founded on objective truth" (*philosophiam "esse," quae quidem in obiectiva veritate innititur*). Continuing the theme in #90, the author warns that "neglect of 'being' inevitably results in losing touch with objective truth and therefore with the very ground that sustains human dignity" (*neglectum ipsius "esse" necessario secum etiam longinquitatem adferre ab obiectiva veritate ac, proinde, ab ipso fundamento illo quod hominis sustinet dignitatem*).

To serve the purposes of dogmatic theology, the author argues here, philosophy must avail itself of a reason capable of grasping objective truth. And to grasp objective truth amounts to genuine knowledge of "being" as such, pertaining both to created things generally and to human dignity in particular. In short, the reason employed by philosophy in support of theology must be capable of grasping real "being" itself.

In #82, knowledge of truth is said to be achieved by an adequation of thing to intellect. Adequation is a relation in which components of the thing known share the same structure as components of the knowing mind. St. Thomas ran afoul of the problem how the incomposite (hence entirely simple) mind of God can share structure with created truth. John Paul II has an obverse problem regarding the adequation of the knowing mind and real being." In #97, being is characterized as active, which is to say something engaged in action. The encyclical leaves us in the dark about how the act of "being" might be structured in a way that permits adequation with a knowing mind.

6.6.2

In the context of *Fides et Ratio*, employment of reason is the hallmark of philosophy. Numerous requirements are laid down in the encyclical which the philosophy it sponsors must meet. These may be repeated in summary form. The philosophy sanctioned by the encyclical is required (1) to assist dogmatic theology in performing its role satisfactorily (##66; 97). This, of course, brings to mind the tradition of philosophy as servant of theology (labelled *philosophia theologiae ancilla* by St. Peter Damian) tracing back to Philo of Alexandria. To serve this purpose, a philosophy must embody (2) a systematic metaphysics (##22; 61; 83) with a number of required features.

Among these features is the mandate (3) that this philosophy must accept the meaningfulness of "being," rejection of which would isolate it from objective truth (#90). Also required (4) is that, as a philosophy of "being" (#97), it will be based on the act of "being" itself. This will give it access to universal reality as a whole (#97). Taking full advantage of this access will push philosophy to its limits (#80), creating a further requirement (5) that the reason it employs must operate with an amended logic. Only with a tailormade logic, the encyclical emphasizes, is philosophy able to comprehend the mystery of the Incarnation.

A philosophy that meets these requirements will confirm the human capacity to know the truth (#82). And the objective truth in question is reached by means of an adequation between intellect and things which is the cornerstone of the account of truth in St. Thomas' *De Veritate*. The final requirement, accordingly, is (6) that philosophy aim at truth conceived in the manner that St. Thomas canonized.

In #49, John Paul II quotes Pius XII's *Humani Generis*, to the effect that the Catholic Church has no "official" philosophy. "The Church makes no philosophy its own" (*Suam ipsius philosophiam non exhibet Ecclesia*), John Paul II claims, "nor does she canonize any one particular philosophy at the expense of others" (*neque quamlibet praelegit peculiarem philosophiam aliarum damno*). This claim is disingenuous, to say the least. The only philosophies known today that meet requirements (1) through (6) trace back to St. Thomas. As far as *Fides et Ratio* is concerned, Neo-Thomism is de facto the official philosophy of the Catholic Church, by dint of its very requirements for an adequate philosophy. To suggest otherwise is like advertising an affirmative-action position (e.g., calling for a woman), after having already filled that position with someone outside the affirmative-action category (a man).

## 6.7 Performance in Title Roles Evaluated

Faith and reason share the title role of John Paul II's *Fides et Ratio*. It is time to assess their joint performance in the roles assigned thein in the preface. Once again, the preface reads: "Faith and reason are like two wings on which the human spirit rises to a contemplation of truth" (*FIDES ET RATIO binae quasi pennae videntur quibus veritatis ad contemplationem hominis attollitur animus*). Wing imagery aside, this sentence affirms that faith and reason are means by which the human spirit reaches truth. There is no suggestion here that there might not be other means (like revelation) as well. Nor is it affirmed that faith and reason must work together (like two wings on a bird) to achieve this goal. In the preface, at least, it is left open whether either could do the job by itself. Since faith and reason are compatible (##17; 43; et al.), however, if they could do the job separately then they could do it together.

Can faith attain truth by itself? The analysis of faith above shows why it cannot. The reason is that faith is an inactive attribute of mind, not capable of acting on its own. In that respect, it is like the attribute of confidence. Being confident might enable someone to do a given thing better, but confidence cannot do anything just by itself. Having faith, likewise, might make doing something easier, but faith by itself can do nothing at all. Literally speaking, faith can move neither mountains nor molehills. Nor, literally speaking, can faith liberate reason (contrary to #20), or assist philosophy in accepting the "foolishness "of the Cross (contrary to #23). Being itself incapable of action, accordingly, faith by itself also is incapable of serving as means by which the human spirit might ascend to truth.

Lest this conclusion seem too quick, let us imagine someone speaking in John Paul II's defense. The defender admits that the preface of *Fides et Ratio* is cast in figurative language. Difficulties have been shown to arise when this language is taken literally. Speaking literally, faith is incapable of acting on its own, and incapable accordingly of helping reason lift the human spirit to a contemplation of truth. The defender argues, however, that this reading misses the intended point of the preface. As far as faith is concerned, the point is that the human spirit can rise to a contemplation of truth, and that faith plays an essential role in that endeavor. It may be granted that its role is not literally active, calling for faith to do something on its own. Faith's role, rather, is to serve as a resource on which the human spirit draws in the course of that endeavor. As a biographer draws on documents sitting (passively) in the archives, so the human spirit draws on the (passive) contents of the faith at its disposal.

By exercising the faith at its disposal, the human spirit engages a resource that contributes to its contemplation of truth. Among the several senses of *fides* discussed above, John Paul II's defense continues, some are more relevant in this regard than others. The several senses in question have been divided into personal and institutional. The Catholic Church as an institution is identified by the doctrines of its Catechism. These doctrines are too numerous and too obscure to be of much service in the ascent to truth of the individual human spirit. The faith that identifies the Catholic Church as an institution, accordingly, is not itself the resource that assists the human spirit in its ascent to truth.

Personal senses of faith, in turn, include (i) the individual's mental state of assent, (ii) faith in divine Persons, and (iii) Christian practices in which the individual person participates. The mind's assent (acceptance) per se obviously is not a resource on which the mind (*animus*) draws in its ascent. Faith (ii), in turn, is an attitude of reliance and confidence. While reliance on God indeed might assist the spirit in its ascent, the attitude of confidence itself that constitutes faith (ii) is not a resource contributing to that ascent. This leaves faith in sense (iii), namely the practices that constitute the Christian way of life. Such practices are pursued within a community of like-minded people who nourish each other in their spiritual growth. Membership in such a community assuredly is an asset in the pursuit of a Christian life. It is participation in the practices of faith (iii), the defender concludes, that provides the resource said to cooperate with reason in the ascent that brings the human spirit to the contemplation of truth.

This understanding of faith in the preface of the encyclical makes sense, and need not be disputed. The fact remains, however, that Christian practices (faith (iii)) are not themselves capable of initiating action. Regardless of the form it takes, faith is a state of mind rather than a source of activity. Just in and by itself, accordingly, faith is incapable of lifting the human spirit to a contemplation of truth. Whether it can effectively team with reason to this effect is another matter, to which we turn presently. Before this, however, we have to consider whether reason can lift the human spirit to truth by itself.

## 6.7.1

The depiction of reason in the encyclical poses serious difficulties for a plausible reading of its prelude. In ways spelled out above, this depiction of reason is conceptually aberrant. The *ratio* of *Fides et Ratio* is a theorical construct, designed to meet theological requirements imposed by a reactionary Neo-Thomism. This postulated *ratio* is endowed with powers that real-life reason, despite its variety, has never possessed. It is not the reason employed by Aristotle, nor the reason critiqued by Kant, nor that behind the critical realism of Lonergan. It is not the reason employed by mathematicians, by scientists, or by philosophers of science. It is not the reason employed by Augustine or Thomas Aquinas in developing their respective accounts. Nor is it the reason employed by John Paul II himself in composing the encyclical. More importantly, it is not the reason employed by ordinary people as they conduct their daily lives in a reasonable manner. And it is not the reason of people who participate in the practices of Christian faith (iii).

The people who participate in faith (iii) are real people. For the most part, although never perfectly, they employ reason in the conduct of their daily lives. The reason that they employ has little to do with the make-believe reason of Neo-Scholastic theologians. It remains possible, nonetheless, that the actual reason these real people employ might cooperate with faith in bringing about a contemplation of the truth of which the preface of the encyclical speaks. It might indeed be the case that neither faith nor reason by itself is capable of bringing this about on its own. Nonetheless, faith might be able to cooperate with actual reason in assisting the human spirit in its ascent to truth. If so, the preface of the encyclical would be at least partially vindicated. In point of fact, there are passages in the body of the encyclical that indicate ways in which actual faith and actual reason might accomplish this together.

### 6.7.2

Section 67 of *Fides et Ratio* draws attention to "the profound conformity between faith and its special need for explanation through reason" (*intimam convenientiam . . . inter fidem eiusque praecipuam necessitatem sese explicandi per rationem*). The conformity here is not mere agreement, but rather a matter of complementarity or synergy. "Faith will be able in this manner" (*Fides poterit hoc modo*), the author says "'to show reason the path fully, when it sincerely seeks the truth'" (*"iter plene demonstrare rationi illi, quae sincere veritatem requirit . . ."*; here the author quotes one of his own epistles). At the same time, the quotation continues, "'it is required that reason be reinforced by faith, in order to discover new horizons that it cannot reach on its own'" (*"exstat necessitas, ut ratio ex fide vim sumat, novosque fines consequatur, ad quos sola pervenire non potest"*).

In our following reflection on these remarks in #67, let us understand the *ratio* in question to be the actual reason of rationally competent people, rather than the fantasized reason of the encyclical. There is a conformity between faith and actual reason. This conformity is synergistic, enabling faith to show reason the way in its search for the truth. Reinforced by faith, the reason of rationally competent people may discover new horizons it cannot reach on its own.

The author returns to the theme of new horizons (*novo fines*) in #73, this time in terms of the relation between theology and philosophy. Through philosophy, the "believer's reason" (*fidelis ratio*) "uses its power of reflection" (*suae cogitationis facultatem exerceat*) to interact "with the word of God to get a fuller understanding of it" (*Dei verbo . . . pleniorem eiusdem comprehensionem*). This involves moving "between two things" (*intra duas res*), namely "God's word and increased understanding" (*Dei verbum . . . altioremque . . . cognitionem*). Theology's role in this transaction is to keep reason from straying, and to help it "explore paths that by itself it would not even have expected it could take" (*explorandas semitas, quas sola ne suspicatur quidem se illas decurrere posse*). This "circular motion" (*circulari motu*) with the word of God leaves philosophy enriched, "insofar as it discovers new and unexpected horizons" (*quia novos et inexspectatos attingit fines*).

In reading #73, we may understand philosophy as a proxy for actual reason (competently employed). Theology, in turn, will give way to the practice of the Christian faith, namely faith (iii) as identified previously. The upshot is a recapitulation of #67. In this synergistic relation, faith and reason help each other along paths that lead to "revealed Truth" (*Veritatem revelatam*, #73). These adjustments make literal sense of the affirmation in the preface that faith and reason lift the human spirit to the contemplation of truth. The sense it makes fits in as well with the assurance in the preface that by knowing and loving God, men and women may come to the fullness of truth about themselves.

The synergy here between faith and reason is reciprocal, which is to say circular as in #73. Their interaction results in an incremental expansion of the limits of human awareness. Faith opens new perspective for reason to explore. And the new territories secured by reason give faith a staging area for launching further ventures of comprehension.

In the illustration of the interaction between faith and reason that follows, both are concerned primarily with the two great commandments. Reason's main contribution is an analysis of key terms and concepts implicated in these commandments. Prominent among these are the concepts of heart and of love. Faith's contribution is an exposition of the two great commandments as they figure in the lives of faithful

Christians. These tasks of analysis and exposition are not mutually exclusive. Rational analyses often will incorporate references to Christian faith, and reason perforce will contribute to the exposition in question.

The results of this synergistic interaction constitute an illustration of what faith and reason can accomplish together. In upshot, they also yield a fuller understanding of the two great commandments than either faith or reason could accomplish separately. By way of caution, these results are not be taken as definitive, either in content or in derivation. Reason takes center stage to get the illustration underway.

### 6.7.2.1

There are approximately 350 occurrences of the term *kardia* (heart) in the NT. Some of these play crucial roles, such as those occurring in the four versions of the First Great Commandment (GC1) found in the Gospels (Matt 22:37; Mark 12:29–30, 33; Luke 10:27). Each of these states that one should love God with all one's heart, in a context suggesting that the heart in some sense is a faculty of knowledge. Other key occurrences of the term appear in Acts and in Paul's letters. In point of fact, the term *kardia* is so central to the core themes of the NT that it some cases it would be difficult to express those themes if the term were not available.

Despite its basic role in the Gospel message, however, the human heart and its attributes are all but ignored in the 1994 *Catechism of the Catholic Church*. Section 2669 endorses repeating the holy name frequently with a humble heart (*corde humiliter*). Section 1439 avers that only the heart of Christ (*Christi cor*) could adequately reveal the depths of his Father's love. There is one other reference to the heart in section 153, which somehow was overlooked by the indexers. Speaking here of faith as a gift of God, the authors attest to the need of help from the Holy Spirit who moves the heart (*qui cor moveat*) and converts it to God.

Mention of the heart of Christ in section 1439 brings to mind the widespread Catholic devotion to the Sacred Heart of Jesus. This devotion is supported by multifarious images of the Sacred Heart, most of which feature an effeminate Jesus with a far-away look in his eyes and a thorn-impaled heart plastered on his chest. Quite frankly, my initial reaction to these images was one of revulsion. After my initial reaction of distaste, however, these unpleasant images led to a general curiosity regarding roles played by the heart in the NT, and in particular regarding what Jesus himself had to say about the human heart. Devotion to the sacred Heart of Jesus was part of my professed faith, and my reason stepped in with an attempt to make it intelligible. I undertook a systematic analysis of the various roles played by the heart in the NT. The results of this analysis turned out to be interesting in their own right.

Four distinct senses of heart figure in the NT. *Kardia*(1) is the seat of the affections, *kardia*(2) is the seat of intellectual activity, *kardia*(3) is a morally engaged aspect of the human person, and *kardia*(4) is the faculty of love. A few examples will be given of each, along with relevant commentary. Translations, for the most part, will be in paraphrase, accompanied occasionally by the original text.

*Kardia*(1) appears in John 16:6 and Rom 9:2. In the former, Jesus speaks of the sorrow (*hē lupē*) that has filled the disciples' heart (*tēn kardian*). In the latter, Paul reports the great anguish he has in his heart (*tē kardia mou*) for the plight of his listeners. Other appearance of *kardia*(1) can be found in John 14:27; Acts 2:26; Rom 10:1.

*Kardia*(2) is the locus of intellectual activity, distinct from the mental faculties that bring that activity about. In Mark 2:6, for instance, the author refers to scribes who were reasoning in their hearts (*dialogizomenoi en tais kardiais autōn*). And in Rom 10:9, Paul urges his audience to believe in their hearts (*pisteusēs en tē kardia sou*). Other passages referring to *kardia*(2) include Mark 11:23; Luke 24:38; Heb 4:12.

*Kardia*(3) is clearly illustrated in Matt 11: 29. Jesus here describes himself as "gentle and lowly in heart" (*praus . . . kai tapeinos tē kardia*), rather than attributing these virtues directly to himself as a person. In Luke 8:15, for another illustration, Jesus explains the parable of the sower by saying that those who hear the word of God will hold it "in an honest and good heart" (*en kardia kalē kai agathē*). In these cases, the moral virtues of gentleness, humility, and honesty are attributed to the hearts of the persons involved. Moral evaluation engages the idiom of a person's heart. This holds for adverse evaluation as well. In its account of the Feast of the Passover, John 13:2 describes the abject intentions of the traitor by saying that the devil put it "into the heart of Judas Iscariot' (*eis tēn kardian . . . Ioudas . . . Iskariōtou*) to betray Jesus. Other passages in which a person's heart serves as a symbol of his or her moral condition include Acts 15:9, Rom 2:15, and Heb 10:22.

*Kardia*(4) differs from the previous three in being itself a human faculty. Paramount among instances are the four statements of the GC1 itemized previously. Each of these affirms that you should love the Lord your God with "all your heart" (*ex holes tēs kardias*; Matt 22:37, *en holē tē kardia*). Whereas *kardia*(1) is the seat, but not the source, of the affections, *kardia*(4) is the cause of love, the faculty by which love is engendered.

This brief analysis of the various uses of *kardia* in the NT, in and by itself, has no immediate bearing on Christian faith. Given the importance of GC1 to Christianity, however, the features of *kardia*(4) disclosed by this analysis prompt further investigation of that faculty within the context of that faith. The next step in the synergistic interaction underway between faith and reason shifts perspective from the latter to the former. This subsequent step is to examine the love mandated by GC1 as a specific exercise of *kardia*(4).

### 6.7.2.2

In Matt 22:37, Jesus is depicted as repeating GC1 in response to a Pharisee's challenge. As Jesus puts it, "You shall love the Lord your God with all your heart and with all your soul and with all your mind" (*Agapēseis kurion ton theon sou en holē tē kardia sou kai en holē tē psuchē sou kai en holē tē dianoia sou*). In the other three NT statements of GC1, mentioned previously, heart is mentioned as the first of several faculties to be addressed unreservedly to God. And all but Mark 12:33 include mind (*dianoia*), whereas Mark 12:53 lists understanding (*suneseōs*) instead. All but Mark 12:33, moreover, include soul (*psuchē*) as well.

The first thing to note about GC1 is that the love of God it calls for is not an emotion. It is not a warm feeling in the heart, nor indeed a feeling of any sort. It is an exercise of *kardia*(4), not of *kardia*(1). A straightforward definition of this love is given in 1 John 5:3: "for this is the love of God, that we keep his commandments" (*hautē gar estin hē agapē tou theou, hina tas entolas autou tērōmen*). Uncomplicated as this definition may appear, however, it is unclear how obedience to commands could be a form of love. A solder obviously might obey a superior officer without loving him in any way.

Help is available in Deut 6:5, which contains the only statement of GC1 in the OT. The (Septuagint) wording in Deuteronomy is the same as that in Matt 22:37, save that *holē tēs dunameōs sou* (all your might) occurs in place of *holē tē dianoia sou* (all your mind). In the preceding chapter 5 of Deuteronomy, Moses had conveyed the Ten Commandments to the assembled people of Israel. Between the Decalogue (5:7–21) and 6:5, Moses exhorts Israel to remain faithful to these commandments. Deut 6.5 is the culmination of this exhortation. It might be thought of as a "meta-commandment," in effect instructing the Israelites to obey the commandments he had written on stone with their entire heart, soul, and might. The love they are ordered to show the Lord their God takes the form of complete obedience to his commandments.

In its NT version, GC1 is more general in its application. It is addressed not only to the warriors (the men) of the Jewish nation, but to men and women of all nations on earth. And the fear of the Lord (*phobēsthe Kurion*, Deut 6:2) that was to motivate obedience by the Israelites is replaced by a motivation rooted in unlimited gratitude. The God toward whom love is to be directed, according to GC1 in the NT, is the God who sent his Son to redeem the entire human race.

With respect to the OT Decalogue, however, the role of GC1 in the NT is less essential than that of GC2. The key to the greater significance of GC2 in this regard is contained in Rom 13:8. Having advised his audience to obey the Roman authorities, Paul turns to their duties as Christians. They are to "love each other, for the one who loves another has fulfilled the law" (*allēlous agapan· ho gar agapōn ton heteron nomon peplērōken*). Paul is quite explicit about the Decalogue being the law in question. "For the commandments 'You shall not commit adultery, You shall not murder, You shall not steal, You shall not covet,' and the other commandments, are summed up in this word 'You shall love your neighbor as yourself'" (*to gar Ou moicheuseis, Ou phoneuseis, Ou klepseis, Ouk epithumēseis, kai ei tis hetera entolē, en tō logō toutō anakephalaioutai (en tō) Agapēseis ton plēsion sou hōs* seauton, 13:9; final phrase emphasized in Greek text).

A shorter statement to the same effect is found in Gal 5:14. "For the whole law is fulfilled in one saying: 'You shall love your neighbor as yourself'" (*ho gar pas nomos en heni logō peplērōtai, en tō Agapēseis ton plēsion sou hōs seauton*, final phrase emphasized in Greek text). The phrase emphasized in the Greek of both Rom 13:9 and Gal 5:14 is a verbatim quotation of (Septuagint) Lev 19:18. The significance of the emphasis emerges from a brief look at this OT passage.

Chapter 19 of Lev is occupied with instructions which Moses is to pass on to the people of Israel, issued by the deity who refers to himself as "the Lord your God" (*Kurios ho Theos humōn*). The people are to revere their fathers and mothers, to keep the sabbath, and to avoid stealing and lying. They are not to hate their brothers (*adelphon*), but may rebuke their neighbors (*plēsion*) if needed to avoid sin. Overall, they are to show the same concern for their neighbors as they have for themselves. In the words of the Lord, the people of Israel are instructed to avoid vengeance against "the sons of your own people" (*tois huiuis tou laou sou*). Moses instructs them instead "to love your neighbor as yourself" (19:18, Greek with highlights above). In verse 34 of the same chapter, they are instructed to show the same deference to a stranger who passes through their land; namely, they are "to love him as themselves" (*agapēseis auton hōs seauton*). Concern for neighbor, deference to stranger, love of self; these are modes of comportment, not exercises of *kardia*(4).

The verbatim quotations of the Lev passage in Rom 13:9 and Gal 5:14 are parts of an interesting pattern in the terminology used to express GC2 in the NT. Incorporated in this pattern are the four NT statements of GC1 in Matt 22:37; Mark 12;30, 33; Luke 10:27. Each of the four is accompanied by a mention of GC2 in the precise terminology of Lev 19:18. These are the only statements of GC1 in the entire NT. All four occur in conversations between Jesus and specialists in Jewish law (chief priests, scribes, Pharisees, lawyers). Inasmuch as these men surely were acquainted with Deut 6:5, which is to say with the OT version of GC1, Jesus could be sure he was interacting with them on common ground.

In the addition of an expression of GC2 to each of these four appearances of GC1 in the Gospels, the terminology used is always that of Lev 19:18. In each case, one is to love one's neighbor as oneself. A reasonable conjecture is that Jesus used the OT terminology to extend the common ground of his interaction with the Jewish legal authorities. Regardless of Jesus' intent, however, it remains an interesting fact that the terminology in which these four Gospel statements of GC2 are expressed invariably is that of the passage from Leviticus.

The terminological pattern becomes more compelling with the realization that the remaining statements of GC2 in the NT exclude reference to love of self. The NT contains more than a dozen such statements, all addressed to followers of Jesus rather than to Jewish authorities. Jesus himself issues the commandment to his disciples in John 13:34; 15:12; 15:17. Paul reminds his audience of Jesus' commandment in Rom 12:10; 13:8; Gal 5:13; 1 Thess 3:12; 4:9. And the later authors do the same in 1 Pet 1:22; 4:8; 1 John 3:11, 23; 4:7, 11; 2 John 5.

In sum, there are four appearances of GC1 in the NT which call for love of neighbor as oneself, and fifteen in which love of self is not mentioned. The four appearances in question constitute verbatim quotations

of Lev 19:18. It was suggested above that the terminology of these four
appearances was part of an effort by Jesus to establish common ground
with the Jewish scholars he was addressing. From the NT perspective,
in any case, the version of GC2 that dictates love of neighbor as oneself
(*hōs seauton*) is defective. One should not love oneself in the first place.
To love oneself is to hold oneself in high regard, which is a form of pride.
In 2 Tim 3:2, Paul links self-love (*philautoi*) with numerous evils, among
which are boasting and pride (*alazones huperēphanoi*). The love cited in
Rom 13:9 and Gal 5:14 as fulfilling the obligations of the Decalogue cannot incorporate pride in any literal sense.

In the synergistic interaction underway between faith and reason,
it is time to reengage the perspective of the latter. The next step is to
examine the terminology of love in which the two great commandments
are expressed.

### 6.7.2.3

Like the first, the second great commandment is formulated in terms of
*agapaō*. As in classical Greek, *agapaō* is sometimes used interchangeably
with *phileō* in the NT (e.g., John 15:12–15; 21:15–17). Usage aside, however, loving another person (engaging *agapaō*) and relating to another
person as a friend (engaging *phileō*) differ in several ways relevant to the
two great commandments.

Friendship is a reciprocal relation. For M to be a friend of N requires
that N be a friend of M as well. The relation between two friends is the
same for both parties. Rather than a relation M has to N coupled with
another relation N has to M, a friendship between M an N is a single
relation in which both parties participate. Several people, moreover, can
participate in a single relation of mutual friendship. Person P might join
M and N as members of a group sharing friendship with one another. In
this respect, a group friendship is like a fellowship. More than a collection of two-person friendships between individual pairs of members, it
is instead a group of individuals sharing in the same common friendship.

The relation of *agapē* in the two great commandments differs in both
respects. In Matt 5:44, while expanding on GC2, Jesus commands his followers to love their enemies. To love one's enemies does not require that
one's enemies return that love. The love of GC2, that is to say, is not a reciprocal relation. If M and N should happen to love each other, moreover, that

mutual love is not a single relation in which both parties participate. Under GC2, a mutual love between M and N would be comprised by the separate loves of M and N for each other. Perforce, the mutual love of M and N is not a relation in which another person P could participate.

Similarly, M's love of God dictated by GC1 is entirely distinct from N's love of God under that commandment. M might love God while N falls short. This is the case regardless of love M and N might happen to hold for each other. Either or both might love God individually, without M loving N or vice versa. The upshot is that a given person's obedience to GC1 does not depend on that person being obedient to GC2. Whether a dependency exists in the opposite direction depends on what one makes of Rom 13:9, in particular of its apparent claim that GC2 sums up commandments other than those specified in the Decalogue. If GC1 is included among those other commandments, then obedience to GC2 constitutes obedience to GC1 as well. Whether GC1 indeed is among those other commandments, it seems fair to say, remains an open question.

The relation between the two great commandments is an interesting question in its own right. One obvious difference is that GC1 mandates love of God on the part of individual believers. This love is to engage the believer's whole heart, whole mind, and so forth, which means that it is to occur without reservation. The love mandated by GC1, accordingly, is unconditional. What is unconditional is one's personal love-relationship with God. In the case of GC2, however, the individual believer is instructed to love other persons beyond number, most of whom the individual will never encounter personally. If there is anything unconditional about this love, it does not involve a personal relationship. And there is no immediately apparent sense in which an impersonal relationship could be unconditional, especially when the person or persons to be loved remain unspecified. We return to this problem presently.

The status of GC2 within the Christian community is logically distinct from that of GC1. This difference in status can be clearly exhibited in terms of quantificational logic. One domain of quantification, applicable is both cases, is that of the Christian community itself (exclusive of babies, the mentally incompetent, etc.). This is the class of individuals mandated to love God by GC1. The status of GC1 within the community of believers is: $(x)(x$ is a Christian believer $\prec$ [implies] $x$ is commanded to love God). Formalizing the status of GC2, however, requires an additional variable $(y)$, ranging over a more extensive domain of quantification, namely that of humankind at large. Expressed in these terms, the status of GC2 is: (x)[x is a Christian believer ⤳ (y)(y is a human person ⤳ x is commanded to love y)].

These formalizations exhibit the respects in which the mandate of GC2 is more complicated than that of GC1. The love itself of GC2 is more complex as well. Let us examine the nature of GC2 love as indicated in the NT. In terms of the ongoing dialectic between faith and reason, the next step re-engages the perspective of faith.

### 6.7.2.4

In his statement of GC2 in John 13:34, Jesus says "just as I have loved you, you also are to love one another" (*kathōs ēgapēsa humas hina kai humeis agapate allēlous*). This instruction is repeated in John 15:12, where Jesus rephrases his commandment as "that you love one another as I have loved you" (*hina agapate allēlous kathōs ēgapēsa humas*). It goes without saying that Jesus loved his disciples in the requisite manner. But no indication is given of what it is in Jesus' complex interaction with his disciples that counts as the love in question.

Uncertainty in this matter is heightened by Jesus' remark in John 15:9 that "as the Father has loved me, so I have loved you" (*kathōs ēgapēsen me ho patēr, kagō humas ēgapēsa*). From the conjunction of John 13:34 and John 15:9, it follows that Jesus' disciples are to love one another in the way that the Father loved the Son. There is no hint in the text as to how divine love of this sort could be duplicated by ordinary people in ordinary circumstances, in the manner that GC2 seems to mandate.

For purposes of comparison, divine love may be thought of as pure in nature, perhaps something like honey dripping fresh from the comb. To make headway toward understanding the love mandated by GC2, we must allow that it is not pure in this manner. It rather is a mixture of various alloys. Several such alloys are clearly distinguished in the NT.

One such is humility. In Eph 4:2, Paul urges his audience to conduct themselves "with all humility and gentleness, bearing with one another in love" (*meta pasēs tapeinophrosunēs kai prautētos . . . anechomenoi allēlōn en agapē*). In Phil 2:1–2, he speaks of the comfort he finds in Christ's love, and hopes his audience might "have the same love" (*tēn autēn agapēn echontes*). This requires that they avoid "selfish ambition and conceit" (*epitheian . . . kenodoxian*), and that they "in humility esteem others more important than themselves" (*tē tapeinophrosunē allēlous hēgoumenoi huperechontas heautōn*). To sum it up, the author of 1 Pet 3:8 instructs his audience to be united in "sympathy, brotherly love, tender heartedness, and humility of mind (*sumpatheis, philadelphoi, eusplanchnoi, tapeinophrones*). These passages indicate that humility is a primary ingredient in the love dictated by GC2.

James 2:8–9 is explicit in opposing the mandate of GC2 to partiality. If indeed you fulfill the great law "You shall love your neighbor as yourself" (*Agapēseis ton plēsion sou hōs seauton*, emphasized in Greek text), we read in 2:8, "you are doing well" (*kalōs poieite*). "But if you show partiality" (*ei de prosōpolēmpteite*), 2:9 adds, "you are committing sin and are convicted by the law as transgressors"' (*hamartian ergazesthe elenchomenoi hupo tou nomou hōs parabatai*). In effect, love of neighbor directly rules out showing partiality in one's dealings with other people, which is deemed a sin. Chapter 2 of James begins with the exhortation "My brothers, show no partiality as you hold the faith in our Lord Jesus Christ" (*Adelphoi mou, mē en prosōpolēmpsiais echete tēn pistin tou kuriou hēmōn 'Iēsou Christou*). The message here is that the impartiality that is part of Christian faith generally enables abiding by GC2 in particular.

Partiality amounts to showing special consideration of one sort or another for a particular person or group of people. Its sinful downside is that partiality to one group results in other groups being treated unfairly. The negative result of partiality is discrimination against those who are excluded from the privileged group. For whatever reason, and in whatever manner, partiality is treating members of a particular group as more important or more deserving than other people excluded from it. The passages from James above state that partiality is to be avoided.

There are several passages in the NT that emphasize God's impartiality. In the opening sequence of Romans, chapter 2, Paul inveighs against those who presume to judge other persons, reminding his readers that God will judge them all on the day of wrath. And God will judge Jew and Greek alike, "for God shows no partiality" (*ou gar estin prosōpolēmpsia para tō theō*, 2:11). In the opening sequence of Ephesians, chapter 6, Paul advises slaves to obey their masters as children obey their parents, knowing that slave and master will be justly treated by their shared Master in heaven "with whom there is no partiality" (*prosōpolēmpsia ouk estin par' auto*, 6:9). In the last few verses of Colossians, chapter 3, participants in a whole bevy of authoritarian relationships are advised that they all are servants of Christ the Lord, and that punishment and reward will be dispensed among them "without partiality" (*ouk estin prosōpolēmpsia*, 3:25). Paul's testimony of God's impartiality is seconded by Peter in Acts 10:34, with his words to Cornelius: "Truly, I understand that God shows no partiality" (*Ep' alētheias katalambanomai hoti ouk estin prosōpolēmptēs ho theos*).

Humility and impartiality are prominent within the amalgam of virtues that constitutes love of neighbor in the NT. Before considering other possible constituents, however, there is a question to be resolved regarding the relationship shared with one's neighbor in fulfillment of GC2. In what respect might that relationship be unconditional? The scope of GC2 extends beyond people one will ever interact with personally. It includes people one will never meet among one's contemporaries, as well as people in subsequent generations. There is a universality in the mandate of GC2 that cannot be cashed out in terms of personal interactions within the lifetimes of individuals bound by it.

This universality goes beyond the way individual Christians interact with other people. It is a matter instead of the way the individual bound by it perceives his or her fellow human beings generally. Obedience to GC2 requires a reorientation of the way one views other people in relation to oneself. One is to view others with impartiality and humility regardless of circumstances, regardless of who they are and when they live. In effect, one does so unconditionally. The unconditional love of GC2 is a matter of how one perceives people generally in relation to oneself.

There is a broad class of character traits pertaining primarily to one's interactions with other people. Examples include the traits of being merciful, benevolent, magnanimous, philanthropic, compassionate, empathetic, and antipathetic. Although one might occasionally show mercy in one's treatment of animals, mercy typically and most often is exercised in one's dealing with other human beings. And it is hard to think of circumstances in which one could properly be said to exercise either magnanimity or philanthropy toward creatures other than one's fellow humans.

Character traits of this sort are latent until they become activated. The trait of being benevolent lies dormant until the person involved actually shows benevolence toward another person. Similarly, the trait of being compassionate is activated by treating other people with compassion, and the trait of empathy is made active by treating other people empathetically. In each case, there is a sharp distinction between the dormant trait and its being activated.

Things are otherwise with the character trait of humility. A humble person remains actively humble even when not interacting with other people. The trait of humility, that is to say, does not have to be exercised in the presence of other people in order for the person possessing it to exhibit humility. Although humility is a character trait bearing on how one interacts with other people, the manifestation of humility does not require that other people be actively involved. One example is that of a person who deliberately refrains from action that would deprive future generations of needed resources, such as draining wetlands for commercial development, and does so for that specific reason. Acting in a way that puts the interests of other people over one's own is an act of humility, which does not require that those others be actually present. A more notable example from the recent past was Pope Francis' choice to live in a guest house (St. Margaret's) rather than in the Apostolic Palace. This was an expression of humility, as it were, heard around the world. But the expression did not implicate other people specifically.

Humility is one component of the neighborly love mandated by GC2. As already noted, another is impartiality, which, like humility, can be actively present in the absence of anyone specifically benefitting from it. A worthy judge can demonstrate impartiality in the procedures of his or her court, independently of particular cases that might be heard in that venue. An impartial judge is one who deliberately avoids biases, and deliberation to that effect can take place in his or her chambers.

Another trait in the mix that constitutes brotherly love is mentioned in Phil 2:3. In this passage, Paul instructs his audience to do nothing from selfishness or conceit, but rather "to esteem others as more significant than yourselves" (*allēlous hēgoumenoi hupechontas heautōn*). A similar instruction is found in 1 Cor 10:24, where Paul says "let no one seek his own [advantage], but that of his neighbor" (*mydeis to heautou zēteitō alla to tou heterou*). There is no specific name for this trait in the NT, although the descriptive phrase "poor in spirit" (*ptōchoi tō pneumatic*) of Matt 5:3 provides an apt characterization. For present purposes, the term "deference" in English will serve as a useful label. Deference joins humility and impartiality as part of the amalgam that comprises brotherly love in the NT.

Like humility and impartiality, deference can be manifest in the person involved independently of the presence of other people to whom deference might be shown. One need not actually exercise the trait of deference in order to exhibit that trait among one's personal characteristics. Deference is an open-ended attitude, directed toward other people regardless of where or when they might possibly be encountered. Among recipients of deference are people never encountered during the deferential person's lifetime, including people of future generations.

This feature of deference corresponds to the fact that the obligation of GC2 extends indefinitely into the future. To meet that obligation requires a readiness to show brotherly love to other people regardless of circumstance in which one might or might not chance to encounter them. In this respect, deference joins humility and impartiality. Constituents of brotherly love are open-ended, in the same manner as the obligation of GC2 itself.


6.7.2.5

Reason moves to the fore again with an examination of the network of love in the NT. This network is established by the divine act recounted in John 3:16. "For God so loved the world, that he gave his only begotten Son" (*Houtōs gar ēgapēsen ho Theos ton kosmon, ōste ton huion to monogenē edōken*). Persons of three categories figure in this transaction: God the giver, Jesus Christ the given, and humankind the recipient (see Matt 18:7 for another passage in which *kosmos* means humanity in general). John 3:16 continues with the affirmation that those who believe in the Son will gain everlasting life.

The NT network of love initiated by God consists of a series of reciprocal love relationships. There are (1) the Father's love of the Son, reciprocated by the Son's love of the Father, (2) Jesus' love of his disciples, which calls for their love of Jesus by way of response, and (3) God's love of the individual person, returned by the individual's love of God. The relationships in (3), of course, have obvious textual bases. God's love of the human individual is part of his love of humanity in general (the *kosmos* of John 3:16), and the individual's love of God is dictated by GC1.

Textual bases for (1) are found in John 15:9 and John 14:31. In the former passage, Jesus tells his disciples "As the Father has loved me, so I have loved you" (*kathōs ēgapēsen me ho patēr, kagō humas ēgapēsa*). In the latter, Jesus says he obeys God's commands so that the world (*kosmos*) may know "that I love the Father" (*hoti agapō ton patera*). Regarding (2), Jesus' love for individual persons is attested by previously quoted John 15:9, where he says explicitly that he loved his people as the Father has loved him. Speaking to his disciples in John 14:15, finally, Jesus indicates that keeping his commandments will attest to their love for him: "If you love me, keep my commandments" (*Ean agapate me, tas entolas tas emas tērēsete*).

The reciprocal relations of (1), (2), and (3) can be visualized as sides of an equilateral triangle. God the Father is at the apex, Jesus the Son at the left base angle, and the human person at the right. The triangle is dynamic. In the course of human time, God's love passes first to Jesus, and next to individual human persons. In obedience to GC1, love then passes from individual persons back to God. On the part of those in full obedience, love flows untrammeled back to God where it originated.

To complete the image of love's flow through time, GC2 must be incorporated within the triangle. The love of neighbor mandated by GC2 is not reciprocal. One may love one's enemies without these enemies loving one in return. This lack of reciprocity keeps neighborly love from joining the main flow of love around the periphery of the triangle. Another respect in which GC2 love differs from love at the periphery is the absence of divine persons among its relata. Neighborly love is a relation among human individuals exclusively. Nonetheless, love of neighbor affects the flow of divinely engaged love. It does so in two distinct ways.

One is that a human person incapable of loving his or her neighbor is incapable of unrestrained love of God as well. Put otherwise, unrestrained obedience of GC1 depends upon obedience of GC2 as well. This dependency is affirmed in 1 John 4:20. In the words of this passage, "for he who does not love his brother, whom he has seen, cannot love God, whom he has not seen" (*ho gar mē agapōn ton adelphon autou hon eōrōken, ton theon hon ouch eōraken ou dunatai agapan*). For most human individuals, however, even the least self-interested, compliance with GC2 is a matter of degree. This makes compliance with GC1 a matter of degree as well. In a sense not entirely metaphorical, compliance with GC2 regulates compliance with GC1.

This influence of GC2 on GC1 can be illustrated by inserting a symbol of a rheostat in the side of the triangle that represents love of God by human individuals. In electrical circuits, a rheostat regulates volume of current flow by varying the resistance through which it flows. An electrical rheostat is commonly depicted by an arrow in contact with the surface of an elongated resistor, only one end of which is connected to the remainder of the circuit. The greater the resistance through which the current flows, the greater the voltage drop over the rheostat, and the less the overall volume of current flow. When the current is love instead of electricity, its flow is regulated by degree of compliance with GC2.

Full compliance with GC1, on the part of a given individual, is enabled by full compliance by that individual with GC2. When this happens, the rheostat of love is at a minimal setting, one imposing no impediment to the flow of love passing through it. Loving God with all one's heart, soul, and mind is enabled by eliminating all self-interest from one's dealings with fellow human beings. Complete absence of self-interest corresponds to the lowest setting of the love rheostat.

The second way in which compliance with GC2 affects divine Love comes to the fore in 1 John 4:12. Neighborly love brings divine love to completion. As this passage puts it, "if we love one another, God abides in us and his love is perfected in us" (*ean agapōmen allēlous, ho theos ev hēmin menei kai hē agapē autou en hēmin teteleiōmenē estin*). In this context, the verb *teleioō* could also be taken to mean "to finish" or "to complete, as well as "to perfect." Regardless of translation, the sense is that God's love is fulfilled in the love that human persons show for each other.

Other occurrences of the verb *teleioō* are found in 1 John 4:17 and 4:18. The immediately preceding passage, 4:16, is essential for understanding 4:17, and is crucially important in its own right. It reads, in part, "God is love, and whoever abides in love abides in God, and God abides in him" (*Ho theos agapē estin, kai ho menōn en tē agapē ev tō theō menei kai ho theos en autō menei*). Given that God is love, the inference that one abides in God if one abides in love is straightforward. The further affirmation that God abides in those who abide in love conveys the primary significance of the passage for present purposes. It is God's presence in those who love that enables God's love to be perfected in the love exercised by those persons.

First John 4:12 says that if we love one another, God abides in us and his love is perfected in us. The following passage 4:16, in turn, says that God abides in those who love because God himself is love. It is because God himself is love that God comes to abide in those who love. Ultimately, it is because God is love that his love is perfected by the love of his people for each other. In short, obedience of GC2 brings God's love for humankind to completion.

First John 4:17 goes on to say "thus it is that love is perfected with us" (*en toutō teteiōtai hē agape meth' hēmōn*), followed by 4:18 and its assurance that "perfect love" (*hē teleia agapē*) casts out fear of punishment "on the day of judgment" (*en tē hēmera tēs kriseōs*, 4:17).

The affirmation "*Ho theos agapē estin*" (God is love), which underlies this conception of perfected love, is conceptually challenging in its own right. The Greek *estin* (third person singular of *eimi*) has several meanings, corresponding basically to those of the English "is." Foremost among relevant meanings are the "is" of identity and the "is" of predication. The sense in which God is love cannot be that of identity, as can be seen by substituting "love" for "God" in John 3:16. If love and God were the same, then "God so loved the world" and "Love so loved the world" would be equivalent expressions. But unlike the former, the latter has no apparent meaning. The "is" of predication is ruled out as well, inasmuch as "love" is not a descriptive adjective. Being a noun rather than an adjective, "love" does not designate a property that can be attributed to other things.

Beyond those of identity and predication, however, there is another meaning that might be conveyed by "is" (*estin*) in the expression "God is love." Let us refer to it as the "is" of personification. Illustrations are easy to find in the ancient Greek pantheon. Athena is the goddess of wisdom. Wise herself, she personifies wisdom. The expression "Athena is wisdom" means that she exemplifies wisdom. Wisdom is typified by this legendary person. Another illustration from the same source is Mercury, who personifies speed. In like manner, Prometheus is foresight, so named for the prescience he personifies.

The affirmation "God is love," understood accordingly, means that God personifies love. God, the first Person of the Trinity, exemplifies love and typifies love. He epitomizes love in the course of human affairs. GC1 instructs us, as human persons, to love the first Person of the Trinity in an unqualified manner responding to that Person's love for us.

God sits at the apex of the triangle representing the network of love relationships connecting human persons with the first two Persons of the Christian Godhead. Love flows from the Person of God through the Person of Jesus, through the individual human person, from whom it returns in due measure to God. Love is perfected to the extent that the individual persons returning it comply with GC2. Both GC1 and GC2 provide instructions for the proper flow of love around and within this triangle of love relationships.

## 6.8 Summary of Chapter

John Paul II's *Fides et Ratio* endorses the cooperation of faith and reason as a means of knowing God. The conception of faith in the encyclical is conceptually murky, and its treatment of reason is unrealistic to the point of make-believe. The author's vision of the combined powers of faith and reason, nonetheless, should be taken quite seriously.

The distortions of faith and reason in the encyclical are due to the author's underlying theological commitments. If we set John Paul II's theology aside, we gain access to the living faith of sincere Christians, and to the reason employed by rational people in their daily affairs. The living faith of actual Christians is a matter of degree. Theology of the Magisterium (bishops and councils) aside, this faith is rooted in the NT; and some Christians are more fully acquainted with the NT than others. Skill in the use of reason is a matter of degree as well. Skill develops with training and practice, a consequence of which is that people differ in their ability to reason accurately.

In the foregoing dialectical interchange between faith and reason, it was assumed that the faith involved was grounded primarily in the NT. It was assumed as well that the reason involved was well trained and competent. If a critic thinks that either faith or reason was misrepresented in the interchange, both factors at least were clearly enough delineated to provide a relevant target for criticism. In any case, it should be borne in mind that the faith and reason involved in the foregoing interchange are not embellished with theological overlays.

Major stages in this dialectical interchange may be summarized. The unifying theme of the interchange is the love called for by the two great commandments. GC1 dictates that one love God with all one's heart, whereas GC2 requires that human individuals love each other. In the context of the NT, heart (*kardia*) is the faculty of love. The first step of the dialectical process is an exercise of reason, concerned primarily with an analysis of the various uses of the term *kardia* in the NT.

*Kardia*(1) is the seat of emotion, *kardia*(2) the seat of intellectual activity, and *kardia*(3) the center of moral virtues and vices. In these three roles, heart does not initiate action. *Kardia*(4), however, is an active faculty. Heart in this fourth sense is the agent of love. The mandate of GC1 is that one exercise this faculty to the utmost in one's love of God. GC2, in turn, mandates that this faculty should be exercised with regard to one's neighbor. Differences between love of God and love of neighbor emerge at a later stage of analysis.

Contributions of faith to this dialectic come mainly in the form of beliefs and attitudes exhibited by faithful followers of Jesus in the NT. In keeping with the unifying theme of the interchange, these contributions pertain primarily to GC1 and GC2. There are four expressions of GC1 in the NT, each accompanied by an expression of GC2. In each case, GC2 calls for loving one's neighbor as oneself. By contrast, there are more than a dozen expressions of GC2 by itself (unaccompanied by GC1) with no mention of self-love by way of comparison. Inasmuch as self-love is a form of pride (a deadly sin), these unaccompanied expressions of GC2 should be taken as normative.

As expressed in the Gospels, the four appearances of GC1 are holdovers from the OT. Precedence of GC2 in the NT is indicated in Rom 13:9 and Gal 5:14, with their joint affirmation that other laws are summed up by that commandment. Rom 13:9 identifies the Decalogue specifically as covered by GC2, whereas Gal 5:14 suggests that GC1 might be covered as well. GC2 is the hallmark of Christian faith in the NT.

Reason again takes the lead with an analysis of the love implicated in the two great commandments. In comparison with *philia* (friendship), the *agapē* of GC1 is unconditional. It is the love of individual persons directed wholeheartedly toward the Person of God. The love of GC2, on the other hand, is not personal. This love pertains to contemporary people one will never meet, as well as people as yet unborn, neither of whom one ever encounters personally. Love of neighbor also is unconditional, but in a sense that does not involve person-to-person commitment.

The lives of faith exhibited by the original Christians in the NT tell us little about the character of the love they learned to exercise with respect to those who counted as their neighbors. We know at least that it was not emotional, being an exercise of *kardia*(4) rather than *kardia*(1). The characteristics of GC2 love for the original Christians have obvious implications for our practice of neighborly love today. As depicted in the NT, this love has several salient characteristics, meaning that it was an alloy of several distinct features.

One such feature was humility. Philippians 2:3, for example, characterizes Christian love as treating others humbly, that is as more significant than oneself. Another component of GC2 love is impartially, in the sense treating all people as equal in importance. James 2:8–9 connects love of neighbor directly with impartiality in this sense. Yet another such component is deference, a term adopted for the preference of one's neighbor's advantage over one's own advocated in 1 Cor 19:24. Humility, impartiality, and deference are all open-ended, in being directed toward an indefinitely large class of people beyond any to be encountered during the relevant person's lifetime.

Humility, impartiality, and deference are built into the perspective from which GC2 instructs us to view other people. Adopting this perspective requires relinquishing a view of the world based on self-interest in favor of a view counting others as no less important than oneself. In effect, GC2 mandates adopting a perspective within which care for others is no less important than care for oneself.

The final step in the dialectical interaction of faith and reason was the formulation of a diagram representing the network of love generated by God's gift of his only Son. The diagram is a triangle with the Person of God at the apex, the Person of Jesus at the left of the base, the individual human person at the right. Love flows counterclockwise from angle to angle, returning from human person to God in fulfillment of GC1. Volume of flow from human individual to God is governed by a rheostat representing GC2. Full compliance with GC2 enables love of God "with all one's heart." Unrestricted love of God brings God's love itself to completion. In upshot, full compliance with GC2 perfects the love that motivated the gift of God's only Son.

## 6.9 Conclusions

This example of cooperative interaction between faith and reason is an obvious departure from the interaction symbolized by the two wings metaphor of *Fides et Ratio*. There are respects, however, in which the present effort shares common cause with the encyclical. It is fitting to finish this critique of John Paul's encyclical by reiterating a few points of departure and a few of common purpose.

Regarding common purpose, both the encyclical and the exercise above address the topic of a cooperative interchange between faith and reason. After all, the exercise above was inspired by the encyclical. Not only that, but the foregoing exploration of faith and reason at earlier stages in Christian thought was part of an effort to understand the contemporary context in which the encyclical was written. I am grateful to St. John Paul II for his motivation of the present study.

A major departure, of course, is that the faith and reason involved in the exercise above share little in common with their counterparts in the encyclical. The concepts of faith and reason at work in *Fides et Ratio* exhibit theological overlays that have accumulated during recent centuries. These theological accoutrements have resulted in concepts radically out of touch with faith and reason in the daily lives of ordinary Christian people today. A priority in developing the illustrative account above, on the other hand, was remaining close to the faith and reason exemplified in the lives of ordinary people.

Another point of divergence, previously neglected, is that *Fides et Ratio* contains no clear examples of faith and reason working together in ways that advance the human mind's "contemplation of truth" (*veritatis . . . contemplationem* in the preface). Reason in the encyclical is a theological construct. And faith operates in domains (e.g., the mystical) from which reason is excluded. Even in theory, it is unclear how they could cooperate in a productive joint endeavor. In the illustrative exercise above, by way of contrast, faith and reason are construed in ways that make working together come naturally. Reason operates within a context of faith, and faith lends itself to rational analysis.

A final difference to be noted is that *Fides et Ratio* has nothing to say about the two great commandments. This is not a criticism of the encyclical per se, which is concerned with theological issues rather than matters of ordinary Christian life. The encyclical, however, constitutes a pronouncement of the Church's Magisterium (teaching authority). And the Magisterium itself has been largely silent on GC2 in particular. GC2 is basic to the conduct of Christian life. It is a criticism of the Magisterium itself to note that it has been more concerned with teaching doctrine than with providing guidelines for a life of neighborly love.

Teachings of the Magisterium are laid out in the *Catechism of the Catholic Church*, the latest edition of which came out in 1994. Neither of the great commandments is listed as such in the index. Both are mentioned in entry 2055, as part of a quotation of Matt 22:37–40. This entry comes toward the beginning of a detailed discussion of the Ten Commandments that goes on for over one hundred pages. Entry 2055 continues by referring to GC1 and GC2 as a "twofold yet single commandment of love," and declares that the Decalogue must be interpreted in its light. Reference to the two as a "single commandment" represents a fundamental misunderstanding of both.

The Catechism makes no clear distinction between the Old and the New Covenant. This despite (1) over a dozen explicit references to the New Covenant in the NT, (2) specific description as the covenant secured by Jesus as a "better covenant" (*kreittonos diathēkēs*) in Heb 7:22, and (3) inclusion of "New Covenant" (*kainē diathēkē*, as in Luke 22:20) in the words effecting consecration of the Eucharist. Neither covenant is cited in the index of the Catichism. There are explicit references to the New Covenant, however, in entries 1964 and 1965. Both pertain to the promise of a new covenant in Jer 31:31. The old covenant was an agreement between God and the Israelites, brokered by Moses, whereas the New Covenant is an agreement between God and the followers of Jesus generally. As the Old Covenant was centered on the Decalogue recorded by Moses, so the New Covenant is centered on the commandment of neighborly love. By overlooking the essential differences between these two covenants, the Catechism fails to provide effective guidance for the conduct of a Christian life.

APPENDIX A

# Alleged Need for Latin as a Fixed
# Language in the Church

FIDES ET RATIO RAISES a problem about the language in which it is expressed. As the author puts it in #96, the problem is one "of the enduring authority and force of the conceptual language used in conciliar definitions" (*de perpetua agitur auctoritate et vi sermonum conceptuumque adhibitorum in conciliorum definitionibus*). The problem is complex, he says, because in addressing it one must seriously consider "the meanings words assume in different times and cultures" (*ipsius significationis quam variis in culturae regionibus temporumque aetatibus verba sibi sumpserunt*).

Having posed the problem, John Paul II then attempts to defuse it with the sanguine remark that "nonetheless the history of human thought" (*Cogitationis humanae historia utcumque*) shows that "some standard universal concepts" (*quasdam principales notiones universalem*) retain meanings assuring the continued "truth of the assertions in which they are expressed" (*veritatem earum affirmationum quam recludunt*). Section 96 concludes with an appeal to philosophy to help solve problems like this. In the words of the encyclical, "philosophy [is called upon] to thoroughly examine the connection between the language of discernment and truth" (*philosophica . . . coniunctio pervestigetur inter sermonem intellectivum et veritatem*). In point of fact, the problem is not resolved in *Fides et Ratio*.

In venturing these remarks, however, John Paul II elicits support from two conservative documents regarding the fixity of Catholic dogma. One is Pius XII's *Humani Generis*, which he quotes (in footnote 112) as asserting that dogmas are based "on principles and notions deduced from a true knowledge of created things" (*principiis ac notionibus ex vera rerum creatarum cognitione deductis*), so that "it is sinful to deviate from them" (*ab eis discedere nefas sit*). The other (in footnote 113) is *Mysterium Ecclesiae*, issued by the Sacred Congregation for the Doctrine of the Faith (previously the Inquisition). The part quoted instructs the faithful "to shun the opinion that dogmatic formulas cannot signify the truth in a determinate way" (*avertant oportet ab opinione secundum quam . . . formulae dogmaticae . . . non possint significare determinate veritatem*). In these footnotes, John Paul II signals his dutiful submission to a highly dubious linguistic thesis. The thesis is that, although language generally changes meaning with changing circumstance, this does not apply to terms in which Church dogmas are expressed. John Paul II affirms that it is dogmatically required that Church dogma retains a fixed meaning.

Section 55 makes clear the branch of philosophy John Paul II relies upon to elucidate the connection between the language of Church dogma and truth. He strongly disapproves of contemporary movements that result in "disdain for the classical philosophy from which the terms of both the understanding of faith and the formulation of dogma itself have been drawn" (*philosophia classica despicatui habetur, ex cuius notionibus sive fidei intellectus sive dogmaticae ipsae formulae verba exceperunt*). The "classical philosophy" in question, of course, is the Neo-Scholasticism that emerged from the Church's attack on Modernism in the early 20th century. John Paul II goes on to draw upon his predecessor, Pius XII, who insisted that the Church hold true to its traditional terminology. In footnote 77 to #55, John Paul II cites Pius XII's *Humani Generis*, specifically section 27, defending terms used by scholastic theologians, and section 30, insisting that truth and its philosophic expression cannot change from day to day. Pope Pius XII had his own reasons for insisting that Church dogma can be expressed in words with fixed and unambiguous meanings. *Humani Generis* was promulgated on August 12, 1950, brief months before Pius XII's dogmatic pronouncement of the Assumption of Mary.

Popes Pius XII and John Paul II both held that the fixity of Church doctrine is grounded in an ecclesiastical Latin which itself retains fixed meanings. From their perspective, a flaw in theological credentials of the

Transcendental-Thomistic Jesuits considered in earlier chapters is that they wrote in languages other than Latin. Rousselot and Maréchal wrote mainly in French. They were aligned with what Neo-Scholastics referred to disparagingly as *le nouvelle theologie* (the new theology), which the arch-conservative Garrigou-Lagrange likened to the Modernism roundly condemned by Pius X. Rahner, in turn, wrote mainly in German, and Lonergan mainly in English. John Paul II had various reasons for hostility toward the Jesuits (summarized in *Time* magazine, "Religion: John Paul Takes on the Jesuits," November 9, 1981). But their choice of theological language was not least among these.

# No Language Is Fixed in the Sense
# Required, including Latin

Pope John Paul II followed his predecessors in relying on Latin as a language with fixed meanings in which fixed doctrines could be reliably expressed. In the case of a given doctrine, the goal is to have a standard version on which the faithful can rely, regardless of what natural language they speak or when they happen to live. The popes in question thought that the unity of the Church depends upon a unity of doctrinal acceptance, which in turn requires a fixed body of doctrine to which the faithful can assent. In providing a body of doctrine expressed in fixed Latin terminology, the goal of these pontiffs was to maintain the unity of its membership as the body of Christ on earth. In effect, they thought that the unity of the Church depends on a universal language in which doctrine can be uniformly expressed.

An integral part of this goal, of course, is that the Latin in which a given doctrine is expressed can be accurately translated into the relevant vernacular. For a vast majority of faithful Christians (those who don't speak Latin), the doctrines to which they actually assent must be translated into their own native languages. It is relevant to recall the profusion of languages represented at Pentecost (Acts 2:9–11): those of "Parthians and Medes and Elamites and residents of Mesopotamia, Judea and Cappadocia, Pontus and Asia, Phrygia and Pamphylia, Egypt and the parts of Libya belonging to Cyrene, and visitors from Rome." The Holy Spirit made the discourse of the twelve apostles (Mathias having replaced Judas Iscariot) available in the many languages of those gathered outside their house. If the Holy Spirit were on hand to render ecclesiastical Latin into myriads of native languages, problems of accuracy presumably would not arise. In these later days, however, the Holy Spirit seems not readily available as a translator, and requirements of accuracy pose serious problems.

As an illustration of the type of problem involved, suppose that a (competent) native speaker from modern Mesopotamia translates a given doctrine from Latin into Arabic, that another native speaker from modern Judea translates the result from Arabic into Hebrew, and that this latter translation is then translated into Italian. When the Italian version is translated back into Latin, it almost certainly would not match the Latin of the original. At various points along the way, the content of the Latin original will have been altered. Assent to the version translated from Italian would be assent to different doctrinal content than assent to the original version in Latin.

In point of fact, loss of fidelity in translation can occur when only two languages are involved. Imagine a group of people highly competent in both Latin and English who are given a sentence in Latin with which none of them was previously familiar. One member of the group translates the expression from Latin to English, and passes the result on to another for translation back into Latin; and then back and forth repeatedly among other members of the bilingual group for further reversals of translation. After several exchanges of this sort, a Latin version very likely will emerge that differs significantly in content from the original version. Even for expert translators, neither the Latin nor the English version has an exact meaning that can be precisely mapped one onto the other.

There are copious examples of such ambiguity within *Fides et Ratio* itself. In the English version issued by the Vatican, the original Latin often is paraphrased rather than translated literally. In some cases, to be sure, the original Latin is so obscure that literal translations might not even be possible. Specific examples are available from the passages from #96 quoted above. If a Latin scholar were to translate the Vatican English back into Latin, it seems unlikely that it would be identical to the Latin of John Paul II. If back-and-forth translations were made by several Latin scholars, moreover, some of the original Latin almost certainly would be lost in the process.

Difficulties of retaining fixed meanings can occur even when only a single language is involved. These difficulties have been studied

extensively by contemporary philosophers, under the label "indeterminacy of translation." According to the indeterminacy thesis, a sentence
with a given meaning (determined by conditions under which standard
users would consider the sentence applicable) could be translated in
different ways, none of which is more accurate than any other within a
relevant context of use. Within a context of mammalian classification,
for (a hackneyed) example, "there is a rabbit," "there is a collection of
undetached rabbit parts," and "there is an instance of rabbithood" are
equivalent and equally correct expressions reporting the presence of an
actual rabbit. Although equivalent in designation, however, these expressions do not mean exactly the same thing.

The nub of the indeterminacy thesis is that, in any given context
of application, sentences admit a plurality of equally acceptable translations. The context of theological doctrine is a case in point. Pope Pius
XII, in the constitution *Munificentissimus Deus*, proclaimed that the "Immaculate Mother of God, the forever Virgin Mary, was assumed body
and soul into heavenly glory" (*Immaculatam Deiparam semper Virginem
Mariam . . . fuisse corpore et anima ad caelestem gloriam assumptam*).
The Latin presumably was translated into most of the several hundred
languages that serve an appreciable number of Catholic believers today.
Given the lack of a completely determinate translation in any particular
case, however, it is unlikely that the content of the dogma remained con-
stant across the many linguistic groups involved. The doctrine of the Assumption expressed in Mandarin most likely will differ in content from
the doctrine expressed in Turkish, in Russian, or in Bengali.

It is even probable, furthermore, that there will be some languages
in which plausible translations cannot be made in the first place. It seems
reasonable to assume that the Nahuati spoken by certain Aztec peoples
has no precise terms for translating *corpore assumptam* (bodily assumption), and that the Māori of New Zealand aborigines is incapable of
translating *caelestem gloriam* (heavenly glory). Although only specially
trained linguists could say for sure, these expressions may also lack literal
counterparts in more prominent world languages, such as Hindi, Urdu,
and Mandarin.

As noted above, one motive for using Latin in the doctrinal formulations of the Church is to provide universal guidelines upon which the
faithful can rely, regardless of time, place, or walk of life. Inasmuch as
these guidelines are formulated in a fixed (i.e., dead) language, they were
thought themselves to remain fixed despite changing circumstances.

For reasons of indeterminacy, however, the goal of formulating fixed doctrines in a single language conveying universally the same meanings turns out to be illusory.

# Practical Ramifications of Demoting Latin from Its Privileged Role in the Church

LATIN HAS BEEN THE official language of Roman Church since the First Council of Constantinople in AD 381. The official doctrines stemming from this and subsequent councils are invariably phrased in Latin. Following the Great Schism of 1054, Greek became the official language of Eastern Christianity, while Latin was retained by the Roman West. The Church's responses to Calvin and Luther were phrased in Latin, whose movements soon came to rely on German, French, and other vernacular languages. Roman Catholicism stood alone in its persistent adherence to the language of its Roman origins.

The so-called "three pillars" of authority in the Catholic Church are sacred scripture, sacred tradition, and the teaching Magisterium. Sacred scripture is represented by the fourth century Vulgate, in which the original Hebrew and Greek are replaced by Latin translations. Sacred tradition is formalized by ecumenical councils and bishops, whose pronouncements have been documented in Latin from the fourth century onward. Subsequent teachings of the Magisterium have been formulated in Latin prior to being released in vernacular languages. Small wonder that recent popes have insisted on the continued use of Latin as the official language of the Church.

Other branches of Christianity also rely on sacred scripture and church history (tradition). The Catholic Church, however, is the only branch with an officially designated teaching authority. Proclamation in Latin is a hallmark of the Church's Magisterium. If Latin were set aside as the official language of the Catholic Church, sacred scripture (in the original Hebrew and Greek) would not be altered. Inasmuch as sacred tradition falls within the competence of the Magisterium, the teaching authority of the Church is the only "pillar" that would be vitally affected. If Latin were abandoned, the Magisterium would lose the symbol of its teaching authority. It would be like an officer without a badge, a king without a crown, a general without a military uniform.

Deprived of Latin, the Magisterium would lose its badge of authority. As far as the ordinary life of the Church is concerned, however, dethronement of Latin from its official status would have few serious ramifications. Consider, for example, the use of Latin in the liturgy of the Mass. This role was significantly altered by Vatican II. Pre-conciliar Masses were celebrated in Latin, with the priest's back to the congregation. As a gesture of *aggiornamento* ("updating"), the council enacted provisions for the priest to face the people and to say Mass in a relevant vernacular. A few Catholic hold-outs joined a few high church Anglicans in continuing to conduct Masses in Latin.

The so-called "Tridentine Mass" has been a bone of contention in the Church since Vatican II. In 2021, the issue came to a head with an Apostolic Letter by Pope Francis, imposing restrictions on the Latin Mass. Previously, priests who wanted to celebrate a Tridentine Mass could do so unless specifically forbidden by their local superiors. Pope Francis changed the rules to require express approval from their Diocesan Bishop on the part of the priests concerned. Although the change seemed minimal for practical purposes by and large, it was a "hot button" issue for the conservative branch of the Church. This branch can be loosely characterized as those who oppose the *aggeriornamento* of Vatican II.

Another practical role of Latin in Church affairs is to facilitate communication among Church officials with different native languages. This use makes sense in theory, but often doesn't work out well in practice. In theory, the idea is that bishops from different cultures, speaking different natural languages, have a common language in which to communicate when gathering for Church business. Since Latin is a "dead" language (without native speakers), it theoretically should not change with use in diverse circumstances over time.

There are practical difficulties, however, with using Latin for communication across native linguistic barriers. People with different native languages tend to pronounce Latin differently, making it hard for others to understand them. A more substantial obstacle is the scarcity of Church officials who speak Latin fluently in the first place. There was an anecdote current during Vatican II regarding a prominent American cardinal who attended the opening meetings. This distinguished person could not understand most of which his fellow prelates (from all over the world) were saying. He requested the help of translators, whom he would pay for himself. After his request had been ignored for weeks on end, he gathered his retinue together and returned to the USA, where bishops generally speak English when communicating with each other.

As far as practical matters of the Church are concerned, there is no need for Latin as an official language. For most practical purposes, exclusive use of vernacular languages would serve as well if not better. What would be lost, if Latin were set aside, is the badge of authority enjoyed by the Magisterium. Those of us whose lives have been given over to teaching, however, know that overt exercise of authority is detrimental to learning. Recall St. Augustine's *De Magistro*, which is a dialogue between Augustine and his son, Adeodatus. The dialogue between them is such that each party learns from the other. It would be ludicrous to think of Augustine, in that conversation, as wearing anything resembling a badge of authority.

In western culture, Latin and Greek are both essential for gaining immediate access to much of its great literature. But Latin has no unique credentials for serving as the official language of the Catholic Church. Christ's earthly Church would still be the Body of Christ if it did its official business in other languages.

Finis